G.C.A. van der Westhuize

FIELD GUIDE

FIELD GUIDE

MUSHROOMS

OF SOUTHERN AFRICA

STRUIK

Cover photographs: (top left) *Gyroporus castaneus*;
(top right) *Ganoderma lucidium*; (bottom left) *Clathrus transvaalensis*;
(bottom right) *Amanita muscaria*
Spine photograph: *Amanita rubescens*

Struik Publishers (Pty) Ltd
(a member of the Struik Group (Pty) Ltd)
80 McKenzie Street
Cape Town 8001

Reg. No.:54/00965/07

First published in 1994

Edited by Pippa Parker, Cape Town
Designed by Tamsyn Ivey and Joan Sutton, Cape Town
DTP by Sue Fortescue and Lyndall Hamilton, Cape Town
Reproduction by Hirt and Carter (Pty) Ltd, Cape Town
Printed and bound by Kyodo Printing Co (Singapore) Pte Ltd

ISBN 1 86825 507 7

WARNING

Eat only those mushrooms which have been positively identified as safe and edible.
Never eat raw field mushrooms. They may contain mild toxins normally destroyed by cooking
causing stomach upsets.

**The authors and publisher do not assume any responsibility for sickness or
death or other misfortune suffered by any person resulting from eating any
mushroom described in this book.**

It is illegal for anybody to collect mushrooms from South African State Forests without a permit, obtainable from the Director-General, Department of Water Affairs and Forestry. In order
to collect mushrooms from a nature reserve, a permit must be obtained from the Director of
Nature Conservation of the province.

FOREWORD

During the past two to three decades an increasing interest in nature and concern for its conservation has been evident among the general public. As a result, many magazine articles and books, including field guides, written in a manner intelligible to the general public, have appeared on mammals, birds, trees and wild-flowers of the region. Also as part of this interest a growing awareness of mushrooms and larger fungi has developed, but articles and popular books on mushrooms of the region have been less prominent. The great bulk of information on mushrooms is still scattered among the pages of scientific works. Consequently the fascinating world of the mushrooms is still unknown and unavailable to many nature lovers.

The Fungi, which include forms with large fruit-bodies such as mushrooms, toadstools, puffballs and others, are probably the least known of the easily visible life forms in nature. As a result, their importance in nature and their potential uses in various industrial activities are still obscure and often surrounded in mystery. Many people know that some mushrooms are poisonous while others are edible and provide tasty protein-rich food. Their importance as food for humans is however not nearly as great as their importance in the food chain of various animals or their role in different natural habitats. Application of some of their qualities in various industrial processes and food production is just beginning to be appreciated. For all these reasons a greater interest in and more intensive studies of mushrooms is justified.

It is therefore of some importance that this book has been produced, although only a small portion of the known species are described and illustrated. Information on the importance in nature of the various species has been included by the authors who, as professional mycologists, have spent their lives in the study of mushrooms and other fungi. Although this guide was prepared for use by the interested layman and nature lover, it is hoped that it will also be useful to readers engaged in professional activities in other fields of biological science. Above all, it is hoped that it will stimulate in all its readers further interest in mushrooms and their fascinating life habits.

N.F. OPPENHEIMER

ACKNOWLEDGEMENTS

It is a pleasure to acknowledge the help and co-operation of the following people and institutions who made preparation of this book possible. Our colleagues, Alice P. Baxter and Dr Cecilia Roux of the National Collection of Fungi, Plant Protection Research Institute, Pretoria, contributed specimens and literature, and assisted with the examination of specimens in the herbarium of the National Collection of Fungi, with the kind permission of Dr I.H. Wiese, Director of the Institute. Dr J. Veldie van Greuning and Dr Martmari van Greuning of the Department of Botany, University of Pretoria actively assisted in collecting specimens.

Professor P.S. Knox-Davies, former Head of the Deparment of Plant Pathology, University of Stellenbosch, assisted us around Stellenbosch.

Dr Derek A. Reid, former Assistant Keeper of the Herbarium, Royal Botanic Gardens, Kew, England, identified a number of specimens and participated in many valuable discussions.

The Director-General of the Department of Environmental Affairs permitted the collection of specimens in the State Forests under his control and the Regional Directors of Forestry of the Eastern Transvaal and the Natal Regions and their staff, made available accommodation in official quarters on a number of collecting trips. The Director of the National Parks Board permitted collecting in the Tsitsikamma Coastal National Park where the Educational officer, Mr Peet Joubert, offered valuable assistance and information.

Mrs Anna Joubert of Meyerspark and Mrs Jackie de Jager of the Department of Botany, University of Pretoria, successfully deciphered handwritings to produce the final typescripts. Miss Ann Pienaar prepared the plates of line drawings.

The senior author is indebted to his wife, Nina, for her help and support in spotting specimens, and running the 'household' during field trips.

Mrs Mitzi Schutte, formerly of the Department of Public Relations of the University of Pretoria, enthusiastically supported the project and offered valuable advice.

We are indebted to our editor, Pippa Parker, for her valuable guidance in the preparation of this book.

We wish to thank Mr Peter Muzzell, Algoa Mushrooms, Port Elizabeth for his keen interest in this project and the role he played in obtaining the sponsorship.

Finally, it is a great pleasure for us to acknowledge the generous financial support of Mr N.F. Oppenheimer which made possible the production of this book at a price that puts it within reach of most nature lovers.

CONTENTS

THE PURPOSE OF THIS BOOK

This book is intended for the nature lover who has an interest in *all* the living organisms in our world. Many strange, even bizarre forms of life share the living world with other apparently uninteresting or common and familiar forms. All living creatures however have some role to play in perpetuating life. Man is inclined to be interested only in those creatures that can readily be seen and used. As mushrooms are frequently inconspicuous and short-lived they have been ignored, even shunned because a number have acquired the reputation of being poisonous when eaten. However, over the centuries some brave souls have taken the trouble to learn to recognize certain edible and poisonous mushrooms and have survived to pass this knowledge on to successive generations. Many, though, have no doubt experienced the frustrations of not being able to name many of the species they find. This book is intended for them as well as for the growing number of people who share an interest in living things and want to know more about the less well-known forms among which the mushrooms are an important group.

Nature lovers are not the only people who may be interested in mushrooms or frustrated by their inability to name them. Professional workers such as doctors, forestry officers, timber technologists, veterinarians, plant pathologists, forest pathologists, entomologists, ecologists and even some professional mycologists may be faced with the problem of identifying mushrooms. Because the mushroom flora of southern Africa has not been studied continuously and systematically very little is known about it, and what information does exist is contained in the pages of numerous scientific journals dating from the last quarter of the previous century to the present time. We have attempted to amalgamate this information and have included in this field guide the common and widely distributed species but also some less common and little-known ones, as well as those which have been found in southern Africa fairly recently.

The species described here represent only about 10-15 % of the total number of mushroom species that have been recorded in southern Africa. The region seems to have a unique mixture of species, many of these known from Europe but also a largely unknown indigenous flora which merges with the flora of tropical Africa.

A vast amount of research is still needed in order to obtain a reasonable knowledge of the mushroom flora of southern Africa. However, this will take many years of hard work. In the meantime this book and others like it will have to partly fill the need.

HOW TO USE THIS BOOK

The aim of this field guide is to provide a ready means of identifying wild mushrooms in the field. In order to do this, the reader must become familiar with the terms used to describe the structures and forms of mushrooms. These are illustrated in plates 1-14 on pages 13-17 and explained further in the Glossary of terms on page 197. Lists of the species occurring in different habitats are given on pages 18-20. By systematically referring to the descriptions and photographs according to habitat and comparing these with the characters of a newly collected specimen, you should be able to arrive at a name for the specimen.

The keys on pages 20-33 offer a quicker way of identifying an unknown specimen. By starting at the beginning of the relevant key and following the numbers after each key entry which agrees with characters present in a mushroom specimen, the reader can arrive at a name for the specimen. Then compare the newly collected specimen with the the species description and photograph(s). If *all* the characters agree, the specimen has been identified.

The species have been grouped according to colour of spore print and have been numbered from 1 to 160 for ease of reference. These numbers refer to species in this book only and do not in any way relate to a system of numbering as in bird and tree species. Each species is illustrated by one or two photographs, one showing the mushroom in its natural environment, the other showing characteristics of individual parts in greater detail. Habitat symbols appearing in the margin alongside the species descriptions provide habitat information at a glance and line drawings (where they appear) highlight distinctive characteristics of the species. Each species entry provides the scientific name which is followed by author citations that is the name(s) of the person(s) who discovered and named the species; the common names are given in English and Afrikaans where they are known to exist. Information on distribution, economic importance and edibility is also provided as a matter of interest. The species descriptions include microscopic characters of the spores to assist professional workers with access to a research microscope to compare specimens. Dimensions given in the form *a* x *b* (in most cases pertaining to stipe and spore measurements) refer to length x diameter, the greater measurement always being given first.

It is essential to remember that the keys, lists of species in different habitats and related descriptions apply only to the species included in this book. As these comprise just a small portion of the known mushroom species of southern Africa, it is likely that the reader may collect species that are not included here. Do not try to 'force' newly collected specimens to fit the descriptions. Rather consult some of the works listed in the Bibliography on pages 201-203.

INTRODUCTION

What is a mushroom?

A mushroom is the visible reproductive structure – in the form of a fruit-body – of a living organism which develops seasonally to produce and disperse spores. Mushrooms belong to a large group of organisms known as the Fungi. The members of this group resemble plants in some ways but all fungi lack chlorophyll and so, unlike plants, are not able to produce their own food. Like animals they draw their sustenance from living and dead plant and animal matter. As such, fungi are regarded as distinct from both plants and animals and are placed in a separate kingdom, the Fungi.

Fungi display a great variety of forms. Only a small proportion produce the large fruit-bodies known as mushrooms. A large number form minute fruit-bodies which are barely visible to the eye but which may be seen with a hand lens if one knows where and when to look for them. The majority of fungi produce fruit-bodies or fruiting structures which are only visible under a microscope with high magnifying power.

The term 'mushroom' originally applied mainly to the edible fruit-bodies of the agarics, that is fruit-bodies shaped like an umbrella with a wide, fleshy cap bearing plate-like appendages underneath and supported on a centrally placed stalk. However, the term eventually came to include the toadstools – a group at first set apart because of their inedibility or poisonous nature. The meaning was gradually extended to include other macrofungi with large fruit-bodies like stinkhorns, puff-balls, the bracket fungi and even the larger cup-fungi. All of these structures are formed to produce and allow the dispersal of the reproductive units, the spores.

Growth and Reproduction

The reproductive unit of all fungi is the **spore** which may be formed asexually or vegetatively, or sexually. Before any fungus can reproduce, it must grow and develop vegetatively. When a fungal spore lands on a suitable base and in favourable conditions of temperature and moisture, it will germinate by sending out a germ tube which becomes attached to the base or substrate. This tube elongates to form the first **hypha** – a filamentous tube which, in most cases, divides up into a series of cells by the formation of crosswalls or **septa**. The first hypha forms side branches which also grow and form septa and further side branches until a web of hyphae develops. This web of hair-like threads is known as the **mycelium** which is the vegetative body of the fungus, responsible for its nutrition and formation. The mycelium will continue growing and branching throughout the substrate for as long as it can obtain nutrients from it and conditions of temperature and moisture remain favourable. In many of the microscopic fungi the mycelium may be seen as a white, grey, greenish, yellow or brown spot of mould or mildew on substrates such as food, leather, textiles, wood, soil and others. When a mushroom is carefully pulled from damp, loose soil, the mycelium may be visible as fine strands of hyphae attached to the base of the stalk and joined to a diffuse network in the soil or on decaying bits of compost.

Under favourable conditions the fungi may grow rapidly and reproduce asexually. At these times vast numbers of spores are formed on special spore-forming branches and the spores are cut off vegetatively from the tips of these structures. The spores vary greatly in size and shape. When conditions unfavourable for growth set in, the fungus may form sexual spores.

These take longer to form, but in many cases are thick-walled and capable of surviving for long periods. In mushrooms sexual reproduction takes place within the fruit-body. Spores are formed through the fusion of two nucleï and subsequent division, a process which occurs in a special spore-bearing structure. The form of this spore-bearing structure is used as a basis for classification of the larger fungi into two subdivsions. In the first group, Subdivision **Basidiomycotina**, the spore-bearing structures are known as **basidia** and are formed in large numbers within a fertile layer, the **hymenium**. The hymenium is positioned in various ways and configurations in the fruit-body, depending on the species, its position and configuration serving as one of the distinguishing characteristics for the different groups of mushrooms. Spores develop on the basidia, each basidium characteristically bearing four spores. As the spores mature they separate from the basidia and are dispersed.

The other group, Subdivision **Ascomycotina**, includes many edible species such as morels and truffles. In this group spores are formed within sac-like structures called **asci**. Asci are also arranged in a fertile layer (the hymenium) which occupies a large part of the fruit-body of these larger species. Each ascus characteristically contains eight, or a multiple of eight, spores, known as **ascospores**. The ascospores are liberated by disintegration of the ascus or are forcibly ejected into the air through a minute opening at its apex. Although most species of ascospore-producing fungi are microscopic organisms, some edible species such as morels, truffles, hare's ears and cup fungi, attain considerable size.

THE ROLE OF MUSHROOMS IN NATURE

Fungi cannot manufacture their own food from simple substances in the way that green plants do. They are totally dependent on ready-made supplies of complex organic nutrients and so derive their sustenance from dead or living plant and animal matter. The role of fungi in Nature is determined by the particular mode of nourishment and growth; this may be saprobic, parasitic or symbiotic.

Saprobic fungi grow on dead organic material, parasitic fungi attack living plants and animals, and fungi living in association with other organisms such as plants and insects in a way that is beneficial to both partners form an association known as symbiosis.

Saprobic fungi are widely distributed and very abundant in nature but most species have rathe specialized habitats. Some grow only on dung, others grow on dead grass, leaves or only on straw. Different species grow on these materials under warm, dry conditions, others grow on them only in cool, moist conditions. Because different species are adapted to grow under different sets of conditions, saprobic fungi are widely distributed geographically. All, however, have one thing in common: they break down their substrates to simpler products which eventually return to the soil as minerals, simple organic compounds and humus. The saprobic fungi thus fulfil important ecological roles. Not all saprobic fungi are beneficial, however. Certain mushrooms and many bracket fungi attack timber used in construction and as transmission poles, causing decay which may lead to disruption of the services.

Parasitic fungi attack living plants causing diseases such as leaf spot, leaf blight, mildew, rust and others. Under natural conditions these fungi have the important function of killing off weaker plants to allow the stronger plants more space and nutrients. When man interferes by planting large areas under one crop, the parasitic fungi may take advantage of this situation b' infecting large numbers of these. Severe food shortages may result and extensive and expensive methods have to be applied to prevent such losses.

The parasitic fungi also attack animals. In man unpleasant diseases such as ringworm or infections of the skin, nails or respiratory tracts may occur. Domestic animals are subject to the same or similar infections which are often difficult to treat successfully. Many insects are also subject to infection by certain parasitic fungi which can attack and kill the larvae, pupae or adult stages. Many harmful insects like flies and mosquitoes are controlled in this natural way which in turn restricts the incidence of infectious diseases spread by these insects.

The **symbiotic fungi** are a very interesting group. Many fungi form symbiotic associations wit' microscopic green algae or blue-green bacteria to produce lichens. The green algae photosynthesize carbon dioxide and moisture from the atmosphere to form starch, and the fungus

8

obtains all its carbohydrate requirements from the alga. On the other hand the fungus protects the alga from desiccation which means that these partners can live under very harsh conditions. Lichens are very important components in the food chains of wildlife in arid regions and also in the maintainance of soil fertility in forests.

An interesting symbiotic association also exists between some groups of wood-destroying termites and mushrooms of the genus *Termitomyces*. These mushrooms are cultivated on specially constructed combs in fungus gardens inside the termite nests. The termites eat wood and woody debris which they collect above ground but only partly digest this food and then excrete it as faecal pellets which the worker termites place at the bottom of the growing mycelium. The mycelium further digests the faecal pellets and grows on the contents to form tiny nodules. These nodules are in turn eaten by the termites and fed to their young. At certain times of the year, usually at the start of the summer rainy season, the fungus gardens are not tended as carefully as usual by the termites, giving the fungus a chance to further develop and finally push upwards through the soil to form the characteristic *Termitomyces* mushroom which is attached to a long, root-like, underground stalk. All *Termitomyces* species are much sought after natural foods and are eaten by many different indigenous peoples, small animals and by insects too.

Many species of mushrooms and other fungi, such as truffles and puff-balls and some microscopic fungi, form symbiotic associations known as **mycorrhizae** with higher plants. These fungi live in the soil and their hyphae penetrate the outer layers of the roots of a mycorrhiza-forming plant. The fungus obtains carbohydrates from the roots which enable it to grow and form extensive mycelial nets in the soil, while the mycelium absorbs mineral elements, especially phosphates, from the soil and makes them available to the host plant.

Herbaceous plants, which include many crops, form mycorrhizae with microscopic fungi. These form the so-called **vesicular-arbuscular mycorrhizae** because the hyphae are coiled, inflated or branched inside the cells of the root. Some woody perennial shrubs and certain species of tree also form vesicular-arbuscular mycorrhizae. Most coniferous trees and many large broad-leafed forest trees, like oaks, form **ectotrophic mycorrhizae** with many species of mushrooms. In this type the fungal hyphae form a mantle-like layer on the outside of the root from where branching hyphae penetrate the outer root layers. The ectotrophic mycorrhizae are present as special structures, often shaped like stunted, bunched, finger-like outgrowths on the roots of these trees. Many species of tree grow very poorly or are unable to grow at all if their roots are not infected with mycorrhizae. Recent studies have shown that it is possible to strongly stimulate growth and vigour of pine seedlings by artificially infecting their roots with selected species of mycorrhizal fungi.

The short phase in the life-cycle of a fungus in which a fruit-body appears is specifically for the purpose of reproduction and perpetuation of the species. However, the role of mushrooms and other fungi goes far beyond this: as rich sources of food, as decomposing agents and in beneficial relationships with some plants. As such they are important components in the food web in Nature.

MUSHROOM POISONING

Mushrooms have been used by man as food for centuries. How safe are they? By far the majority of macrofungi are not poisonous and many are edible and delicious. Of the about 10 000 different species of fleshy fungi the vast majority are harmless. However, there are poisonous fungi and some can even be fatal. The most important precaution against mushroom poisoning is to be able to positively identify the fungi you want to eat. There is no simple test or rule to indicate whether a mushroom is edible or deadly poisonous. All known so-called tests are irrelevant and false and to rely on them is like playing Russian roulette. One should never take unnecessary chances by eating unfamiliar mushrooms.

Fortunately the number of really dangerous mushrooms is small and confined to just a few genera. There are also a number of fungi that are not deadly poisonous but do cause a variety of symptoms when eaten. All these poisonous fungi produce toxins and it is possible to classify them in a few basic groups based on the chemicals involved in the poisoning.

Protoplasmic toxins (cyclopeptides)

The genus *Amanita* is principal amongst poisonous fungi; it includes the notorious Death Cap, *Amanita phalloides* – reponsible for over 95 % of cases of fatal mushroom poisoning – and the equally fatal *Amanita virosa*. Both species have numerous and extremely complex toxins which hamper the development of suitable treatment techniques. The toxin molecules are made up of amino-acids arranged in a double ring and known as cyclopeptides. They fall into two main groups, the amatoxins and the phallotoxins, differing in their mode of action on the body and the speed at which they act. The amatoxins, the real toadstool poisons, are extremely poisonous, 0,1 mg per kilogram of body mass being sufficient to kill the eater. They are slow working causing death several days after ingestion. The phallotoxins, the quick-acting toxins, can cause death in rats two to five hours after administration. In tests with toxins injected into mice it was found that phallotoxins are 10 times more lethal than cyanide and that 2 mg per kilogram is enough to kill the victim. Fortunately the phallotoxins are much less poisonous when taken by mouth. *Amanita phalloides* has at least five amatoxins and six phallotoxins and all these produce different and variable symptoms. It is said that the Death Cap is a tasty mushroom! After eating a meal of it the first signs of poisoning are felt after five to 30 hours. By this time the toxins have been taken up in the blood stream, rendering stomach pumping ineffectual. The victim starts to suffer from abdominal pains, diarrhoea and vomiting. If treatment is not administered immediately the victim may die from shock, fluid loss and exhaustion. If treated, the patient may revive for a day or two and then suddenly relapse, with a weakening pulse, a drastic drop in blood pressure and even hallucinations. Death usually occurs as a result of kidney and liver damage and weakening of the heart muscles. Up till fairly recently treatment was usually futile. New techniques of blood filtration by carbon-column haemodialysis and high therapeutic doses (up to 900 mg per day) of the drug thioctic acid are effective provided poisoning is diagnosed in time. Although none of the other *Amanita* species are as deadly as the Death Cap, they should all be approached with suspicion, particularly the white amanitas.

The genus *Galerina* contains amatoxins but no phallotoxins and should also be avoided.

Muscimol toxins (ibotenic acid)

Many mushrooms produce toxins that affect the central nervous system, causing hallucinogenic effects. These toxins act rapidly, usually within five to 30 minutes, but rarely last longer than eight hours. They cause dangerous but usually not fatal poisonings. Symptoms include blurred vision, profuse sweating, vomiting, lowered heart beat and blood pressure and sometimes hallucinations, delirium and convulsions. The well-known and characteristic Fly Agaric, *Amanita muscaria*, often used by fairy-tale illustrators, is an excellent example of this group of mushrooms. It has been known for centuries for its hallucinogenic properties and has been reported to be eaten deliberately in some regions. Tribes in Siberia have been using it for centuries as a religious and recreational intoxicant. In India it is known as 'Soma' and references to it can be found in the 3 000-year-old sacred book, *Rig Vefa*. At first it was thought that muscarine was the active toxin. However, this toxin is present in inconsequential concentrations and the isoxazoles, ibotenic acid, and its decarboxylation product, muscimol, and the weakly toxic oxazole, muscazone, are in fact the active ingredients. Although the Fly Agaric is very rarely fatal, readers are warned not to experiment with this mushroom. Other mushrooms in this group include the Warted Agaric, *Amanita pantherina*, and species of the genera *Clitocybe*, *Inocybe* and *Panaeolus*. Many authors consider these species more poisonous than the Fly Agaric. Cases of death due to eating *Amanita pantherina* have been recorded in southern Africa.

Hallucinogenic toxins (psilocin and psilocybin)

The Aztecs of Mexico described their sacred mushroom (*Psilocybe* species) as the 'flesh of the Gods'. They have been using these mushrooms for thousands of years in Central America for religious rites; Wasson's (1957) description of the rediscovery of this practice makes fascinating reading.

Psilocybe species and members of the genera *Conocybe, Gymnopilus, Panaeolus and Stropharia* contain hallucinogenic indole alkaloids called psilocin and its phosphoric acid, ester psilocybin. An effective dose is 4-8 mg representing about 2 g of dried mushroom. The psychoactive principles contained in these mushrooms are in the LSD (lysergic acid) family of hallucinogenic compounds which have a strong effect on the central nervous system, producing visions and smothering sensations, optical distortions and even, reportedly, religious and mystical experiences. Some of these drugs are very potent and the ingestion of as little as 5 mg of the mushroom *Psilocybe cubensis* can cause visual hallucinations in 15 minutes. The ingestion of larger quantities of any of these mushrooms could therefore be fatal.

Gastrointestinal toxins

Some mushroom toxins, though seldom fatal, can cause severe digestive upsets, such as nausea, hallucinations or alcohol-like intoxication. Symptoms develop within 30-90 minutes after eating. They can be dangerous to children or to adults if ingested in quantity. Species of genera such as *Boletus, Chlorophyllum, Entoloma, Hebeloma, Lactarius, Marasmius, Pholiota, Russula, Scleroderma* and *Tricholoma* are included in this group. Even some true mushrooms, such as *Agaricus xanthodermus* with its characteristic bright yellow staining when bruised (page 108), can cause upsets. Many mushrooms can cause some kind of intoxication when eaten raw. Fortunately many of these irritant substances are destroyed in cooking.

Other toxins

The False Morel, *Gyromitra esculenta*, is often eaten in Europe where it is confused with the eminently edible and good *Morchella esculenta*, the True Morel. The False Morel is responsible for about 4 % of all fatal mushroom poisonings. It produces the deadly toxin monomethyl hydrazine (MMH) which causes blood poisoning and affects the central nervous system. Symptoms include diarrhoea, vomiting, loss of muscle co-ordination and severe headaches. Cases of fatal poisoning are known principally from Europe.

One of the common ink caps, *Coprinus atramentarius*, which is an edible species, can be quite harmful to some people, particularly when consumed with alcoholic beverages. Symptoms include a deep reddening of the face, an acceleration of the pulse, loss of strength, nausea and vomiting. It is now known that this mushroom contains coprine, a unique amino acid that blocks the metabolism of ethyl alcohol at the acetaldehyde stage. The action of coprine is very similar to that of antabuse (disulfiram) used in treating alcoholics!

FORM AND CLASSIFICATION

The fruit-bodies of mushrooms and other higher fungi display a great diversity of forms. The form and other characteristics of the fruit-bodies, are used to classify the fungi into groups which share common features. These groups have different ranks, according to the number of common features, in the system of classification. The highest rank, Division, has the smallest number of common characters, only one or two, and the lower ranks of Genus and species have the largest number of common features. Thus the number of shared features increases with decreasing rank from Division to Class, Order, Family, Genus and Species. Fungi are known by their genus and species names (always Latin names), which mostly indicate some characteristic feature of the form or habit of the fruit-bodies.

Classification

The species included in this book belong to one of two subdivisions, the **Basidiomycotina** which produce and bear spores on a microscopic structure, the **basidium**, and the **Ascomycotina**, the members of which produce ascopores in elongated sacs called **asci**. Within these two larger groupings fungi are further classified according to the form of the fruit-body and characteristic features of it (see plates 1-14). In the true mushrooms, Order Agaricales, the fruit-body generally consists of a **cap** which is supported on a stalk, or **stipe** (Plate 1). The stipe is usually attached at the centre of the cap, or to one side of it, that is, **excentrically**; in some cases it may be attached at the margin of the cap, that is **laterally**. In a few species there is no stipe and the fruit-body is then **sessile** on the substrate (plates 3 & 9).

On the lower surface of the cap flat, plate-like appendages – the gills or **lamellae** – hang downwards and radiate outwards from the stipe or, in the case of a sessile cap, from the point of attachment to the substrate. The hymenium (see page 8) is situated on the sides of the lamellae and the spores which are set free from the basidia, drop downwards until they are caught by air currents and carried to new localities. The shape of the cap, its colours, the nature of its upper surface, whether it is smooth, dry, sticky, gluey, scaly or hairy, are important features used in classification. So too, are the colours of the lamellae, their shape, spacing and extent of their attachment to the stipe (Plate 8).

In some mushrooms the fruit-bodies are enclosed in their young stages in a membrane known as the **universal veil**. This membrane is ruptured as the fruit-body grows and remains around the base of the stipe as the **volva**. The volva takes the form of a sac-like membrane, or a number of coarse, raised ridges or warts which are attached to the stipe base. Over the cap surface the remains of the universal veil appear as as loose, thick scales. In many species, another membrane, the **partial veil** covers the lamellae in the young stages. As the cap expands, the partial veil is stretched between the stipe and cap margin until it ruptures, leaving a **ring** of tissue or **annulus** around the upper part of the stipe.

The shape, colour and texture of the stipe, and the presence of a volva or volval remains and/or a ring, are important macroscopic characters used in the classification of mushroom species (plates 10-13). Microscopic features, such as the nature of the hyphae, the shape and size of basidia, spores, and sterile structures in the hymenium – the cystidia – are also of great value in classification. Different combinations of macroscopic and microscopic characters distinguish the different families, genera and species.

In one family of fungi, the Boletaceae, the fruit-bodies resemble those of the Agaricales but the hymenium is located inside minute tubes which hang vertically from the underside of the cap and open as small pores on its lower surface. This tissue resembles foam rubber.

Fungi in the Order Aphyllophorales, produce fruit-bodies in a variety of forms. The simplest of these grow on wood or bark, and consist of a thin, more or less smooth layer of hyphae forming a skin-like or crust-like layer on which the hymenium is borne. In some species the sur face may be wrinkled or covered with wart-like or spine-like projections. These are the **resupinate** forms (Plate 3). In more complex forms the fruit-bodies may consist of club-shaped or branching finger-like or even spine-like structures with the hymenium covering the entire surface. In others, fruit-bodies may be **effused-reflexed**, that is, consisting of a resupinate part and a reflexed part projecting outwards horizontally and away from the substrate (Plate 3). In such forms the hymenium is mostly present as a smooth layer on the lower surface of the reflexed part and continuing downwards on the resupinate part.

In some species the hymenium is present on spines that project downwards while in many others it is located in minute tubes that hang vertically from the resupinate and reflexed parts. In still other species, the fruit-bodies are **dimidiate** or shelf-like (Plate 5), consisting entirely of tissue projecting horizontally from the substrate with the hymenium covering the lower surface in a smooth layer, or, with the hymenium present in tubes attached vertically to the lower surface. Sometimes the tubes are elongated radially and as such may resemble lamellae.

Fungi in the Class Gasteromycetes are characterized by basidia that develop in enclosed structures. The spores are released at maturity by rupturing or disintegration of the enclosing tissues. In many cases the fruit-bodies are large and often spectacular structures such as the stinkhorns, earth-stars and puff-balls.

Although the Aphyllophorales and Gasteromycetes are not mushrooms in the strict sense, many of the species in these groups produce quite conspicuous and interesting fruit-bodies. Further, very many of them are of economic importance; we have therefore included these groups in this book.

Identifying mushrooms

To identify an unknown mushroom one must carefully observe all the important characters of form, texture, colour and odour of the fruit-body, as well as its locality and the substrate on which it is growing. These characters are expressed in various terms and, together with the re evant shapes of different parts of the fruit-body, surface characters and textures, are given ar illustrated in plates 1-14. Although most of these characters are discernible to the naked eye, hand lens giving 10 x magnification is a most valuable aid.

ASPECTS OF MUSHROOM FORM AND SHAPE

Plate 1

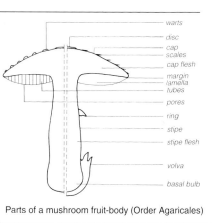

warts
disc
cap
scales
cap flesh
margin
lamella
tubes
pores
ring
stipe
stipe flesh
volva
basal bulb

crust
upper surface
flesh
margin
tubes
pores
lower (hymenial) surface
substrate (wood)

Parts of a mushroom fruit-body (Order Agaricales)   Parts of a pore fungus (Order Aphyllophorales)

Plate 2 Types of growth habit

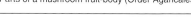

Solitary/single (with stipe)

Scattered (with stipe)

Clustered/tufted (with stipe)

Grouped (with stipe)

Solitary/single (sessile)

Scattered (sessile)

Grouped (sessile)

Rosette

Multiple fans

Plate 3 Means of attachment to substrate

Stipitate (with stipe)

Sessile

Substipitate

Imbricate/overlapping

Effused-reflexed

Resupinate

13

Plate 4 Cap shapes

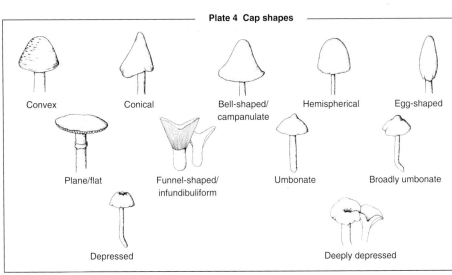

Convex

Conical

Bell-shaped/
campanulate

Hemispherical

Egg-shaped

Plane/flat

Funnel-shaped/
infundibuliform

Umbonate

Broadly umbonate

Depressed

Deeply depressed

Plate 5 Forms of fruit body
(viewed from above)

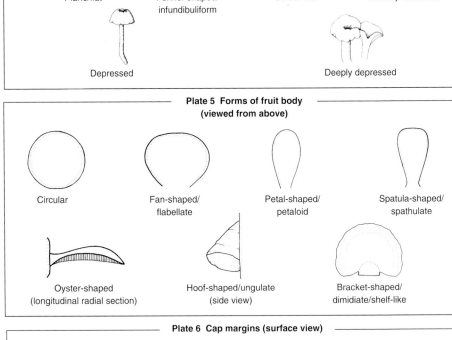

Circular

Fan-shaped/
flabellate

Petal-shaped/
petaloid

Spatula-shaped/
spathulate

Oyster-shaped
(longitudinal radial section)

Hoof-shaped/ungulate
(side view)

Bracket-shaped/
dimidiate/shelf-like

Plate 6 Cap margins (surface view)

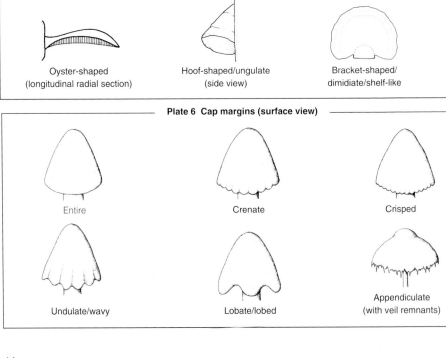

Entire

Crenate

Crisped

Undulate/wavy

Lobate/lobed

Appendiculate
(with veil remnants)

Plate 7 Cap margins (sectional view)

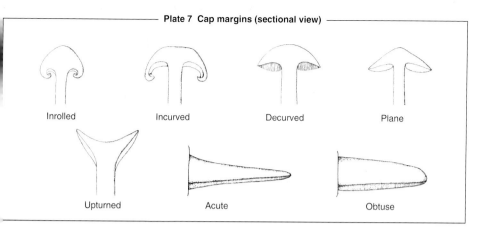

Inrolled Incurved Decurved Plane

Upturned Acute Obtuse

Plate 8 Lamellae
Attachment

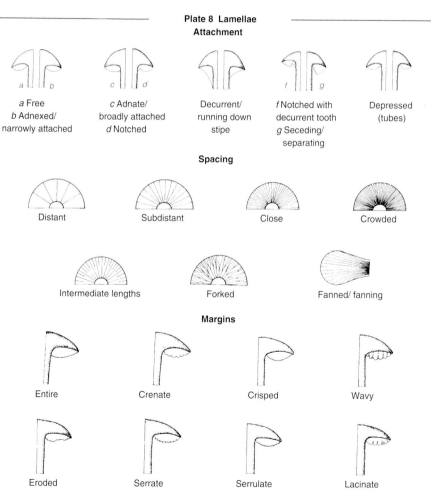

a Free
b Adnexed/
narrowly attached

c Adnate/
broadly attached
d Notched

Decurrent/
running down
stipe

f Notched with
decurrent tooth
g Seceding/
separating

Depressed
(tubes)

Spacing

Distant Subdistant Close Crowded

Intermediate lengths Forked Fanned/ fanning

Margins

Entire Crenate Crisped Wavy

Eroded Serrate Serrulate Lacinate

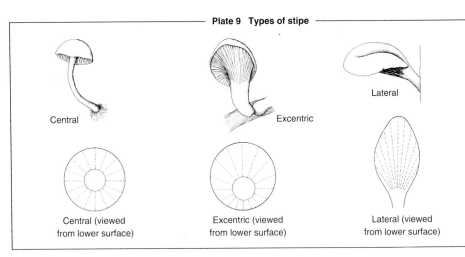

Plate 9 Types of stipe

Central

Excentric

Lateral

Central (viewed from lower surface)

Excentric (viewed from lower surface)

Lateral (viewed from lower surface)

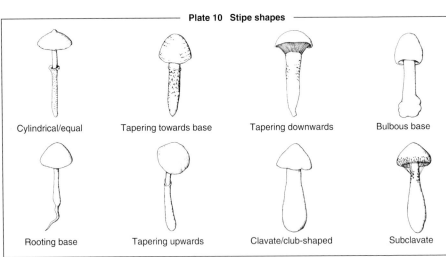

Plate 10 Stipe shapes

Cylindrical/equal

Tapering towards base

Tapering downwards

Bulbous base

Rooting base

Tapering upwards

Clavate/club-shaped

Subclavate

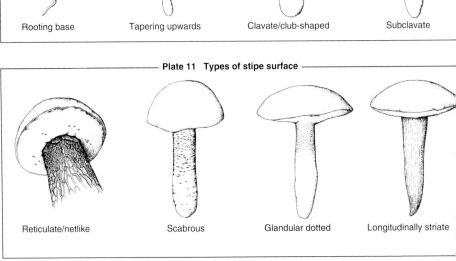

Plate 11 Types of stipe surface

Reticulate/netlike

Scabrous

Glandular dotted

Longitudinally striate

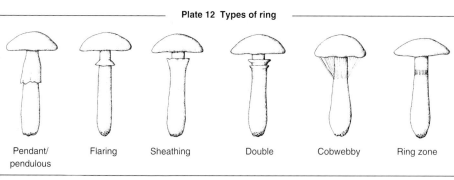

Plate 12 Types of ring

| Pendant/ | Flaring | Sheathing | Double | Cobwebby | Ring zone |
| pendulous | | | | | |

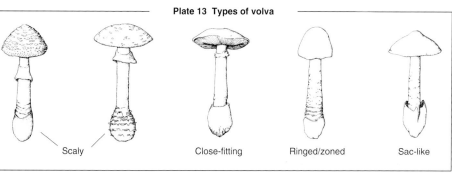

Plate 13 Types of volva

Scaly   Close-fitting   Ringed/zoned   Sac-like

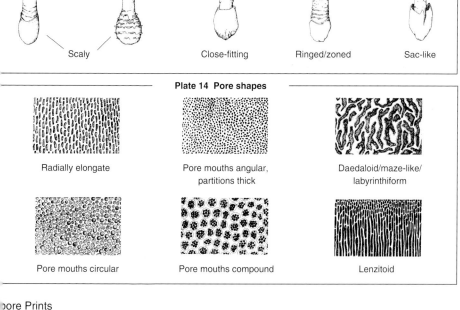

Plate 14 Pore shapes

Radially elongate

Pore mouths angular, partitions thick

Daedaloid/maze-like/ labyrinthiform

Pore mouths circular

Pore mouths compound

Lenzitoid

ɔore Prints

ʝe colour of the spores is an important characteristic in the identification of mushrooms. This
best seen in a spore print which yields a good supply of spores for microscopic examination
ɩd experimentation in the laboratory. Because spore prints can be stored for many years,
ey also provide a permanent record for use in future scientific research.

Spore prints are easily made in the following way and as illustrated in Plate 15. Remove a
ɘdge-shaped piece from the cap of a freshly collected, mature fruit-body and place it with
ɘ lamellae or tubes downwards on a piece of white paper. In smaller fruit-bodies (10-50 mm
ɑm.) cut off the stipe as close to the cap as possible and place the entire cap on the paper.
ᴠert a small cup over the cap to allow a damp atmosphere to develop and leave undisturbed
ʳ 6-10 hours (overnight). Lift the cap carefully from the paper, taking care not to smudge or
ɔ over the surface. A deposit of spores which mirrors the pattern of the lamellae or pores

should be present on the paper. Let the spore print dry, preferably in a gentle draught. Once dry, you will be able to see the spore colour and microscopic characters of the spores.

Instead of the cup, a small polythene freezing bag (25 x 15 cm) may be used. Paper squares of 7 x 7 cm are ideal for making spore prints. Place the paper square with the cap selected for printing on it inside the plastic bag. Fold the open end over and seal with a small weight; then leave overnight. Treat the spore print in the manner described above, and label the specimen. This method allows a large number of paper squares to be carried on a collecting trip. Many such spore prints can be stored in a small space and the paper squares have ample space for marking the name of the mushroom as well as other relevant information.

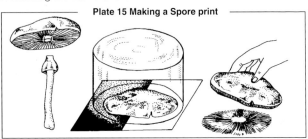

Plate 15 Making a Spore print

SPECIES IN DIFFERENT HABITATS

Habitat and substrate are important factors in distinguishing groups of mushrooms. These two aspects of mushroom ecology are the ones we have chosen to group the mushrooms in this book and also form the basis of the keys to identification (pages 21-33).

Species listed as growing under pines or broad-leafed trees are those which appear in the ground and among leaf-litter under and close to these trees, usually in small groves and plantations. Species found on dead wood grow mostly either on pine wood (softwood) or wood of broad-leafed trees (hardwood) only. A few species grow on both. The wood may be present at stumps or dead logs, including thin branches and twigs, or may occur in groves or plantations of different trees. Structural timber such as fence posts and transmission poles may also be attacked. Such lignicolous species cause decay in the wood, seen as softness, increased brittleness and colour changes. A bleached appearance in the wood indicates a white rot whereas darkening indicates a brown rot. In both cases the wood is weakened. The type of rot is an important feature in the identification of wood-rotting fungi. This colour change is best seen by cutting away the discoloured surface wood around the fruit-body to reveal fresh surfaces.

 Species occurring in ground, among grass or low, scattered shrubs

2. *Amanita foetidissima*	47. *Termitomyces schimperi*	80. *Coprinus plicatilis*
8. *Amanita pleropus*	48. *Termitomyces umkowaani*	83. *Panaeolus papilionaceu*
12. *Chlorophyllum molybdites*	50. *Agrocybe semiorbicularis*	93. *Phlebopus sudanicus*
16. *Hygrocybe nigrescens*	51. *Bolbitius vitellinus*	118. *Lignosus sacer*
24. *Lepiota cristata*	52. *Conocybe tenera*	141. *Phallus rubicundus*
25. *Leucoagaricus bisporus*	60. *Lepista caffrorum*	142. *Itajahya galericulata*
26. *Leucoagaricus leucothites*	61. *Lepista sordida*	143. *Aseroë rubra*
27. *Leucocoprinus birnbaumii*	67. *Agaricus arvensis*	145. *Clathrus transvaalensis*
28. *Macrolepiota procera*	68. *Agaricus bitorquis*	146. *Scleroderma cepa*
29. *Macrolepiota rhacodes*	69. *Agaricus campestris*	148. *Scleroderma*
30. *Macrolepiota zeyheri*	71. *Agaricus semotus*	*verrucosum*
43. *Termitomyces clypeatus*	72. *Agaricus diminutivus*	149. *Pisolithus tinctorius*
44. *Termitomyces*	74. *Agaricus trisulphuratus*	151. *Calvatia lilacina*
microcarpus	75. *Agaricus xanthodermus*	152. *Vascellum pratense*
45. *Termitomyces reticulatus*	76. *Coprinus comatus*	155. *Battarrea stevenii*
46. *Termitomyces sagittiformis*	78. *Coprinus micaceus*	156. *Podaxis pistillaris*

Species occurring under broad-leafed trees

1. *Amanita excelsa*
3. *Amanita muscaria*
4. *Amanita pantherina*
5. *Amanita phalloides*
6. *Amanita phalloides* var. *alba*
7. *Amanita phalloides* var. *umbrina*
9. *Amanita rubescens*
10. *Armillaria mellea*
17. *Laccaria laccata*
24. *Lepiota cristata*
36. *Russula sororia*
43. *Termitomyces clypeatus*
44. *Termitomyces microcarpus*
45. *Termitomyces reticulatus*
46. *Termitomyces sagittiformis*
47. *Termitomyces schimperi*
48. *Termitomyces umkowaani*
55. *Gymnopilus junonius*
57. *Hebeloma crustuliniforme*
62. *Paxillus involutus*
65. *Agaricus augustus*
70. *Agaricus placomyces*
71. *Agaricus semotus*
73. *Agaricus sylvaticus*
77. *Coprinus disseminatus*
78. *Coprinus micaceus*
79. *Coprinus lagopus*
81. *Hymenagaricus luteolosporus*
82. *Hypholoma fasciculare*
86. *Stropharia aurantiaca*
88. *Boletus aestivalis*
89. *Boletus edulis*
91. *Gyroporus castaneus*
92. *Leccinum duriusculum*
99. *Amauroderma rudé*
122. *Pseudophaeolus baudonii*
131. *Ramaria formosa*
142. *Itajahya galericulata*
144. *Clathrus archeri*
148. *Scleroderma verrucosum*
149. *Pisolithus tinctorius*
150. *Lycoperdon perlatum*
153. *Geastrum triplex*
154. *Myriostoma coliforme*

Species occurring under pine trees

1. *Amanita excelsa*
3. *Amanita muscaria*
4. *Amanita pantherina*
5. *Amanita phalloides*
9. *Amanita rubescens*
10. *Armillaria mellea*
13. *Collybia distorta*
17. *Laccaria laccata*
18. *Lactarius deliciosus*
19. *Lactarius hepaticus*
31. *Marasmius androsaceus*
33. *Russula caerulea*
34. *Russula capensis*
35. *Russula sardonia*
36. *Russula sororia*
38. *Tricholoma albobrunneum*
39. *Tricholoma saponaceum*
41. *Clitopilus prunulus*
55. *Gymnopilus junonius*
57. *Hebeloma crustuliniforme*
58. *Hebeloma cylindrosporum*
59. *Inocybe eutheles*
62. *Paxillus involutus*
65. *Agaricus augustus*
71. *Agaricus semotus*
73. *Agaricus sylvalicus*
89. *Boletus edulis*
90. *Chalciporus piperatus*
94. *Suillus bellinii*
95. *Suillus bovinus*
96. *Suillus granulatus*
97. *Suillus luteus*
102. *Coltricia perennis*
119. *Phaeolus schweinitzii*
122. *Pseudophaeolus baudonii*
130. *Clavulina cristata*
132. *Thelephora terrestris*
140. *Rhizopogon luteolus*
143. *Aseroë rubra*
147. *Scleroderma citrinum*
159. *Rhizina undulata*

Species occurring on dead wood (standing trunks, logs, thinner branches on soil, stumps, buried wood)   B: broad-leafed; P: pine

1. *Campanella capensis* B
4. *Cyptotrama asprata* B
5. *Favolaschia thwaitesii* B
0. *Lentinus sajor-caju* B
1. *Lentinus stupeus* B
2. *Lentinus velutinus* B
3. *Lentinus villosus* B
7. *Leucocoprinus birnbaumii* B
2. *Pleurotus ostreatus* B
7. *Schizophyllum commune* B
0. *Trogia cantharelloides* B
2. *Pluteus salicinus* B
3. *Crepidotus mollis* B
4. *Crepidotus variabilis* B
6. *Gymnopilus penetrans* P
3. *Paxillus panuoides* P
4. *Tubaria furfuracea* B
77. *Coprinus disseminatus* B
78. *Coprinus lagopus* B
79. *Coprinus micaceus* B
82. *Hypholoma fasciculare* B
84. *Psathyrella candolleana* B
98. *Fistulina africana* B
99. *Amauroderma rudé* B
100. *Ganoderma applanatum* B
101. *Ganoderma lucidum* B
103. *Phellinus gilvus* B
104. *Phellinus rimosus* B
105. *Coriolopsis polyzona* B
106. *Coriolus hirsutus* B
107. *Coriolus versicolor* B
108. *Daedalea quercina* B
109. *Favolus spathulatus* B
110. *Fomitopsis lilacino-gilva* B
111. *Funalia protea* B
112. *Funalia trogii* B
113. *Gloeophyllum sepiarium* P
114. *Hexagona tenuis* P
115. *Laetiporus sulphureus* B
116. *Lenzites betulina* B
117. *Lenzites elegans* B
119. *Phaeolus schweinitzii* P
120. *Polyporus arcularius* B
121. *Polyporus dictyopus* B
123. *Pycnoporus sanguineus* BP
124. *Trametes cingulata* B
125. *Trametes meyenii* B
126. *Trichaptum byssogenus* B
127. *Tremella mesenterica* B
128. *Calocera cornea* BP
129. *Serpula himantioides* P

Species occurring on dead wood (cont.)

133. *Laxitextum bicolor B*
134. *Cymatoderma elegans B*
135. *Podoscypha parvula B*
136. *Stereum australe B*

137. *Stereum hirsutum B*
138. *Stereum ostrea B*
139. *Hymenochaete*
    ochromarginata B

147. *Scleroderma citrinum P*
158. *Cyathus olla BP*

Species occurring on living trees   *B:* broad-leafed; *P:* pine

11. *Campanella capensis B*
98. *Fistulina africana B*
99. *Amauroderma rudé B*
100. *Ganoderma*
    applanatum B

101. *Ganoderma lucidum B*
104. *Phellinus rimosus B*
115. *Laetiporus sulphureus B*
116. *Lenzites betulina B*
119. *Phaeolus schweinitzii P*

122. *Pseudophaeolus*
    baudonii BP
159. *Rhizina undulata P*

Species occurring on compost and plant litter

25. *Leucoagaricus bisporus*
31. *Marasmius androsaceus*
49. *Volvariella speciosa*
66. *Agaricus bisporus*
79. *Coprinus lagopus*
86. *Stropharia aurantiaca*

118. *Lignosus sacer*
130. *Clavulina cristata*
131. *Ramaria formosa*
143. *Aseroë rubra*
144. *Clathrus archeri*
145. *Clathrus transvaalensis*

150. *Lycoperdon perlatum*
153. *Geastrum triplex*
154. *Myriostoma coliforme*
157. *Tulostoma albicans*
158. *Cyathus olla*

Species occurring on herbivore dung

51. *Bolbitius vitellinus*
83. *Panaeolus papilionaceus*

85. *Psilocybe coprophila*
87. *Stropharia semiglobata*

Species occurring on or around termite nests

43. *Termitomyces clypeatus*
44. *Termitomyces microcarpus*
45. *Termitomyces reticulatus*
46. *Termitomyces sagittiformis*

47. *Termitomyces schimperi*
48. *Termitomyces*
    umkowaani
156. *Podaxis pistillaris*

KEYS FOR IDENTIFICATION OF SPECIES

These keys are applicable only to the species described in this book. To use the keys, first
determine the habitat in which you found the specimen, then select the relevant key (A,B,C, D,
E, etc.). Keys A to H distinguish groups or individual species according to morphological features of the fruit-body. Match your specimen to the descriptions in the key and progress
numerically as indicated until you arrive at an individual species.

A specimen identified with the use of these keys must be carefully compared with the relevant description of the species. **Caution in exercising judgement and careful observation are
essential when attempting identification.**

Species in different habitats

Fruit-bodies on open ground or in grass   Key A   Fruit-bodies on living trees   Key E
Fruit-bodies under broad-leafed tree   Key B   Fruit-bodies on compost or plant litter Key F
Fruit-bodies under pine trees   Key C   Fruit-bodies on herbivore dung   Key G
Fruit-bodies on dead wood   Key D   Fruit-bodies on termite nests   Key H

A   B   C   D   E   F   G   H

KEY A Species occurring on open ground, among grass, or near small shrubs, not under a grove of trees 1

1 Fruit-bodies umbrella-shaped with cap and central stipe 2
1 Fruit-bodies consisting of a globose to egg-shaped or bell-shaped spore-bearing part upon a stipe 26
1 Fruit-bodies with a prominent, porous, fragile stipe or supporting arms and dark-coloured, slimy, smelly spore masses 29
1 Fruit-bodies more or less globose or with globular lobes; without stipe 31
1 Fruit-bodies not as above 37
2 Cap with lamellae on underside 3
2 Cap with tubes and pores on underside 36
3 Lamellae white to cream and remaining so 4
3 Lamellae white at first, turning to pink, green or tan at maturity 7
3 Lamellae white to pink at first, soon turning dark brown to black at maturity 13
3 Lamellae rusty brown at maturity 23
4 Cap and stipe coarsely scaly; volval remains at base of stipe 5
4 Cap with fine scales; no volval remains at base of stipe 6
5 Cap and stipe brick-red and covered with brick-red, wart-like scales 8. *Amanita pleropus*
5 Cap and stipe white, covered with loose, fluffy, white scales; emitting sweetish, nauseating odour 2. *Amanita foetidissima*
6 Fruit-bodies small, white, with reddish-brown, appressed scales and reddish-brown disc over large, rounded umbo; stipe fragile, bruising reddish; ring disappearing 24. *Lepiota cristata*
6 Lamellae white to pale yellow, darkening slightly with age; cap with small, appressed, pale yellow to pale tan scales on surface but pale tan over prominent, flattened umbo 25. *Leucoagaricus bisporus*
6 Fruit-bodies small, finely scaly, bright sulphur-yellow bleaching later; stipe club-shaped 27. *Leucocoprinus birnbaumii*
7 Stipe with basal bulb and movable ring 8
7 Stipe without ring 11
8 Cap smooth, white; lamellae white to pinkish; ring fixed when young but later free, movable 26. *Leucoagaricus leucothites*
8 Cap large, covered with brown scales 9
9 Scales large, irregular, over upper part of cap; lamellae with greenish tints maturing to drab green 12. *Chlorophyllum molybdites*
9 Lamellae white, maturing to pale tan 10
10 Cap white, covered with numerous pale brown scales; stipe tall (to 35 cm), slender, covered with fine greyish-brown scales 28. *Macrolepiota procera*
10 Cap covered with small white scales and large, polygonal reddish-brown scales arranged concentrically; flesh turning reddish when cut 29. *Macrolepiota rhacodes*
10 Cap white, covered with soft, white and harder, pale brown scales, often with central umbo, margin often fringed; stipe slender, white, mealy or covered with small soft, white scales 30. *Macrolepiota zeyheri*
11 Stipe normal, not elongated into root-like underground extension 12
11 Stipe with root-like extension underground; lamellae turning pink; associated with termites. *Termitomyces* spp. .... KEY H
12 Fruit-bodies scattered or grouped, medium to large, white, thick, fleshy, smooth, without umbo; lamellae turning pale brown 60. *Lepista caffrorum*
12 Fruit-bodies small, white, with prominent, pointed umbo; lamellae turning pink; clustered on termite soil casts 44. *Termitomyces microcarpus*
13 Lamellae becoming wet and inky, or deliquescing from the cap margin at maturity; spores black 14
13 Lamellae remaining dry at maturity; spores purplish brown to black 16
14 Fruit-bodies large, white; cap egg-shaped, at first shaggy with coarse white scales, later deliquescent, cap turns black and dissolves 76. *Coprinus comatus*
14 Fruit-bodies small; cap and lamellae becoming inky, not deliquescent 15

15 Fruit-bodies delicate; cap ochreous over the centre, surface appearing conspic-
    uously grooved or folded   80. *Coprinus plicatilis*
15 Fruit-bodies small, clustered; cap acorn-shaped, brownish with glistening mica-like
    particles over the upper parts; on buried, decaying wood   78. *Coprinus micaceus*
16 Stipe without ring; lamellae never pink, black at maturity..   17
16 Ring on stipe; immature lamellae pinkish, turning purplish brown to black..   18
17 Fruit-bodies waxy, small; cap conical, bright orange to red, with black streaks,
    finally black   16. *Hygrocybe nigrescens*
17 Fruit-bodies not waxy; stipe tall, slender, fragile; cap greyish, conical to bell-shaped;
    lamellae mottled as groups of spores mature, finally black with white edges
    83. *Panaeolus papilionaceus*
18 Cap white, smooth, medium-sized, thick with margin inrolled; stipe short with two
    separate rings   68. *Agaricus bitorquis*
18 Stipe with one ring; cap smooth or scaly..   19
19 Cap smooth, medium-sized, white; lamellae bright rose-pink when young, soon
    puplish brown; ring membranous   69. *Agaricus campestris*
19 Cap smooth, large, yellowing slightly where bruised; ring double, thick; odour of
    aniseed   67. *Agaricus arvensis*
19 Cap scaly, brightly coloured or turning yellow on bruising   20
20 Cap scaly, brightly coloured, not bruising yellow..   21
20 Cap scaly and bruising yellow..   22
21 Cap small to medium, cap surface and stipe below ring covered with orange-
    coloured, soft, wart-like scales; lamellae soon purplish brown
    74. *Agaricus trisulphuratus*
21 Cap small, less than 40 mm diam., surface and stipe below ring covered with small,
    wine-red to purplish scales   72. *Agaricus diminutivus*
22 Cap small to medium, soon covered in small, lilac scales and wine-red fibres
    radiating to the white margin, finally dirty brownish; stipe with double membranous ring,
    yellowing at the bulbous base   71. *Agaricus semotus*
22 Cap medium to large, smooth white at first, later brownish or covered with fine,
    blackish, powdery scales, staining bright chrome-yellow on bruising; odour of carbolic
    acid   75. *Agaricus xanthodermus*
23 Cap and stipe concolorous: lilac, purplish or brownish; stipe without ring   24
23 Cap and stipe not concolorous; pale-coloured   25
24 Fruit-bodies smooth, lilac to purplish; lamellae slightly decurrent, turning rusty
    brown at maturity   61. *Lepista sordida*
24 Fruit-bodies small, deep yellow-brown to rusty brown, smooth; cap hemispherical;
    stipe tall, slender with bulbous base   50. *Agrocybe semiorbicularis*
25 Cap small, conical, smooth, ochreous-brown drying pale beige; stipe tall, slender,
    whitish; lamellae cinnamon at maturity   52. *Conocybe tenera*
25 Cap small, conical, smooth, margin grooved, chrome-yellow at first, fading brownish
    grey; lamellae pale yellow, maturing rusty brown   51. *Bolbitius vitellinus*
26 Fruit-bodies medium-sized to large; spore-bearing part egg-shaped   27
26 Fruit-bodies small with spore-bearing part globose, or medium-sized with spore-
    bearing part hemispherical..   28
27 Fruit-bodies white, shaggy with large, loose, white scales and white to greyish
    lamellae inside next to stipe   76. *Coprinus comatus*
27 Fruit-bodies greyish white, later brownish grey; spore sac tearing away from stipe
    at lower part and releasing olivaceous-brown to reddish-brown powdery spore
    mass; no lamellae inside   156. *Podaxis pistillaris*
28 Fruit-bodies small with ashy grey, globose spore sac with pimple-like apical pore,
    resting in a brownish cup on a narrow, erect, brown stipe   157. *Tulostoma albicans*
28 Fruit-body medium to large, consisting of a thick, bell-shaped brownish structure
    bearing a brown, powdery spore-mass on its convex upper surface, and covered
    at first by a glossy white to ochreous cap-like membrane; this structure supported
    on a tall stipe covered with shaggy, brownish scales.   155. *Battarrea stevenii*

29 Fruit-bodies with a single, porous, erect stipe bearing an apical, foul-smelling, dark-coloured spore mass 30

29 Fruit-bodies consisting of reddish upright arms branching and united at their upper parts into a lattice-like structure; arms bear dark-coloured and slimy spore masses on small projections on their inner surfaces.   145. *Clathrus transvaalensis*

30 Stipe medium-sized, bright golden yellow to apricot-orange, with apical, thimble-shaped cap covered with fetid, slimy, dark green spore mass   141. *Phallus rubicundus*

30 Stipe medium-sized to large, creamy white, bearing fetid, dark grey to greenish-black, slimy spores on small, cauliflower-like branches suspended from a white, apical disc.   142. *Itajahya galericulata*

31 Fruit-bodies underground, under surface cracks in sandy soil and under dunes of the northern Cape Province   160. *Terfezia pfeilii*

31 Fruit-bodies above ground; spores produced internally 32

32 Fruit-bodies white, globose, small, smooth or with small conical warts; spore mass finally ochreous-olive   152. *Vascellum pratense*

32 Fruit-bodies grey or brown... 33

33 Fruit-bodies medium to large, grey, soon chocolate to bay brown and fragile, breaking up to release purplish-grey to purplish-brown spores   151. *Calvatia lilacina*

33 Fruit-bodies pale greyish brown to blackish brown 34

34 Fruit-body surface smooth 35

34 Fruit-body surface rough, pale brown to bay brown or umber, covered with darker scales or flattened warts   148. *Scleroderma verrucosum*

35 Fruit-body medium-sized, flattened globose, pinkish pale brown, leathery, smooth at first, later finely scaly, splitting to reveal violet-grey spores   146. *Scleroderma cepa*

35 Fruit-bodies medium to large, globose to egg-shaped or irregular with rounded protuberances; surface smooth, ochreous brown streaked with black, resembling horse droppings   149. *Pisolithus tinctorius*

36 Fruit-body large; cap thick, fleshy, surface smooth, olive-brown; stipe thick, inflated towards the base, excentric; tubes deep, greenish yellow to yellowish olive; pores angular, small   93. *Phlebopus sudanicus*

36 Fruit-body with thin, leathery cap; cap surface greyish brown to brown, zonate, hairy, and with creamy white, shallow, circular pores underneath; stipe arising from subterranean sclerotium   118. *Lignosus sacer*

37 Fruit-bodies small, funnel-shaped with globose 'eggs' inside, resembling bird's nest; clustered on decaying twigs and other plant debris   158. *Cyathus olla*

KEY B Species occurring under broad-leafed trees..   1

1 Fruit-bodies umbrella-shaped with cap and central stipe   2

1 Fruit-bodies more or less globose, egg-shaped or pear-shaped, without a stipe 20

1 Fruit-bodies composed of a globose spore sac upon a star-shaped base 22

1 Fruit-bodies not as above 23

2 Cap with lamellae on lower surface   3

2 Cap with pores on lower surface 16

3 Lamellae white to cream, remaining so   4

3 Lamellae white at first changing to pink or salmon   7

3 Lamellae white or yellow to pink, changing to dark purplish brown or black   8

3 Lamellae some shade of red or brown, unchanging or darkening with age; spores white or brown.. 13

4 Fruit-bodies medium to large; stipe with prominent ring, and volval remains..............   5

4 Fruit-bodies small to medium; stipe without basal bulb or ring   6

5 Cap surface smooth, white or yellowish green, olive-green to olive-brown; prominent sac-like volva   5. *Amanita phalloides*

5 Cap surface pale brown with white, pyramidal warts, margin striate; stipe white; volva composed of two ridges at base of stipe   4. *Amanita pantherina*

5 Cap surface bright orange-yellow to red with loose, white, pyramidal warts   3. *Amanita muscaria*

5   Cap surface greyish brown, covered with greyish-white mealy patches, margin smooth; stipe widening downwards, brownish grey below ring; volva reduced to zone of small scales   1. *Amanita excelsa*

5   Cap surface reddish brown, covered with greyish-pink wart-like scales; stipe widening downwards, reddish brown, with large, membranous, striate ring; volval remains in form of a few white or faintly greenish warts scattered over top of basal bulb   9. *Amanita rubescens*

6   Fruit-body small, white; surface covered with appressed, reddish-brown scales, and central disc over a rounded umbo; stipe slender, cylindrical, fragile, almost smooth, with membranous ring which disappears later   24. *Lepiota cristata*

6   Fruit-body medium-sized; cap surface hazel-brown, sticky, depressed at centre, paler at striate, down-turned margin; stipe cylindrical, without ring, white to pale brownish grey, flared below lamellae, brittle   36. *Russula sororia*

7   Fruit-bodies small, white, with prominent, pointed umbo; stipe without ring; clustered on termite soil casts   44. *Termitomyces microcarpus*

7   Fruit-bodies white or greyish brown; stipe elongated into underground root-like pseudorhiza; associated with termites *Termitomyces* spp. ....KEY H

8   Lamellae maturing inky, black 9

8   Lamellae maturing greyish brown to purplish black; dry.. 10

9   Fruit-bodies small; cap acorn-shaped, brownish with glistening, mica-like particles over upper part, clustered on or near rotting wood   78. *Coprinus micaceus*

9   Fruit-bodies very small; caps pale buff, deeply grooved; occurring in large groups on stumps and/or adjacent soil   77. *Coprinus disseminatus*

9   Fruit-bodies small; caps long, conical, expanding flat, grey, covered with whitish to pale grey fibrils; stipe tall widening downwards   79. *Coprinus lagopus*

10 Fruit-bodies medium to large, whitish, surface covered with coloured scales........... 11

10 Fruit-bodies small to medium, yellow or orange, with or without scales on cap 12

11 Cap medium to large, covered with small, greyish-black scales; stipe tall, narrow, white, with ring; cap and stipe bruising vivid yellow   70. *Agaricus placomyces*

11 Cap small to medium, smooth and white at first, covered with small, lilac scales and with wine-red fibres radiating to the white margin, finally dirty brownish; stipe with double, membranous ring, yellowing at bulbous base   71. *Agaricus semotus*

11 Cap medium-sized, covered with numerous, small, brown, appressed scales; brownish scales on stipe below thick ring; flesh white, reddening when cut 73. *Agaricus sylvaticus*

11 Cap medium to large, covered in chestnut-brown, fibrous scales; lamellae white at first, later brown; cap and stipe bruising yellowish; flesh reddish with age; odour of bitter almonds   65. *Agaricus augustus*

12 Fruit-bodies small; cap sulphur-yellow with dark brown central disc and dark brown, wart-like scales in concentric circles over upper surface; occurring in dense clusters in ground next to stump   81. *Hymenagaricus luteolosporus*

12 Fruit-bodies small; cap bell-shaped, smooth, orange-red; stipe tall, slender, pale brownish orange, attached by yellow mycelial threads to woody debris 86. *Stropharia aurantiaca*

13 Cap depressed or funnel-shaped; lamellae decurrent... 14

13 Cap convex to umbonate.. 15

14 Cap small, centrally depressed, ochreous to tawny, margin striate, lamellae deep pink, maturing dusty with white spores   17. *Laccaria laccata*

14 Cap medium to large, centrally depressed to funnel-shaped, margin strongly inrolled; lamellae pale ochre to sienna, decurrent on cylindrical stipe 62. *Paxillus involutus*

15 Cap small to medium, convex, margin incurved, pale ochreous tan; stipe whitish, granular over upper part   57. *Hebeloma crustuliniforme*

15 Cap medium to large, rich golden tawny, surface covered with small, appressed, fibrous scales; stipe widest near its middle; found clustered at base of tree or stumps 55. *Gymnopilus junonius*

16 Fruit-bodies medium-sized, woody or corky, brown; stipitate; pore surface white, bleeding red when bruised; associated with *Acacia* spp. 99. *Amauroderma rudé*
16 Fruit-body fleshy; stipe central or excentric or lateral.................................... 17
17 Stipe shorter than diameter of cap, excentric or lateral; fruit-bodies large, bright yellow to orange-yellow, surface irregularly lumpy; stipe excentric and attached to root, or lateral and attached to pad of mycelium at base of tree 122. *Pseudophaeolus baudonii*
17 Stipe central, length equal to or exceeding cap diameter 18
18 Stipe surface smooth, cinnamon to rusty tawny, concolorous with smooth cap surface; pores whitish to pale yellow; occurring under oaks 91. *Gyroporus castaneus*
18 Stipe surface scaly or reticulate.. 19
19 Stipe buff-coloured, covered with small brownish-black to black, rounded scales, often tinted bluish green at the base, cap surface light cinnamon-buff, smooth, medium to large; pores whitish, bruising olive-brown; occurring under poplars 92.*Leccinum duriusculum*
19 Stipe surface covered with net-like pattern of raised, brownish threads; cap medium to large, surface smooth, pale straw to pale snuff-brown; pores greenish yellow; occurring under oaks 88. *Boletus aestivalis*
19 Stipe thick and white, surface covered over upper part with netlike pattern of white threads; cap medium to large, surface smooth, fawn to light brown, sticky when wet; pores cream, maturing olive-green; occurring under oaks and pines 89. *Boletus edulis*
20 Fruit-bodies medium to large, more or less globose to top-shaped or irregularly lumpy; surface smooth, ochreous brown streaked with black but bright orange yellow at the base; occurring under eucalyptus and black wattle 149. *Pisolithus tinctorius*
20 Fruit-bodies small, flattened globose or inverted pear-shaped...................... 21
21 Fruit-bodies scattered, flattened globose, pale brown to bay-brown or umber, covered with darker scales or flattened warts, and with short, thick, furrowed pillar-like base 148. *Scleroderma verrucosum*
21 Fruit-bodies clustered, pear-shaped, white, later pale greyish brown; surface studded with wart-like granules which are more numerous, taller and darker around the raised, apical pore 150. *Lycoperdon perlatum*
22 Spore sac with single apical pore and rays of star-shaped base often transversely cracked and forming a collar around the spore sac 153. *Geastrum triplex*
22 Spore sac with several pores on the upper part 154. *Myriostoma coliforme*
23 Fruit-bodies small, orange-yellow, consisting of clusters of erect, repeatedly branching, cylindrical branches 131. *Ramaria formosa*
23 Fruit-bodies otherwise.. 24
24 Fruit-bodies medium-sized, consisting of a white, erect, spongy stalk bearing a dark greenish-grey, slimy, foul-smelling spore mass on whitish, much branched structures attached to an apical disc 142. *Itajahya galericulata*
4 Fruit-bodies composed of four or five red, spongy, tapering arms, radiating from a short, central stipe and bearing greenish black, slimy, stinking spore masses on their upper surfaces; occurring under oak and eucalyptus trees 144. *Clathrus archeri*

KEY C Species occurring under pine trees... 1
1 Fruit-bodies umbrella-shaped with cap and central stipe 2
1 Fruit-bodies otherwise.. 34
2 Cap with lamellae on lower surface 3
2 Cap with pores on lower surface 27
3 Lamellae white to pale cream or pinkish, not darkening 4
3 Lamellae white to pink, turning dark purplish brown to black; 18
3 Lamellae clay-brown, rusty or cigar-brown 20
4 Ring present on stipe... 5
4 Ring not present on stipe.. 10
5 Fruit-bodies single; volva or volval remains on basal bulb of stipe; growing on ground under healthy trees.. 6

5 Fruit-bodies clustered, nearby, at the base of or on trunks of dead trees; caps small to medium, covered with small brownish scales; lamellae broad, pinkish cream 10. *Armillaria mellea*

6 Stipe with basal bulb and sac-like volva; cap surface smooth olive-green to brownish olive 5. *Amanita phalloides*

6 Stipe with basal bulb but volval remains present as warts or ridges over upper surface of basal bulb 7

7 Cap surface in brownish colours 8

7 Cap surface red or brownish pink 9

8 Cap with white pyramidal warts on surface, margin striate, volva composed of two ridges over basal bulb; stipe white 4. *Amanita pantherina*

8 Cap with greyish, mealy patches over surface, margin smooth, stipe brownish grey below ring; volva remains as a zone of small scales over basal bulb 1. *Amanita excelsa*

9 Cap surface reddish brown to brownish pink covered with greyish pink, wart-like scales; stipe reddish brown, widening downwards; volva remains as a few scattered warts on basal bulb 9. *Amanita rubescens*

9 Cap surface bright scarlet, orange-red to orange-yellow with scattered, white, pyramidal warts; stipe white; volva remains as concentric rings of wart-like scales over basal bulb 3. *Amanita muscaria*

10 Fruit-bodies white, firm, fleshy; lamellae gradually pink, decurrent on stipe; odour of fresh meal 41. *Clitopilus prunulus*

10 Fruit-bodies fleshy firm or cheesy brittle; cap surface reddish or brownish...................11

11 Cap surface in reddish colours; lamellae yellow 12

11 Cap surface in pale or dark brown colours, lamellae white to pale brownish 14

12 Cap surface sticky, purplish pink to vermilion, depressed at centre; lamellae yellowish 34. *Russula capensis*

12 Cap surface not sticky 13

13 Surface with prominent, broad umbo, deep violet, bluish purple to brownish purple; stipe tall, slender, white 33. *Russula caerulea*

13 Cap surface violet red, purplish red to brownish red, stipe flushed lilac to greyish rose; lamellae slightly decurrent 35. *Russula sardonia*

14 Cap depressed at centre... 15

14 Cap with central umbo.. 16

15 Fruit-bodies small to medium-sized, greyish sepia, margin downturned and deeply grooved; lamellae adnexed, creamy, edges browning 36. *Russula sororia*

15 Cap depressed to funnel-shaped, margin smooth, strongly inrolled, rusty brown to snuff-brown; lamellae decurrent, pale ochre or darker 62. *Paxillus involutus*

16 Cap medium-sized, clustered, surface smooth, reddish brown; stipe slender, whitish, longitudinally grooved, appearing twisted, tough fibrous 13. *Collybia distorta*

16 Stipe not grooved and fibrous 17

17 Cap smooth, fawn to smoky brown or blackish with odour of soap 39. *Tricholoma saponaceum*

17 Cap rusty-brown to dark brown, shiny and oily when moist; stipe white over upper third, streaked brown over lower part 38. *Tricholoma albobrunneum*

18 Cap medium-sized, white, covered with numerous, small, appressed, brown scales; stipe with brownish scales below ring, not bruising yellow 73. *Agaricus sylvaticus*

18 Cap and/or stipe bruising yellow 19

19 Cap medium to large, white, covered with chestnut-brown fibrous scales; flesh reddish in age; odour of bitter almonds 65. *Agaricus augustus*

19 Cap small to medium, white at first, covered with small, lilaceous scales with wine-red fibres radiating towards white margin, finally dirty brownish; stipe with double membranous ring, yellowing at bulbous base 71. *Agaricus semotus*

20 Stipe without ring 21

20 Stipe with thin, membranous ring, swollen in middle part but narrowing towards base; fruit-bodies clustered, medium-sized, bright golden tawny to brownish orange 55. *Gymnopilus junonius*

21 Stipe thin, tall, shiny black, hair-like, tough; cap small, pinkish brown, radially grooved; occurring in large numbers on fallen pine needles   31. *Marasmius androsaceus*

21 Stipe fleshy... 22

22 Fruit-bodies exuding milky fluid when cut 23

22 Fruit-bodies not exuding milky fluid when cut 24

23 Fruit-bodies medium-sized, mostly shallow funnel-shaped, orange to apricot-coloured with greenish tints which increase with age; stipe short, spotted with small depressions of brighter colours; sap carrot-coloured   18. *Lactarius deliciosus*

23 Fruit-bodies small, shallow funnel-shaped, surface liver-coloured to dull chestnut; stipe tall, reddish brown; lamellae pale buff to pale ochre; sap milky white
   19. *Lactarius hepaticus*

24 Fruit-bodies small to medium; cap pale brownish, surface smooth, sticky; upper part of stipe scaly.. 25

24 Fruit-bodies small; cap surface pale brownish to brownish pink; surface not sticky; upper part of stipe smooth 26

25 Cap smooth, sticky or shiny, pale beige to brownish, margin inrolled; lamellae pale brownish to rust-coloured; upper part of stipe with mealy appearance; odour of radishes   57. *Hebeloma crustuliniforme*

25 Cap smooth, pale cream at striate margin, darkening to light brown or cinnamon over centre, covered with clear, sticky fluid; stipe with small, granular scales over upper part, fibrous, hollow   58. *Hebeloma cylindrosporum*

26 Cap small, tawny to brick-red, depressed at centre; stipe same colour as cap, tough, fibrous; lamellae broad, pink, appearing powdered white with spores at maturity   17. *Laccaria laccata*

26 Cap small, bell-shaped with prominent umbo, pale buff with coarse, fibrous scales; stipe whitish, surface finely powdery   59. *Inocybe eutheles*

27 Cap thin, leathery, small to medium, depressed to funnel-shaped, surface zoned in brown shades; stipe thin, rusty-brown, velvety   102. *Coltricia perennis*

27 Cap thick, fleshy or spongy 28

28 Stipe short, central or excentric... 29

28 Stipe central, well developed, equal to or longer than diameter of cap...................... 30

29 Stipe short to longish or absent in sessile forms; cap large, surface velvety to finely hairy, orange brown to brown, margin ochre; pores large, pale greenish brown when fresh, bruising and drying brown   119. *Phaeolus schweinitzii*

29 Stipe short, central when in soil, excentric when cap is appressed to tree trunk; cap large, bright yellow to orange-yellow to ochre-buff, surface lumpy, hairless; pores small, bright yellow to ochre-buff   122. *Pseudophaeolus baudonii*

30 Stipe thick, whitish, bulbous, upper part covered by network of thin, white threads; cap medium to large, surface smooth, brown   89. *Boletus edulis*

30 Cap small to medium-sized; stipe surface smooth or covered with tiny granules or dots 31

31 Stipe smooth, pores large, compound, with several tubes opening into each pore   95. *Suillus bovinus*

31 Stipe smooth, cinnamon to sienna but chrome-yellow around the base; cap small, pores small, rust-coloured   90. *Chalciporus piperatus*

31 Stipe surface granular or spotted 32

32 Stipe surface pale-coloured, with dark-coloured spots and white ring; cap surface chestnut, sticky   97. *Suillus luteus*

32 Stipe without ring 33

33 Stipe tapering downwards, pale yellowish, streaked and spotted dark red; cap surface brown, pale towards margin   94. *Suillus bellinii*

33 Stipe of even thickness, yellow, upper part covered with yellow granules exuding milky droplets; cap surface rusty brown, smooth, sticky   96. *Suillus granulatus*

34 Fruit-bodies more or less globose, without stipe 35

34 Fruit-bodies otherwise.. 36

35 Fruit-bodies subglobose, potato-like, partly or entirely underground, pinkish to

yellow-brown; thread-like rhizomorphs attached to lower sides
140. *Rhizopogon luteolus*

35 Fruit-bodies above ground and on pine stumps, medium-sized, globose, yellow, covered with polygonal warts over the tough, outer skin, narrow, short, column of rhizomorphs at base   147. *Scleroderma citrinum*

36 Fruit-bodies irregularly shaped, crust-like, hairless, dark yellow-brown to blackish brown, with root-like threads attaching the lower surface to soil   159. *Rhizina undulata*

36 Fruit-bodies composed of clusters of branches or fan-shaped lobes or horizontal radiating arms 37

37 Fruit-bodies composed of clusters of white, erect, branches arising from a thicker base   130. *Clavulina cristata*

37 Fruit-bodies composed of four to nine bright orange-red to red arms, split towards their tips, radiating from a central disc, covered with patches of slimy, dark, greenish black, foul-smelling spore masses   143. *Aseroë rubra*

37 Fruit-bodies composed of clusters or rosettes of small, fan-shaped, thin, purplish brown to umber lobes; occurring among pine needles   132. *Thelephora terrestris*

KEY D Species occurring on dead wood.. 1
1 Cap soft, fleshy, lamellate.. 2
1 Cap thin, leathery, lamellate 14
1 Cap with pores underneath, fleshy, thick 18
1 Cap with pores underneath, woody or corky, thick 21
1 Cap with pores underneath, thin, leathery... 28
1 Fruit-bodies otherwise.. 37
2 Fruit-bodies sessile.. 3
2 Fruit-bodies with stipe.. 4
3 Fruit-bodies overlapping; cap fan-shaped, surface smooth, beige to flesh-brown with purplish to blue-grey tints; occurring on dead stumps of broad-leafed trees 32. *Pleurotus ostreatus*

3 Fruit-bodies grouped, fan-shaped, white to yellowish with greyish, water-soaked margin; lamellae white to brownish; occurring on dead hardwood logs and stumps 53. *Crepidotus mollis*

3 Fruit-bodies grouped, fan to kidney-shaped with lobate margins; surface smooth, white; lamellae white to yellowish-flesh colour; occurring on thin, dead branches 54. *Crepidotus variabilis*

3 Fruit-bodies clustered; cap petal-shaped, margins incurved, surface velvety, buffy yellow to darker with a lilac to mauve hairy area near attachment; occurring on pine stumps only   63. *Paxillus panuoides*

4 Fruit-bodies small, bright yellow; lamellae white 5
4 Fruit-bodies small to large; lamellae coloured.. 6
5 Cap lemon-yellow; stipe concolorous, club-shaped; occurring on thin, hardwood branches or on soil   27. *Leucocoprinus birnbaumii*

5 Cap small with yellow-orange, tuft-like scales; stipe cylindrical, bright yellow-orange, scaly below ring; occurring on dead hardwood logs   14. *Cyptotrama asprata*

6 Cap umbonate, greenish grey to bluish grey; lamellae white turning brownish pink; occurring on dead hardwood logs   42. *Pluteus salicinus*

6 Lamellae brown or black at maturity 7
7 Lamellae brown... 8
7 Lamellae black 10
8 Cap cinnamon to buff, small, with white, woolly mycelium at base of stipe; occurring on hardwood logs   64. *Tubaria furfuracea*

8 Cap in orange-brown colours, mostly on pine wood...................................... 9
9 Cap large, golden yellow to tawny; lamellae rust-coloured; stipe spindle-shaped; occurring in clusters at base of trunks and stumps of pine trees and occasionally broad-leafed trees   55. *Gymnopilus junonius*

9 Cap small to medium, brownish orange with paler margin; lamellae yellowish,

darkening to tawny; occurring on pine logs 56. *Gymnopilus penetrans*

10 Cap greyish, greyish brown to brownish 11
10 Cap white or bright yellow 13
11 Cap very small, 10 mm diam.; occurring in large groups on stumps of broad-leafed
    trees or adjacent soil 77. *Coprinus disseminatus*
11 Cap 10-40 mm diam.; occurring in groups at base of broad-leafed trunks, stumps
    or buried wood.. 12
12 Cap conical, greyish with greyish scales; margin splitting and inrolled upwards
    as spores mature with production of inky fluid 79. *Coprinus lagopus*
12 Cap small, brownish buff to rusty yellow, covered in young stage with glistening,
    mica-like particles; clustered on ground and at bases of trunks and stumps of broad-
    leafed trees 78. *Coprinus micaceus*
13 Cap sulphur-yellow, darker to orange-tan over centre; occurring in dense clusters on
    broad-leafed stumps and logs 82. *Hypholoma fasciculare*
13 Cap white when dry, pale beige to buffy brown over centre; stipe silvery white,
    smooth, fragile, without ring; grouped on logs and stumps of broad-leafed trees
    or on adjoining soil 84. *Psathyrella candolleana*
14 Fruit-bodies sessile or with indistinct stipe 15
14 Fruit-bodies with stipe.. 16
15 Cap small, surface greyish, densely hairy; lamellae split longitudinally; occurring
    mostly on broad-leafed logs and stumps, occasionally on pine logs
    37. *Schizophyllum commune*
15 Cap medium to large, surface hairy, whitish to greyish brown; lamellae anastomosing,
    branching, elongate, forming pores in places; solitary, grouped or compound and
    overlapping on dead hardwood logs and stumps 116. *Lenzites betulina*
15 Cap small to large, surface coarsely hairy, zoned dark brown to blackish with
    bright yellow-brown margin; lamellae brownish ochre to reddish brown,
    anastomosing, and forming elongate pores in places; grouped or compound
    on pine logs and stumps 113. *Gloeophyllum sepiarium*
16 Lamellae edges entire; fruit-bodies small, funnel-shaped, cream to straw-coloured,
    surface smooth; grouped on dead, thinner branches of hardwood trees
    40. *Trogia cantharelloides*
16 Lamellae narrow, edges finely serrated.. 17
17 Fruit-bodies medium to large, deeply depressed to funnel-shaped; surface smooth,
    white to cream to pale ochre, darker in centre; stipe short and thick with ring near
    its apex; scattered or grouped on dead trunks and logs of broad-leafed trees
    20. *Lentinus sajor-caju*
17 Fruit-bodies small to medium; cap deeply depressed to funnel-shaped, margin
    strongly inrolled; surface densely hairy especially towards margin, dark reddish
    to purplish brown to almost black; stipe scaly; grouped on dead logs of broad-leafed
    trees 21. *Lentinus stupeus*
17 Fruit-bodies small to medium, resembling those of *Lentinus stupeus* but with long,
    curly hairs forming scattered, erect scales over centre of cap; surface cream at first,
    darkening to pale blackish brown 23. *Lentinus villosus*
17 Fruit-bodies small to medium; cap deeply depressed to broadly funnel-shaped,
    surface uniformly velvety, without zones and uniformly pale greyish cinnamon to tawny
    brown; stipe tall, slender, velvety, same colour as cap 22. *Lentinus velutinus*
18 Fruit-bodies small, yellow-orange to brownish orange, gelatinous-fleshy with large,
    shallow pores of different sizes on lower surface; stipe lateral; grouped on twigs
    15. *Favolaschia thwaitesii*
18 Fruit-bodies large, with short, lateral stipe; pores formed by numerous separate
    tubes 98. *Fistulina africana*
    Fruit-bodies large, pores not formed by separate tubes 19
19 Fruit-bodies with stipe or sessile and compound on pine stumps; surface hairy,
    bright yellow to brown; pores greenish yellow, browning on bruising
    119. *Phaeolus schweinitzii*

19 Upper surface of fruit-bodies hairless to finely downy 20
20 Fruit-bodies compound, sessile; cap sulphur-yellow to yellow-orange, suede-like,
    surface uneven, fading to white in age; occurring on trunks and stumps of oak and
    eucalyptus   115. *Laetiporus sulphureus*
20 Fruit-bodies large, single or compound, bracket-shaped; surface irregularly lumpy,
    hairless, orange-yellow when young, drying to buff or brownish; closely appressed
    to wood surface, arising from a pad of tissue at its base; occurring on dead stems
    of pines, eucalyptus and other trees and plants   122. *Pseudophaeolus baudonii*
21 Fruit-bodies bracket-shaped; upper surface covered by a crust 22
21 Fruit-bodies bracket-shaped or hoof-shaped; upper surface otherwise...................... 23
22 Crust thick, hard, dull brown; pore surface white   100. *Ganoderma applanatum*
22 Crust thin, lacquer-like, yellow to deep red   101. *Ganoderma lucidum*
23 Upper surface hairy, at least in younger parts 24
23 Upper surface hairless... 26
24 Surface hair white to cream, greenish in older parts; fruit-body hard, thick; pores
    narrow, elongated, maze-like, creamy white; occurring on logs and stumps of broad-
    leafed trees, often *Acacia* spp.   125. *Trametes meyenii*
24 Surface and hairs some other colour... 25
25 Surface hair long, tawny to rust-coloured, turning grey and disappearing in age;
    hymenial surface brownish cream, pore mouths angular; fruit-body closely appressed
    to logs of willow   112. *Funalia trogii*
25 Surface and hairs lilac on younger parts but greyish fawn to brownish in older parts
    which may also be hairless; pores bright rose to lilac-mauve; fruit-bodies occurring
    on oak or eucalyptus logs   110. *Fomitopsis lilacino-gilva*
26 Fruit-bodies bracket-shaped; upper surface white or coloured.................................... 27
26 Fruit-bodies hoof-shaped, upper surface dark grey to blackish, abundantly
    cracked both radially and concentrically; margin rounded, velvety, yellowish brown;
    pores yellowish brown, minute; occurring on hardwood stems   104. *Phellinus rimosus*
27 Upper surface smooth, pure white to creamy white; pores concolorous, elongated,
    maze-like; occurring on indigenous hardwood logs   117. *Lenzites elegans*
27 Upper surface shiny, smooth; fruit-bodies bright orange-red throughout; occurring
    on pine and hardwood logs, stumps and thinner branches 123. *Pycnoporus sanguineus*
27 Upper surface beige to pale brown; pore surface creamy white with wide, coarse,
    elongated, maze-like pores; occurring on oak logs   108. *Daedalea quercina*
27 Upper surface dark grey to brownish black; margin and pores creamy white;
    occurring on logs of indigenous broad-leafed trees   124. *Trametes cingulata*
28 Fruit-bodies circular, with stipe.. 29
28 Fruit-bodies bracket-shaped, substipitate or sessile.. 30
29 Stipe hairy or slightly scaly, central; cap circular, margin fringed with fine, short
    hairs; pores large, hexagonal to angular, radially elongated; occurring on dead
    wood of broad-leafed trees   120. *Polyporus arcularius*
29 Stipe excentric, cylindrical, dull dark brown; cap circular to fan-shaped, depressed,
    surface hairless, dark reddish brown to black, merging with stipe in fan-shaped
    specimens; pores minute, whitish; occurring on dead wood of indigenous hardwood
    trees   121. *Polyporus dictyopus*
30 Flesh and pores white to creamy white when fresh... 31
30 Flesh and pores pale brownish to dark brown when fresh... 33
31 Pores large, 1-2 per mm, angular, radially elongated   109. *Favolus spathulatus*
31 Pores small, 3-4 per mm, circular to angular, not radially elongated 32
32 Surface hairy, concentrically zoned in whitish to greyish to greenish cream
    106. *Coriolus hirsutus*
32 Surface velvety, with bluish, greyish to brown zones   107. *Coriolus versicolor*
33 Flesh yellow to pale yellow-brown 34
33 Flesh dark brown, umber or reddish brown.. 35
34 Surface velvety to hairy, concentrically zoned in yellowish buff to greyish; flesh thin,
    yellow, fibrous; occurring on dead stumps, logs and branches of broad-leafed trees

105. *Coriolopsis polyzona*

34 Surface yellow-brown to pale reddish brown, at first velvety later hairless, usually rough with stiff projections; flesh tough, yellow-brown in upper layer, sometimes darker below; occurring on logs and branches of dead hardwood trees 103. *Phellinus gilvus*

35 Upper surface of fruit-body smooth, hairless, reddish brown; pores shallow, hexagonal, 0,5-1 mm diam. 114. *Hexagona tenuis*

35 Upper surface of fruit-body dark brown, hairy.. 36

36 Surface hairs soft, brown, velvety to hairy; flesh corky, fibrous, olive-brown; pores angular to elongate, with greyish bloom inside when fresh 111. *Funalia protea*

36 Surface densely covered with dark yellowish-brown to greyish-brown hairs; lower surface with circular pores near margin, but radially elongate in older parts and bright lavender to lilac or purplish when fresh 126. *Trichaptum byssogenus*

37 Fruit-bodies bracket-shaped, shelf-shaped, fan-shaped or with partly reflexed cap; hymenial surface without lamellae or pores.. 38

37 Fruit-bodies otherwise.. 44

38 Entire fruit-body rusty brown, with ochre margin, effused-reflexed; hymenium smooth; occurring on dead hardwood logs 139. *Hymenochaete ochromarginata*

38 Fruit-bodies not rusty brown; surface umber to buff or ochre or other colours.......... 39

39 Hymenial surface white or creamy white 40

39 Hymenial surface creamy buff to greyish brown 41

40 Hymenial surface smooth, white; upper surface dark brown, hairy; fruit-bodies fan-shaped, often overlapping 133. *Laxitextum bicolor*

40 Hymenial surface covered with conspicuous, radiating ribs and warts; fruit-body woody, fan-shaped 134. *Cymatoderma elegans*

41 Upper surface hairless, smooth, zoned pale orange-brown to golden brown; hymenium smooth; fruit-bodies strap-shaped to fan-shaped, mostly with reduced base or short lateral stipe; translucent when fresh 135. *Podoscypha parvula*

41 Upper surface velvety to hairy, concentrically zoned in different colours.................. 42

42 Surface zoned in yellow-brown to reddish brown or greyish; hymenial surface reddish brown to greyish buff and 'bleeding' red when cut 136. *Stereum australe*

42 Hymenium not bleeding red when bruised or cut 43

43 Surface covered with bundled or matted hairs, zoned in greyish, light yellow-brown to light reddish brown; hymenium smooth, cream to buffy cinnamon to light orange; fruit-bodies often occurring in large groups 137. *Stereum hirsutum*

43 Fruit-bodies thin, fan-shaped; surface velvety, zoned in grey, greenish grey, light yellow-brown, hazel or chestnut brown; some zones hairless; hymenial surface cream to pale buff; often occurring in large groups 138. *Stereum ostrea*

44 Fruit-bodies small, finger-like, sparingly branched; gelatinous-tough, bright orange-yellow; grouped 128. *Calocera cornea*

44 Fruit-bodies otherwise.. 45

45 Fruit-bodies subglobose or pear-shaped enclosing a dark-coloured, powdery spore mass 46

45 Fruit-bodies otherwise.. 47

46 Fruit-bodies subglobose, lemon-yellow to ochre; outer surface covered with large, irregular, flattened, wart-like protuberences; basal column consisting of root-like threads; occurring on and near pine stumps and around pine trees 147. *Scleroderma citrinum*

46 Fruit-bodies pear-shaped, white; upper part thickly studded with tiny, persistent warts interspersed with darker, erect warts which disappear and leave small depressions; grouped on or around pine stumps 150. *Lycoperdon perlatum*

47 Fruit-body spreading skin-like over surface of dead log; margin white; older part lilac to brown and covered with irregular ridges in a net-like or angular pore-like pattern 129. *Serpula himantioides*

47 Fruit-body a yellow-orange, jelly-like mass with numerous contorted lobes and folds 127. *Tremella mesenterica*

KEY E Species occurring on living trees* 1
1 Fruit-bodies large, fleshy or woody.. 2
1 Fruit-bodies very small, delicate, fleshy, white with short lateral stipe and lamellae
  with lateral branches giving a coarsely pore-like appearance near the margin
  11. *Campanella capensis*
2 Fruit-bodies with a hard, shiny or dull crust on upper surface 3
2 Fruit-bodies without crust.. 4
3 Fruit-bodies with lateral stipe and a horny, dark brownish-red to maroon crust;
  hymenial surface with pores formed by numerous, short, separate, ochre tubes
  98. *Fistulina africana*
3 Fruit-bodies sessile, bracket-shaped, thick; upper surface with hard, dull brown
  crust, concentrically grooved; hymenial surface white, pores small; tubes brown
  and in layers   100. *Ganoderma applanatum*
3 Fruit-bodies sessile, substipitate or stipitate with lacquer-like, yellowish to red to dark
  chestnut-brown crust over upper surface and stipe   101. *Ganoderma lucidum*
4 Fruit-bodies sessile 5
4 Fruit-bodies with short or long stipe... 6
5 Fruit-bodies tough, leathery, hairy, whitish to pale ochre; hymenial surface
  appearing lamellate, with circular to elongated pores   116. *Lenzites betulina*
5 Fruit-bodies large, compound, with numerous bright, yellow to orange-yellow,
  fleshy, overlapping lobes, fading to white with age; pores small, angular
  115. *Laetiporus sulphureus*
5 Fruit-bodies large, single or compound, bright orange-yellow, fading to buff; spongy-
  cheesy, brittle, pores small, angular; loosely attached and arising from a pad of tissue
  attached to underground parts of the trunk   122. *Pseudophaeolus baudonii*
5 Fruit-bodies hoof-shaped, hard, with grey to black, cracked upper surface; margin brown,
  velvety; hymenial surface with minute, circular pores   104. *Phellinus rimosus*
6 Stipe central or excentric, well developed, dark brown, bearing inverted conical
  cap; cap surface velvety, zonate, brown, plane or depressed; hymenial surface
  silvery white, poroid, bleeding red when bruised   99. *Amauroderma rudé*
6 Stipe excentric, poorly developed, attached underground to root or trunk; cap thick,
  bright orange-yellow to buff, spongy-cheesy, brittle; hymenial surface with tiny,
  yellowish pores   122. *Pseudophaeolus baudonii*
6 Stipe excentric, lateral or absent; cap circular to fan-shaped, tough, with velvety
  to woolly, ochre to rust-brown surface; pores angular, greenish yellow, darkening
  to brown on bruising; occurring on or near pine stumps and trunks
  119. *Phaeolus schweinitzii*

  * The fruit-bodies may actually occur on a dead branch or part of a trunk

KEY F Species occurring on compost and plant litter 1
1 Fruit-bodies mushroom-like with cap, lamellae and stipe 2
1 Fruit-bodies otherwise 3
2 Fruit-bodies white, with salmon-pink lamellae and sac-like volva   49. *Volvariella speciosa*
2 Fruit-bodies brownish, lamellae at first rose-pink, soon turning purplish-brown;
  stipe with membranous ring   66. *Agaricus bisporus*
2 Fruit-bodies with smooth, shiny, orange-red to reddish-brown cap; stipe tall with
  disappearing ring; lamellae adnate, creamy white changing to dark olivaceous
  yellow and finally greyish brown   86. *Stropharia aurantiaca*
3 Fruit-bodies resembling tiny bird's nest with eggs   158. *Cyathus olla*
3 Fruit-bodies otherwise.. 4
4 Fruit-bodies with short, spongy stipe arising from membranous egg-like structure,
  and bright orange-red, radiating arms; emits a foul odour.. 5
4 Fruit-bodies otherwise.. 6
5 Arms 4-6 in number, tapering towards the tips, covered with irregular patches of
  greenish-black, slimy, foul-smelling spore masses   144. *Clathrus archeri*

5 Arms 5-9 in number, tapering and splitting into two thinner arms towards the tips; dark, greenish black; slimy spore mass emitting foul odour over central disc at the base of the arms   143. *Aseroë rubra*
6 Fruit-bodies consisting of subglobose spore-sac with a single apical pore, and sessile on a star-shaped base with 4-8 thick, sharp-pointed, recurved rays   153. *Geastrum triplex*
6 Fruit-bodies consisting of subglobose spore-sac with 4-8 pores, and supported on a number of short columns on a star-shaped base   154. *Myriostoma coliforme*

KEY G Species occurring on herbivore dung

Fruit-bodies mushroom-shaped, with cap, lamellae and stipe.................................... 1
1 Cap and stipe in bright yellow colours 2
1 Cap and stipe grey or brown... 3
2 Cap shiny egg-yellow, conical to bell-shaped, margin grooved; stipe slender, finely powdery, without ring 51. *Bolbitius vitellinus*
2 Cap shiny, light yellow, hemispherical, smooth, margin even; stipe smooth, tall, with thin, appressed, membranous ring 87. *Stropharia semiglobata*
3 Fruit-bodies small; cap smooth, shiny, tan, pale reddish brown; lamellae grey-brown, darkening evenly to dark brown 85. *Psilocybe coprophila*
4 Fruit-bodies small on tall stipes; cap smooth, pale grey to dark brownish grey when wet; lamellae mottled by uneven maturation of spores, finally evenly black 83. *Panaeolus papilionaceus*

KEY H Species occurring on or around termite nests*.. 1

1 Fruit-bodies mushroom-shaped with cap, lamellae and stipe....................................... 2
1 Fruit-bodies tall; stipe carrying elongated, egg-shaped, spore-bearing part which releases dark brown spores from its base at maturity   156. *Podaxis pistillaris*
2 Cap small, whitish, with sharp-pointed umbo; stipe without rooting base; occurring in troops on termite soil casts on soil surface   44. *Termitomyces microcarpus*
2 Cap medium to large; stipe elongated into underground rooting base (pseudorhiza).. 3
3 Pseudorhiza concolorous with portion of stipe above ground 4
3 Pseudorhiza dark greyish brown to black 5
4 Cap greyish brown with prominent, sharp-pointed umbo; stipe slender, very tough, slightly or not at all thickened underground 43. *Termitomyces clypeatus*
4 Cap white, with slight, rounded umbo greyish to brown and surrounded by scale-like patches of adhering sand grains in concentric circles; pseudorhiza long, even, or tapering gradually downwards 45. *Termitomyces reticulatus*
4 Cap thick, fleshy, white, with thick, brownish to dark brown scales over centre and more or less concentrically around it; stipe with thick sheath-like ring; surface below ring coarsely scaly   47. *Termitomyces schimperi*
5 Cap greyish brown with prominent, sharply conical umbo; stipe thickened below ground and tapering to a dark brownish pseudorhiza 46. *Termitomyces sagittiformis*
5 Cap large, evenly ochre-brown or paler towards the margin, slightly to markedly umbonate; stipe cream-coloured, thickened underground; pseudorhiza tapering down wards, covered by dark grey to black, longitudinal striae 48. *Termitomyces umkowaani*

* Certain species of fungus-growing termites do not build conspicuous mounds. In such cases the presence of a long underground pseudorhiza will indicate a *Termitomyces* spp.

ABBREVIATIONS AND SYMBOLS

mm: millimetre	mg: milligram	☠ ☠: Deadly poisonous
iam.: diameter	kg: kilogram	
cm: centimetre	/: per	? ☠: Suspected
µm: micrometre (1/1000 mm)	☠ : Poisonous	Poisonous

SUBDIVISION: BASIDIOMYCOTINA

1. Amanita excelsa (Fr.) Kummer

Edibility unknown

Amanita excelsa has been recognized in southern Africa only recently – in the eastern Cape and in the Transvaal. It may be mistaken for the similar *A. pantherina* but differs from this species by having dull greyish scales over the cap, a smooth margin, and greyish-brown colours on the underside of the ring and scaly lower stipe. The distinct ridges of volval remains characteristic of *A. pantherina* are absent from *A. excelsa.*

A. *excelsa* forms mycorrhizae with pines but grows under broad-leafed trees as well. The fruit-bodies appear in late summer and autumn after good rains. Its edibility is unknown, but in view of the danger of confusing it with the poisonous *A. pantherina* it is not recommended for eating.

Fruit-bodies attached to substrate by stipe (stipitate)

Fruit-bodies single or scattered under pine trees. ***Cap:*** 60-120 mm diam., fleshy, convex at first expanding to flat; margin even, smooth, splitting with age and turning upwards. Surface brownish grey to almost umber with the cuticle smooth and dry but ornamented with irregular, whitish-grey to beige, mealy to hoary scales. ***Stipe:*** Central, stout, widening downwards towards the bulbous base; 45-100 x 7-20 mm but up to 30 mm diam. in the bulbous base. White and striate above the ring, ashy grey to pale olive-grey below; one to two ridges of scales (the remains of the volva) over the upper parts of the bulbous base; fleshy-tough, solid. Ring membranous, persistent, white and striate on upper surface, ashy grey to pale olive-grey on under surface. ***Lamellae:*** Free, crowded, full and intermediate lengths, thin, margins entire; white. ***Flesh:*** White, firm, thick, unchanging when cut; with a slight, unpleasant odour. ***Spore print:*** White. ***Spores:*** Hyaline, broadly ellipsoidal to ovoid, smooth, amyloid; 8-10 x 5-8 μm.

2. Amanita foetidissima Reid & Eicker   *Stinke*

Edibility unknown

Amanita foetidissima occurs in the eastern Cape, Natal and eastern Transvaal in summer to early autumn. Heavy rain may wash the scales off the cap making recognition difficult. The scaly stipe and characteristic odour may then indicate its identity.

A. *foetidissima* has been known as *A. strobiliformis* and even *A. solitaria* in southern Africa but research has shown that it differs from both of these in microscopic characters. The strong, sickly sweet odour from which this species derives its name is not present in *A. strobiliformis.* As most *Amanita* species are poisonous, this species is best regarded as dangerous. (*Afrikaans:* Stinksampioen.)

Cap margin appendiculate (with adhering veil fragments)

Fruit-bodies usually grouped in grassy places. ***Cap:*** 45-120 mm, fleshy, somewhat conical when young expanding to convex; margin regular, incurved, extending slightly beyond the lamellae and appendiculate with adhering veil fragments. Surface scaly with large, thick, soft, irregular, cream to buff scales, occasionally with pale brown tinges; in more or less concentric circles over the pale creamy-white cap surface; slightly sticky and adhering to fingers when handled. ***Stipe:*** Central, 90-180 x 12-22 mm, widening downwards to a bulbous, short-rooting base; pale cream to pale buff, area below ring covered with soft, cream to pale brownish, irregular scales; upper surface of basal bulb with faint rings of wart-like scales; fleshy-tough, solid. Ring persistent, fixed, membranous, striate on upper surface. ***Lamellae:*** Free, crowded, full and intermediate lengths, thin, edges entire, up to 8 mm broad; creamy white or with a pale pinkish tinge. ***Flesh:*** Firm, creamy white, unchanging, up to 10 mm thick; with cloying, sickly-sweet, fetid odour. ***Spore print:*** White. ***Spores:*** Hyaline, ovoid to subglobose or ellipsoidal, smooth, thin-walled, amyloid; 7-10 x 6-8 μm.

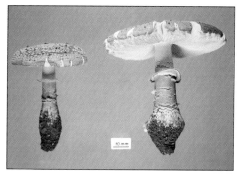

Amanita excelsa showing scaly cap surface, white lamellae, and grey stipe below ring with volval remains on bulbous base.

Amanita excelsa

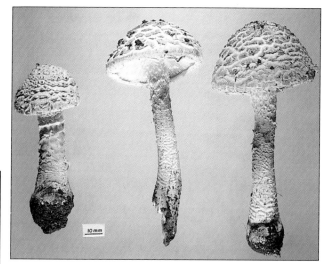

Amanita foetidissima showing coarsely scaly cap and stipe, incurved cap margin with adhering veil remnants and wart-like scales on bulbous base of stipe.

Amanita foetidissima **Stinker**

Poisonous

3. Amanita muscaria (L.:Fr.) Hooker　　　　　*Fly Agaric*

Amanita muscaria is widespread throughout southern Africa, occurring under pines and occasionally oaks, with which it forms mycorrhizae. Fruit-bodies appear in summer and autumn, either singly or in scattered groups under older trees. The striking fruit-bodies with bright red, white-warted caps make this the most easily recognized species of mushroom.

　　A. muscaria is poisonous, but seldom fatal. It causes nausea, vomiting, giddiness, hallucinations, convulsions and even loss of consciousness one to three hours after eating. Arctic people use the dried fruit-bodies as an inebriant, and reindeer are known to become addicted to them. Duiker and probably also porcupines eat the fruit-bodies in southern African plantations. The common name of this species derives from the centuries-old practice of using broken pieces of the fruit-body in a saucer of milk to attract and kill flies. (*Afrikaans:* Vlieëgifswam.)

Fruit-bodies single or grouped under pines and oaks. *Cap:* Up to 200 mm diam., fleshy, globose at first, opening to flat; margin even, sometimes with adhering veil fragments, usually striate at maturity. Surface vermilion, scarlet, orange-red to orange-yellow, covered with conspicuous white to faintly yellowish warts; smooth, sticky when young, later dry. *Stipe:* Central, 90-200 x 10-30 mm, white to yellowish, mostly cylindrical or widening to a bulbous base; usually covered with shaggy, loose scales and with a series of partial ridges or warts over the upper parts of the basal bulb; firm, solid or stuffed. Ring membranous, soft, white or yellowish, often drying and disappearing. *Lamellae:* Free, crowded, full and intermediate lengths, thin, edges entire, broad; white. *Flesh:* Thick and soft, white but yellowish under the red skin, unchanging; odourless but with increasingly bitter taste with age. *Spore print:* White. *Spores:* Hyaline, subglobose, smooth, thin-walled, non-amyloid; 10-12 x 7-10 μm.

Fruit-bodies with flat caps

Poisonous

4. Amanita pantherina (DC.:Fr.) Kummer.　　　*Warted Agaric*

Amanita pantherina is widely distributed throughout the region. It is common in pine plantations, forming mycorrhizae with pines although it may also form them with oaks and *Eucalyptus* species. Fruit-bodies appear in late summer to autumn after good rains. The greyish-brown cap with white warts, striate cap margin and volval rings and ridges around the basal part of the stipe make this species easy to recognize.

　　A. pantherina is poisonous, causing nausea, vomiting and loss of consciousness one to three hours after eating; death may occur if the patient is not treated promptly. It is known to have caused a number of deaths as well as serious illness in southern Africa. (*Afrikaans:* Tiersampioen.)

Fruit-bodies solitary, scattered or grouped under pines, *Eucalyptus* spp., and oaks. *Cap:* 50-130 mm diam., fleshy, hemispherical at first, later flattened with margin turning upwards; margin even, striate. Surface smooth, sticky and pale greyish brown at first, later smoky brown, yellowish brown or brownish olive and covered with large, white, floccose warts, often in more or less concentric rings. *Stipe:* Central, 70-130 x 10-20 mm, widening towards the basal bulb; white, firm, smooth; fleshy-tough, solid at first, soon hollow. Ring tattered, persistent and membranous without striae or grooves, and attached high up on stipe. Basal bulb with one or two, white, belt-like rings above it and closely wrapped by the volva which forms a distinct free rim. *Lamellae:* Free, crowded, thin, edges entire; white. *Flesh:* Thin, firm, white, unchanging; with odour and taste of raw potato. *Spore print:* White. *Spores:* Hyaline, broadly ovoid, smooth, thin-walled, non-amyloid; 9-10,5 x 6,2-8 μm.

Stipe with volval rings around base

Amanita muscaria showing central stipe with bulbous base, distinctive red cap, and membranous ring attached to apex of stipe.

☠ *Amanita muscaria* **Fly Agaric**

☠ *Amanita pantherina* **Warted Agaric**

Amanita pantherina showing striate cap margin, membranous ring, and belt-like rings above basal bulb wrapped by volva which forms a free rim around it.

5. Amanita phalloides (Vaill.:Fr.) Secr. *Death Cap*

Amanita phalloides is known throughout the region. The fruit-bodies develop after rains in summer to autumn under oaks, pines and poplars with which it forms mycorrhizae. It is not as common as other species of *Amanita* however. The species is readily recognicable by the olivaceous yellow-green colours of the cap surface, the white lamellae and stipe, and the white, sac-like volva which envelopes the basal bulb below ground level.

A. phalloides is the most deadly poisonous mushroom known. It is reported that 30 g of fresh cap, when eaten, is sufficient to cause death in an adult. This mushroom contains amatoxins which cause extensive liver and kidney damage resulting in 50-90 % mortality. The symptoms, which include violent abdominal pains, vomiting, thirst and diarrhoea, appear from six to 24 hours after ingestion during which time the cells of the liver and kidneys are damaged. Unless the symptoms are recognized early and treated promptly, death occurs after a few days. No effective antidote to the amatoxins has been developed as yet. (*Afrikaans:* Duiwelsbrood; Slangkos.)

Fruit-bodies single or scattered on ground under oaks, pines and occasionally poplars. *Cap:* 50-150 mm diam., fleshy, subglobose at first expanding to convex, later flattened; margin even, downturned, splitting and often with adhering veil fragments. Surface smooth, sticky when wet, satiny when dry; in various shades of greenish yellow-olive, smoky brownish green to smoky olive, darker towards the centre, often streaked with radiating, dark fibrils. *Stipe:* Central, white, more or less cylindrical, 50-150 x 8-20 mm, widening into a bulbous base which is enveloped in a large, white, sac-like volva; smooth or faintly banded; fleshy-tough, solid at first, later hollow. Ring white, persistent, membranous and attached near the apex. *Lamellae:* Free, crowded, full and intermediate lengths, thin, edges entire; white. *Flesh:* Thin, white with faint yellowish flush under the skin, unchanging; with a faint, sickly sweetish odour when young, stronger and unpleasant when old. *Spore print:* White. *Spores:* Hyaline, broadly ellipsoidal to subglobose, smooth, thin-walled, amyloid; 8-10 x 7-9 μm.

Stipe with sac-like volva

6. Amanita phalloides var. alba

This mushroom resembles *A. phalloides* in all morphological characters except that the cap surface is white and occasionally faintly yellowish over the central part. This mushroom was found growing in the leaf-litter under *Eucalyptus cloeziana* at Sabie in early December and again in March, together with *A. phalloides* var. *umbrina* (described below). It corresponds closely with descriptions of *Amanita verna*, the Spring Amanita, which appears in Europe in early spring, but which has not been reported from southern Africa.

A white Amanita was reported to occur in spring in the south-western Cape Province by the late Miss Edith L. Stephens who referred to it as *Amanita capensis*. As a formal description was never published, this name is invalid, and because no type specimen exists, its identity cannot be determined.

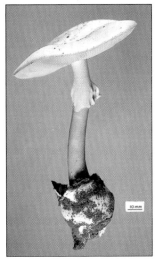

Amanita phalloides showing persistent, membranous ring and white, sac-like volva around basal bulb of stipe.

 *Amanita phalloides*
Death Cap

Amanita phalloides
var. *alba*

Deadly poisonous

Edibility unknown

7. Amanita phalloides var. umbrina

This mushroom resembles *A. phalloides* in all morphological characters except that numerous dark grey-brown radiating fibrils are present in the whitish surface of the cap so imparting a greyish-brown colour. This colour may be deeper over the central part or towards the margin or more or less even over the cap surface.

A. phalloides var. *umbrina* was found at the same time and localities as *A. phalloides* var. *alba*. For this reason these collections are regarded as varieties of *A. phalloides* which has the characteristic olivaceous yellow-green cap colours.

These specimens were described as a distinct new species recently, namely, *Amanita reidii* Eicker & van Greuning.

8. Amanita pleropus (Kalchbr. & MacOwan) Reid

Amanita pleropus is a rare and little-known species. It was recorded during the last century from Inanda, Natal, and Boschberg, Somerset East, and has been found around Pretoria during the last few years. The fruit-bodies appear in mid-summer in lawns and may well be more widely distributed than is presently known.

This species resembles *A. rubescens,* which is common in pine planta-tions, but may be distinguished by the absence of whitish warts on the cap, its creamy coloured lamellae that do not bruise red, and its habitat in grassy places, away from trees. Its resemblance to *A. rubescens* might have caused confusion in the past which may account for its low rate of record-ings. As most species of *Amanita* are known to be poisonous, *A. pleropus* is best avoided.

Fruit-bodies grouped or clustered in grassy areas, often forming fairy rings. *Cap:* 50-160 mm diam., hemispherical at first expanding to convex, finally flat with a slightly depressed centre; margin even, smooth, incurved, pro-jecting beyond lamellae, with remnants of veil attached. Surface brick-red to reddish brown, rough, scaly to warty, the warts flattened, irregular or somewhat pyramidal. *Stipe:* Central, 40-110 x 10-25 mm, cylindrical or widening somewhat towards a short spindle-shaped, rooting base; white to creamy white and smooth above the ring, smooth or somewhat scaly below the scales being mostly reddish brown; with two to four slight warty ridges (the remains of the volva) on the upper half of the basal swelling. Ring creamy white, membranous, somewhat granular on under surface, pendu-lous and persistent. *Lamellae:* Free, close to crowded, full and intermediate lengths, thin, edges entire; white to translucent creamy. *Flesh:* Creamy white to cream, brownish under cuticle, firm, unchanging, up to 10 mm thick; with faint, sickly sweet odour. *Spore print:* White to yellowish. *Spores:* Hyaline, ellipsoidal, smooth, thin-walled, amyloid; 10-14 x 7,7-9,7 μm

☠☠ *Amanita phalloides*
var. *umbrina*

Amanita pleropus

Amanita pleropus showing brick-red, wart-like scales on cap surface and stipe, creamy white lamellae, and warty ridges on upper part of basal swelling, above the rooting base.

9. Amanita rubescens (Pers.: Fr.) S.F. Gray   *Blusher*

Edible

Amanita rubescens is distributed throughout southern Africa. It is fairly common under pines and oaks during summer and autumn and forms my-corrhizae with both of them. It differs from other species of *Amanita* by the reddish colours of the fruit-bodies, the slightly greenish, striate, pendulous ring, and the tendency of the flesh to turn pink (blush) when cut or bruised.

    A. rubescens is edible and tasty but in the Transvaal soon becomes infested with maggots. Because of the danger of mistaking the poisonous *A. pantherina* and suspect *A. excelsa* for this species, it is not recommended for eating however. (*Afrikaans:* Vals tieramaniet.)

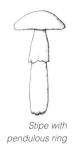

Stipe with pendulous ring

Fruit-bodies single, scattered or grouped on ground under pine trees and oaks. *Cap:* 60-150 mm diam., fleshy, hemispherical at first expanding to flat; margin even, smooth or faintly striate. Surface smooth, rosy brown to reddish brown or pinkish fawn, covered in patches of irregular, loose, wart-like scales that come off easily. *Stipe:* Central, 60-140 x 10-15 mm at the top, widening to 25-40 mm at the bulbous base where faint, concentric ridges mark the remains of the volva; smooth, white at the top, but concolorous with the cap below the ring and somewhat scaly; fleshy-tough, hollow in age. Ring thin, soft, pendulous, membranous; pale cream to faintly greenish and conspicuously striate, appearing pleated, the striae continuing on the the upper part of the stipe. *Lamellae:* Free, crowded, full and intermediate lengths, thin, edges entire; white but staining reddish when cut or bruised. *Flesh:* White, turning pink when cut or bruised, especially in the stipe; faint, indistinct odour and mild to later acrid taste. *Spore print:* White. *Spores:* Hyaline, broadly ellipsoidal, smooth, amyloid; 7,2-9 x 5-7 µm.

10. Armillaria mellea *sensu lato*   *Honey Mushroom, Bootlace Fungus*

Edible

Armillaria mellea is widely distributed throughout southern Africa. It causes a serious disease of the roots and lower parts of the trunks of both broad-leafed and coniferous trees and shrubs. Its presence is indicated by death of the infected tree and the presence of a sheet of creamy-white mycelium underneath loose bark around the base of the trunk. Copious resin flow occurs in affected pines. On some dead trees dark, shoelace-like rhizomorphs are also present under the bark, on the roots and in the soil.

    At least five species are now being recognized in the *A. mellea* complex of species. Fruit-bodies appear mostly in autumn but seem to occur infrequently. All species in the *A. mellea* complex are edible when cooked but flavour varies according to species. (*Afrikaans:* Heuningswam.)

Fruit-bodies clustered on ground, on stumps or tree trunks. *Cap:* 30-60 mm diam., fleshy, convex at first becoming centrally depressed, later shallow funnel-shaped; margin wavy, striate, downturned at first, finally upturned. Surface cream to dark cream with centre honey-coloured, later streaked to spotted with dark tan; matt, dry, radially grooved or striate, with minute scattered, dark brown, pointed scales. *Stipe:* Central, long, cylindrical and bent 35-90 x 3-8 mm; creamy white but darkening towards the base; striate, the striae often appearing spirally twisted, becoming somewhat shaggy with loose, white, woolly scales to which spores adhere. Ring thin and membranous. *Lamellae:* Subdistant, decurrent on the stipe, full and intermediate lengths, up to 6 mm wide, thin, with slightly irregularly bayed edges; cream white at first, later darkening to pinkish brown. *Flesh:* Soft, creamy white, unchanged, thin to very thin over lamellae; with faint, pleasant, mushroomy odour. *Spore print:* White. *Spores:* Hyaline, ovoid to ellipsoidal, smooth, thin-walled; 8-10 x 5-7 µm.

Amanita rubescens
Blusher

Amanita rubescens at three
stages of growth, showing
warted cap surface,
pendulous ring and free,
crowded lamellae.

10 mm

Armillaria mellea **Honey Mushroom**

10 mm

Armillaria mellea showing depressed cap with
dark brown scales, decurrent lamellae and
tall, slender stipe with loose, woolly scales.

11. Campanella capensis (Berk.) Reid

The tiny fruit-bodies appearing in the photograph were found grouped on the bark of a living indigenous, broad-leafed tree in the Tsitsikamma Forest in early summer. The species was described originally, however, from decayed stalks of herbaceous plants from Table Mountain, and later from Natal. These records indicate wide distribution throughout the south-western, southern, and south-eastern Cape Province and southern Natal. It appears to be mostly associated with dead plant material.

The pure white, bonnet-shaped fruit-bodies with the characteristic lamellae visible as depressions on their upper surfaces were quite conspicuous against the dark brown bark. *C. capensis* is probably associated with the decay of dead plant material. The edibility of the species is unknown.

Fruit-bodies scattered or grouped on living trees or dead plant material. *Cap:* 7-12 mm diam., thin, fleshy, bonnet-shaped, pure white; margin regular. Surface smooth to slightly depressed over lamellae, semi-matt, dry. *Stipe:* Lateral, reduced, 1-2 x 1 mm, continuous with cap; cap appearing pendulous; white; fleshy-tough, solid. *Lamellae:* Distant ridges or folds radiating from stipe, forked, reticulate towards furtherest parts, with lateral branches giving a coarsely pore-like appearance; full and intermediate lengths; free, entire, narrow; white. *Flesh:* Thin, membranous, white; no odour. *Spore print:* Creamy white. *Spores:* Hyaline, subglobose to ovoid, smooth, thin-walled, non-amyloid; 6,1-7,6 x 4,4-5,6 μm.

12. Chlorophyllum molybdites (Meyer: Fr.) Mass.   *False Parasol*

Chlorophyllum molybdites is widely distributed and common in Natal, the Transvaal and tropical Africa, appearring on lawns and in grassy areas in summer and autumn. It does not occur in the south-western and southern Cape. It can be recognized by the large, irregular, amber-brown scales over the white surface of the cap and the stipe which widens downwards to the basal bulb. Below the ring the stipe surface soon darkens to brown, but the appearance of greenish tints which progressively darken on the maturing lamellae is the most striking characteristic of this species.

C. molybdites is poisonous and may be confused with the edible Parasol Mushroom, *Macrolepiota zeyheri* (p. 62), which grows in similar localities. *C. molybdites* causes severe intestinal pain, nausea and diarrhoea when eaten. The symptoms may last for about three days. (*Afrikaans:* Valse Sambreelsampioen.)

Fruit-bodies mostly in groups, sometimes forming fairy rings in lawns and grassy places. *Cap:* 100-250 mm diam., fleshy, subglobose at first, later hemispherical to convex with a central umbo; margin even, striate, splitting and occasionally turning upwards in wet weather. Surface white to creamy, covered at first with a bright, dark brown skin which breaks up into coarse, irregular, brown, scattered scales but remains unbroken over the central umbo. *Stipe:* Central, up to 250 mm x 25 mm, swollen at the base and tapering somewhat upwards; white, silky, darkening to brownish below the ring and staining reddish brown when cut or wounded; firm, fleshy-tough, solid. Ring conspicuous, movable, white, membranous on upper part and with a thickened brownish margin below. *Lamellae:* Free, crowded, full and intermediate lengths; broad, thin, fragile, margins entire; white at first turning greenish to dull olive-green and drying greenish-khaki. *Flesh:* White, thick, firm, staining brownish red in stipe when cut. *Spore print:* Pale bright green turning to dull sordid green. *Spores:* Hyaline to greenish, ovoid to broadly ellipsoidal, truncate with germ pore, smooth, thick-walled, dextrinoid; 9-11 x 6,5-8 μm.

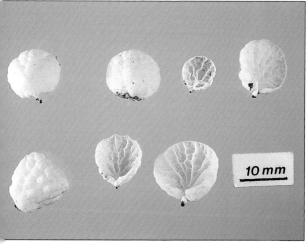

...ampanella capensis (above
...ght and left) Fruit-bodies on
...e trunk (above right), and
...owing short, lateral stipe,
...nnet-shaped cap, and
...diating, pore-like lamellar
...ds (above left).

☠ *Chlorophyllum molybdites*
False Parasol

Chlorophyllum molybdites
showing dark brown
scales on cap surface,
green lamellae and
large, prominent ring
on brownish stipe.

Edible

*Stipe
longitudinally
striate*

Edibility suspect

13. Collybia distorta (Fr.) Quél.

Collybia distorta has been collected in the Weza State Forest, southern Natal and near Sabie in the eastern Transvaal. It seems to be rare but may occur in between these two widely separated localities.

C. distorta grows in clusters among pine needles under the trees. The fruit-bodies are joined at the bases of the stipes and appear in late summer to autumn. The reddish-brown caps attached to tough, cartilaginous and spirally grooved stipes are characteristic. The role of this species in nature is unknown. The fruit-bodies are edible but tasteless.

Fruit-bodies grouped and clustered in ground under pines. *Cap:* 25-80 mm diam., fleshy, convex at first, expanding to flat with a low, broad umbo; margin wavy, downturned. Surface smooth, dry, reddish brown but lighter with age and towards margin. *Stipe:* Central, cylindrical, 40-70 x 4-8 mm, whitish and tinged with cap colour, striate to finely grooved and strongly spirally twisted; tough-cartilaginous, solid; joined at the base with other stipes; without ring. *Lamellae:* Adnate, crowded, full and intermediate lengths, thin, narrow with slightly uneven edge; white at first staining reddish brown. *Flesh:* Pale pinkish beige, soft, up to 4 mm thick; with faint mushroomy odour and flavour. *Spore print:* White. *Spores:* Hyaline, subglobose, smooth, thin-walled; 3-4,5 μm.

14. Cyptotrama asprata (Berk.) Redhead & Ginns

Formerly known as *Collybia chrysopepla*, this species grows on dead hardwood twigs and logs, especially oak. It prefers damp conditions and is known from the south-western and eastern Cape Province and southern Natal. It is not common but may be more widely distributed in the region than is known at present as it also occurs in tropical East Africa.

Cyptotrama asprata is readily recognized by the small, bright, yellow-orange fruit-bodies with coarsely scaly caps and lower stipes. It is involved in the conversion of dead wood and woody debris to humus. Its edibility is unknown but is probably suspect.

Fruit-bodies scattered to grouped on dead, hardwood logs. *Cap:* 10-45 mm diam., thin, fleshy, globose, expanding to convex or almost flat; margin even to slightly undulate, striate. Surface covered with bright yellow-orange tuft-like scales, darker towards the centre but falling off to leave a dry, smooth, yellow-orange surface. *Stipe:* Central, cylindrical, 10-50 x 1-3 mm, with a ring-like ridge on the upper part; smooth and white above the ridge with fine hairs near the apex, but rough below ridge with yellow to yellow-orange, pustular scales; solid, tough-cartilaginous. *Lamellae:* Adnate to slightly decurrent, subdistant, broad, margins entire; white. *Flesh:* Thin, white, unchanging; odourless. *Spore print:* White. *Spores:* Globose to broadly lemon-shaped, smooth, thin-walled with granular contents; 6-7,5 x 5-7 μm.

46

Collybia distorta

Cyptotrama asprata

Cyptotrama asprata showing scaly,
orange-yellow cap and lower stipe,
and adnate, broad, white lamellae.

Edibility unknown

15. Favolaschia thwaitesii (Berk. & Br.) Singer

Favolaschia thwaitesii is known to occur in the south-western Cape where it forms fruit-bodies in winter. It is also known from Natal and has recently been collected in the eastern Transvaal in autumn. It also occurs in tropical East Africa and is probably more common in southern Africa than the records indicate but its small fruit-bodies are easily overlooked.

F. thwaitesii grows on dead, decaying twigs and thinner branches of broad-leafed trees under wet conditions. Apparently it assists in the break-down of woody debris to humus, forming its fruit-bodies in large groups. The small orange-coloured fruit-bodies with lateral stipes and shallow pores on the lower surface make this pretty little fungus easy to recognize. Although the hymenium of this species is inside shallow pores instead of over lamel-lae, the micromorphological characters correspond with those of true mush-rooms and therefore it is classified in the Family Tricholomataceae together with many other species. The edibility of *F. thwaitesii* is unknown.

Fruit-bodies small, laterally stipitate, in groups on dead wood. ***Cap:*** 5-15 mm diam., small, delicate, gelatinous-fleshy, circular to broadly kidney-shaped; margin entire, undulate and crenulate. Surface convex to flat, gelatinous and marked with a mosaic design; yellow-orange at first darkening to orange or brownish orange, translucent, finally finely powdered. ***Stipe:*** Absent or lateral, cylindrical, 2-15 x 1-2 mm, attached to cap obliquely from below and arising from a pad of mycelium on the substrate; without ring; surface mealy, concolorous with the cap, translucent. ***Tubes:*** In lower sur-face approx. 0,5 mm deep, concolorous with cap. Pores large 0,5-1,5 mm diam., circular to angular, larger at the centre of the cap; edges of separat-ing walls mealy. ***Flesh:*** Up to 1 mm thick, gelatinous, tough, cap colour but paler; odourless. ***Spore print:*** White. ***Spores:*** Hyaline, broadly ellip-soidal to subcylindrical, smooth, thin-walled, with refringent guttules, amyloid; 7,5-11,5 x 4-6,5 µm.

Edible

16. Hygrocybe nigrescens (Quél.) Kühner   *Blackening Wax Gill*

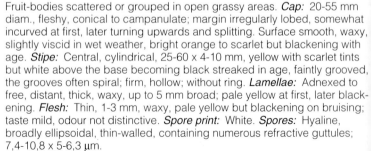

Hygrocybe nigrescens grows in lawns and other naturally grassy places during autumn. It occurs in the south-western Cape Province and the Trans-vaal but may be widely distributed throughout the eastern and southern parts of southern Africa. This species may be readily recognized by the bright red, waxy caps that turn black with age. The very similar *H. conica* has been reported from Pretoria. It has a more strongly conical cap and differs slightly in microscopic characters from *H. nigrescens* although many mycologists regard them as one species. *H. nigrescens* is edible but appar-ently tasteless and is not recommended. (*Afrikaans:* Verkoolwaslamel.)

Fruit-bodies scattered or grouped in open grassy areas. ***Cap:*** 20-55 mm diam., fleshy, conical to campanulate; margin irregularly lobed, somewhat incurved at first, later turning upwards and splitting. Surface smooth, waxy, slightly viscid in wet weather, bright orange to scarlet but blackening with age. ***Stipe:*** Central, cylindrical, 25-60 x 4-10 mm, yellow with scarlet tints but white above the base becoming black streaked in age, faintly grooved, the grooves often spiral; firm, hollow; without ring. ***Lamellae:*** Adnexed to free, distant, thick, waxy, up to 5 mm broad; pale yellow at first, later black-ening. ***Flesh:*** Thin, 1-3 mm, waxy, pale yellow but blackening on bruising; taste mild, odour not distinctive. ***Spore print:*** White. ***Spores:*** Hyaline, broadly ellipsoidal, thin-walled, containing numerous refractive guttules; 7,4-10,8 x 5-6,3 µm.

Fruit-bodies with conical caps

Favolaschia thwaitesii (above and left) on dead branch (above), and showing lateral stipe and large shallow pores of hymenial surface (left).

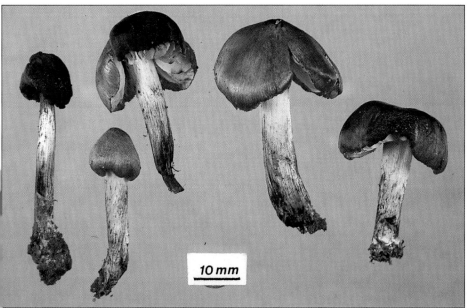

Hygrocybe nigrescens showing bright red, blackening caps and ringless, yellow, blackening stipes.

Hygrocybe nigrescens
Blackening Wax Gill

Edible

17. Laccaria laccata (Scop.: Fr.) Berk. & Br. *Deceiver*

This species is common and widely distributed in the south-western, southern and eastern Cape Province, Natal and Transvaal. The fruit-bodies always occur in groups in leaf-litter under trees, especially pines, during late summer to autumn. The variability in the colours and appearance of the fruit-bodies has earned for this species the common name 'Deceiver'. However, the closely grouped, smallish fruit-bodies with pink lamellae that acquire a white, powdery appearance with the formation of spores serve to distinguish this species.

Laccaria laccata is edible but tasteless. It is more important as a mycorrhizae-forming species with pine trees. (*Afrikaans:* Verkulswam.)

Fruit-bodies grouped in leaf-litter under trees, mostly pines. *Cap:* 10-65 mm diam., fleshy, convex at first, later flat, often depressed at the centre; margin finely striate, wavy, downturned but finally turning upwards. Surface smooth, tawny to brick red when wet, ochreous yellow and finely flaky when dry. *Stipe:* Central, tall, cylindrical, 30-95 x 3-8 mm, concolorous with cap but whitish around the slightly swollen base, smooth, often somewhat flattened and twisted; tough-fibrous, hollow; without ring. *Lamellae:* Adnate and notched, subdistant, up to 8 mm broad, margin thin, even; pink, becoming whitish and powdery with mature spores. *Flesh:* Thin, 0,5-2 mm, soft, reddish brown, unchanging; with indistinct odour and taste. *Spore print:* White. *Spores:* Hyaline, globose, spiny, 7-10 μm.

18. Lactarius deliciosus (L.:Fr.) S.F. Gray *Orange Milk Cap; Pine Rings*

Edible

Lactarius deliciosus is common in pine plantations in the south-western and southern Cape Province during the rainy season from April to September. The fruit-bodies usually occur in groups of scattered individuals after good rains but seem able to develop even under dry conditions. This species forms mycorrhizae with pines.

L. deliciosus is easily recognized by its characteristic shape, colours and the production of orange-coloured sap when some part is broken or cut. It is edible and has a good flavour but young, fresh fruit-bodies should be eaten rather than older ones which tend to be tough and tasteless. (*Afrikaans:* Oranje Melkswam.)

Fruit-bodies solitary or scattered under pines. *Cap:* Up to 120 mm diam., fleshy, fragile, at first flattened dome-shaped, opening to plane and slightly depressed at the centre with margin curled inwards, finally shallow funnel-shaped. Surface smooth, matt, slightly sticky when moist; carrot-red to orange or reddish orange, often with tan-coloured concentric zones, turning dull greyish green in age and when touched. *Stipe:* Central, up to 70 mm x 10-20 mm, smooth, even, stiff and brittle; concolorous with cap or lighter, and spotted orange, turning green and exuding orange sap where cut or bruised; solid at first, becoming spongy to hollow and showing a bright orange-red zone underlying the outer layer; without ring. *Lamellae:* Decurrent, unequal lengths, forked, thick, deep, fragile; orange to reddish orange, becoming greenish in age and exuding an orange-coloured sap when broken. *Flesh:* Thick, firm, brittle; whitish at first but young specimens soon bright orange-red, older ones more orange; exuding orange sap when cut or broken; odourless or faintly aromatic. *Spore print:* White to pale ochre. *Spores:* Hyaline, ellipsoidal, covered by a network of thin ridges; 7-9 x 6-7 μm.

Laccaria laccata
Deceiver

Laccaria laccata showing hygrophanous cap with finely striate margin, pink lamellae, and central stipe – paler around the slightly swollen base.

10 mm

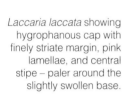

Lactarius deliciosus showing funnel-shaped cap with greyish-green upper surface, orange lamellae, and short, orange-spotted stipe.

Lactarius deliciosus
Orange Milk Cap

Inedible

19. Lactarius hepaticus Plowright *apud* Boudier

Lactarius hepaticus occurs sporadically under pines in the south-western, southern and eastern Cape Province and eastern Transvaal in late summer to autumn. Like most species of *Lactarius* it forms mycorrhizae with pines. It is readily recognized by the brownish funnel-shaped fruit-bodies with the dark, liver-coloured cap and stipe surfaces, and the white, milky sap which readily oozes from the brownish lamellae when damaged.

    L. hepaticus is inedible because of the bitter flavour of its sap.

Fruit-bodies scattered to grouped under pines. *Cap:* 20-70 mm diam., fleshy, convex at first, expanding to flat, finally funnel-shaped; margin undulate, downturned, slightly striate, finally slightly lobate. Surface smooth, dry, matt, liver-coloured to dull chestnut. *Stipe:* Central, cylindrical, straight or slightly curved, 25-70 x 3-8 mm, smooth, same colour as cap or more reddish and often pale below the cap; brittle, at first solid, later hollow; without ring. *Lamellae:* Slightly decurrent, close, full and intermediate lengths, thin, edges entire; pale buff to deeper buff and later powdery white with spores; fragile, exuding a milky white sap where damaged. *Flesh:* Pinkish buff, thin, darker and more reddish in stipe and exuding milky white sap when cut; with a bitter, acrid taste in cap. *Spore print:* Pale cream. *Spores:* Hyaline, broadly ellipsoidal, covered with large warts which are joined by thin to thick ridges forming an incomplete network; 8-9 x 6-7 µm.

20. Lentinus sajor-caju (Fr.) Fr.   *Funnel Woodcap*

Edible

Lentinus sajor-caju forms fruit-bodies in groups or as scattered individuals on decaying logs or dead stems of broad-leafed trees mostly during early summer. It is known from the southern and eastern Cape, southern Natal and the eastern Transvaal. It is also widely distributed throughout sub-Saharan Africa, south-east Asia, Australasia and the Philippines.

    This species is readily recognized by its large, conspicuous, mostly funnel-shaped fruit-bodies set upon short stipes and growing on dead wood. It is active in the decay of dead wood in which it causes a white rot. Species of *Lentinus* are related to the wood-rotting pore fungi because of their micromorphological characters, and many mycologists classify them with those species. Because of their mushroom-like appearance they are grouped with the mushrooms in this book. The fruit-bodies are edible while young but with age become very tough. (*Afrikaans:* Tregterhoutswam.)

Fruit-bodies single, scattered or grouped on dead wood of broad-leafed trees. *Cap:* 50-160 mm diam., soft-leathery at first, becoming tough and drying hard-horny; convex at first and deeply depressed in the centre but later cup-shaped to funnel-shaped; margin inrolled, later straight, smooth, thin, wavy and slightly lobed. Surface smooth, dry, often finely radially striate and cracking in age; occasionally partly covered with small, appressed, darker-coloured scales especially towards the centre; colour variable: at first white, changing to cream, pale ochreous or smoky and brownish, often darker in the centre. *Stipe:* Central, excentric or occasionally lateral, short, cylindrical, 8-30 x 5-15 mm; concolorous with cap; tough and solid. Ring near the apex, white to yellowish brown or blackish, disappearing. *Lamellae:* Decurrent on stipe, densely crowded, full and intermediate lengths, thin, narrow, up to 3 mm wide, edges entire or finely denticulate; whitish to concolorous with cap. *Flesh:* White, firm, up to 8 mm over the centre but thin over the lamellae, tough and pliable, drying hard and horny; without distinctive odour. *Spore print:* White. *Spores:* Hyaline, narrowly cylindrical, often curved, smooth, thin-walled; 5-9 x 1,5-2,5 µm.

Fruit-bodies with funnel-shaped caps (infundibuliform)

Lactarius hepaticus

Lentinus sajor-caju showing funnel-shaped cap, and densely crowded lamellae running into short stipe attached to wood.

Lactarius hepaticus showing funnel-shaped cap, lamellae exuding milky sap, and ringless, liver-coloured stipe.

Lentinus sajor-caju
Funnel Woodcap

Inedible

21. Lentinus stupeus Klotzs   *Bluegum Woodcap*

Lentinus stupeus – known earlier as *L. stuppeus* – forms fruit-bodies in small groups on dead hardwood logs during summer and early autumn. It is known to occur from Stutterheim in the eastern Cape Province northwards through Natal to the eastern, north-eastern and northern Transvaal and northwards from here throughout tropical and East Africa.

The fruit-bodies may be recognized by their dark, tough, hairy caps with strongly inrolled margins and relatively short, thin stipes. *L. stupeus* is an active wood-decaying fungus which causes a white rot in dead wood of broad-leafed trees. The fruit-bodies are too tough for eating. (*Afrikaans:* Bloekomhoutswam.)

Fruit-bodies with deeply depressed caps

Fruit-bodies growing in groups on dead wood. *Cap:* 10-50 mm diam., tough-leathery, deeply depressed to funnel-shaped; margin strongly and persistently inrolled. Surface densely hairy but less hairy to smooth over the centre; dark reddish to purplish brown to almost black. *Stipe:* Central, cylindrical, widening towards the apex, 15-40 x 2-4 mm; densely covered with fine cinnamon-brown hairs at the apex but with small, blackish scales over the dull, yellowish-brown surface elsewhere and somewhat hairy at the base; tough-fibrous, solid; without ring. *Lamellae:* Crowded, shortly decurrent and anastomosing at the stipe apex, full and intermediate lengths, narrow, thin, edges strongly denticulate; pale yellowish buff. *Flesh:* Whitish to pale beige, tough, fibrous, unchanging, 1-2 mm thick; without distinctive odour. *Spore print:* Deep cream colour. *Spores:* Hyaline, cylindrical, smooth, thin-walled; 6-8,5 x 2,2-3,2 μm.

22. Lentinus velutinus Fr.   *Velvet Woodcap*

Inedible

Lentinus velutinus is widely distributed throughout tropical Africa, Asia and the Americas. It is known in southern Africa mainly from collections in the southern and eastern Cape, Natal and the north-eastern Transvaal. It is a variable species that forms fruit-bodies singly or in groups on dead tree stumps, trunks and branches, or on rotting, buried wood of broad-leafed trees during summer. It differs from the other species of *Lentinus* described here by the velvety, uniformly coloured upper surface of the cap and the velvety surface of the slender stipe which is usually much longer than the diameter of the cap.

L. velutinus forms a pseudosclerotium, that is, a mixture of mycelium and substrate tissue hardened into a more or less egg-shaped resting body which survives long after the wood substrate has rotted away. New fruit-bodies may develop from this at a later stage. The thin, tough fruit-bodies are inedible. (*Afrikaans:* Fluweelhoutswam.)

Fruit-bodies grouped on dead wood. *Cap:* 20-80 mm diam., thin, tough-leathery, deeply depressed to broadly funnel-shaped; margin thin, at first strongly inrolled, later turned outwards, wavy, densely covered with short hairs. Surface uniformly velvety, without zones, uniformly pale greyish cinnamon to tawny brown or darker brown. *Stipe:* Central, slender, elongate cylindrical, 20-100 x 2-10 mm, expanding slightly at both apex and base; surface concolorous with cap or slightly darker, uniformly velvety, the hairiness extending into the bases of the lamellae; tough, solid; often arising from a thickened pad of mycelium; without ring. *Lamellae:* Shortly decurrent, crowded, full and intermediate lengths, not anastomosing, very narrow, thin, edges entire; pale buff to greyish brown. *Flesh:* White, thin, up to 1 mm thick, fibrous, drying rigid; without distinctive odour. *Spore print:* Cream to pale buff. *Spores:* Hyaline, cylindrical, smooth, thin-walled; 5-7 x 3-3,7 μm.

Lentinus stupeus
Bluegum Woodcap

Lentinus stupeus showing densely hairy cap surface, inrolled margin, yellowish-buff lamellae, and scales on stipe.

Lentinus velutinus **Velvet Woodcap**
Fruit-bodies showing velvety cap surface, decurrent lamellae and velvety stipe.

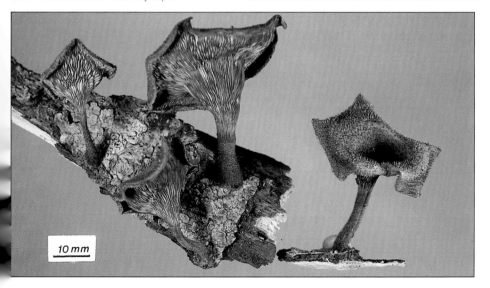

23. Lentinus villosus Klotzsch

Lentinus villosus forms fruit-bodies in small groups on the dead wood of broad-leafed trees. It is the most common species of *Lentinus* in tropical Africa but rare in southern Africa. It is known in Zimbabwe but in South Africa from one collection in the eastern Transvaal only. It closely resembles *L. stupeus* and may be confused with this species, but can be distinguished by its lighter-coloured cap with pale-coloured lamellae, its stipe which is taller than the diameter of the cap, and its lighter spore print. It causes a white rot of dead wood.

L. villosus is inedible because of its tough texture.

Fruit-bodies grouped on dead wood. *Cap:* 10-50 mm diam., tough-leathery, deeply funnel-shaped to broadly cup-shaped; margin strongly inrolled. Surface densely covered with long curly hairs especially at the margin but hairs forming scattered, erect scales toward the centre; white to cream at first, darkening to bistre. *Stipe:* Central, cylindrical, expanding at the apex, 30-60 x 3-9 mm; surface concolorous with cap, densely hairy towards the apex but with ochreous-brown, small, appressed, fibrillose scales below; tough, solid; without ring. *Lamellae:* Shortly decurrent, crowded, full and intermediate lengths, slightly anastomosing at the stipe apex, narrow, thin, edges denticulate; white turning to ivory. *Flesh:* Whitish, tough-fibrous, up to 2 mm thick; without distinctive odour. *Spore print:* White to cream. *Spores:* Hyaline, cylindrical, thin-walled, smooth; 5,7-8,5 x 2,4-3,5 μm.

24. Lepiota cristata (Bolt.:Fr.) Kummer   *Stinking Parasol*

Lepiota cristata prefers localities with abundant organic material in and on the soil and is mostly found under broad-leafed trees in woods. It is known to occur in the south-western and eastern Cape and in the Transvaal. These widely separated localities may indicate its occurrence elsewhere in suitable habitats.

The small size, delicate appearance, small deciduous ring and reddish-brown scales over the white, umbonate cap distinguish this species. *L. cristata* is probably one of the mushroom species which help to convert organic litter to compost and humus. Its edibility is unknown but it is best regarded with suspicion. (*Afrikaans:* Stink Sambreel.)

Fruit-bodies with bell-shaped caps (campanulate)

Fruit-bodies scattered in humus-rich soil, garden refuse or leaf-litter under trees. *Cap:* 20-50 mm diam., thin, fleshy, irregularly bell-shaped and umbonate; margin regular, smooth, finally somewhat irregularly lobed in some caps. Surface silky, white, covered with small, reddish-brown scales which form an unbroken layer over the umbo. *Stipe:* Central, cylindrical, 20-40 x 3-4 mm; white, tinged with flesh colour, smooth, fleshy, hollow. Ring narrow, membranous and deciduous. *Lamellae:* Free, crowded, full and intermediate lengths, thin, edges entire, 2-4 mm broad; white, ageing brownish. *Flesh:* Thin, white; with pleasant taste but unpleasant fungusy odour. *Spore print:* White. *Spores:* Hyaline, bullet-shaped to wedge-shaped, smooth, thin-walled, dextrinoid; 6-7 x 3-3,5 μm.

ntinus villosus

Lentinus villosus showing depressed, hairy cap surface and scaly, ringless stipe.

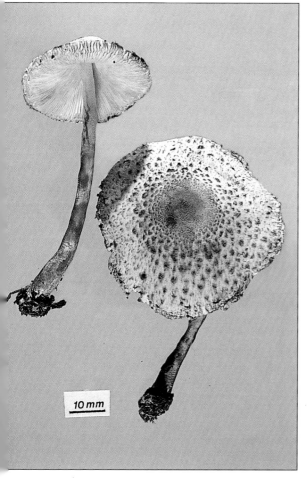

Lepiota cristata **Stinking Parasol** Fruit-bodies showing white cap with small reddish-brown scales.

25. Leucoagaricus bisporus Heinem.

Edibility suspect

Leucoagaricus bisporus is known mainly from collections around Pretoria, the eastern Transvaal and Natal. It grows on decaying organic debris, and probably takes part in the conversion of organic material to humus.

The species may be recognized by its clustered, pale-coloured fruit-bodies with a flattened, more deeply coloured umbo surrounded by minute scales, the striate cap margin, tall stipe and flesh which turns reddish when cut. A tropical fungus, it seems to be at the southern limits of its range in southern Africa and is quite rare here. Its edibility is unknown but species of *Lepiota*-like fungi with flesh discolouring reddish on cutting are best regarded as poisonous.

Fruit-bodies single or clustered on ground among grass. *Cap:* 20-80 mm diam., fleshy, conical, expanding to bell-shaped with a prominent flattened umbo; margin even or wavy by way of pressure from adjacent caps, striate downturned and slightly ragged. Surface scaly with small, appressed scale more or less concentrically arranged, silky below the scales; pale yellowish but darkening to tan over the umbo, scales cream coloured or darker. *Stip* Central, cylindrical, 30-75 x 4-8 mm; smooth, often slightly bulbous at the base, fused below ground level with other stipes and with rhizoids attache creamy white above to pale fawn below ring, darkening when handled and discolouring brownish when cut; fleshy-tough to slightly fibrous, hollow. Rir membranous, persistent, fixed; white above but brownish from adhering sc below. *Lamellae:* Free, crowded, full and intermediate lengths, thin, edge: entire, up to 6 mm broad; pale yellowish white at first darkening slightly wi age. *Flesh:* Firm, white, discolouring reddish on cut surfaces, 1-5 mm thick; without distinctive odour. *Spore print:* White to pale yellow. *Spores:* Hyaline ellipsoidal, smooth, thin-walled, dextrinoid; 8,4-9,9 x 5,5-6,9 μm.

Cap with broad umbo

26. Leucoagaricus leucothites (Vitt.) Wasser.   *Smooth Lepio*

Edible

Leucoagaricus leucothites – previously known as *Lepiota naucina* and *Lepiota cretaceus* – occurs in the Transvaal, Orange Free State, eastern Cape, and south-western Cape where it seems to be most common. It appears after rains in late summer to autumn.

L. leucothites resembles the Field Mushroom, *Agaricus campestris*, in sor respects but may be distinguished by the movable ring and the lamellae which never turn brown. The pale pinkish mature lamellae and the absence of a volva distinguish this species from some of the deadly poisonous *Amar* species. *L. leucothites* is edible and tasty but beware of confusing it with poisonous species. (*Afrikaans:* Gladde sambreel.)

Fruit-bodies solitary or grouped in open fields and pastures. *Cap:* 40-100 n diam., fleshy, at first somewhat egg-shaped but expanding to broad conve and finally almost plane sometimes with a slight umbo; margin incurved at first, even, smooth, occasionally with adhering remnants of veil. Surface smooth, matt, like chamois leather, sometimes cracking with age; silvery white but buff or smoky in age. *Stipe:* Central, 60-100 x 8-15 mm, tapering upwards from a bulbous base, silky, smooth or slightly striate on the lower parts; firm, at first stuffed in the centre, later hollow. Ring prominent, white, pendulous, membranous with frilly edges; movable, often disappearing wi age. *Lamellae:* Free, crowded, separated from stipe by a collar, full and intermediate lengths, thin, fragile, margins entire or minutely uneven; white at first, soon turning to pink. *Flesh:* White, thick, soft and slightly fibrous in the stipe; with a faintly fruity odour. *Spore print:* White or with a slightly pin tinge. *Spores:* Hyaline, almond-shaped to obovoid, apiculate, smooth, thin walled with germ pore, 1-guttulate, dextrinoid; 8-9 x 5-6 μm.

Leucoagaricus bisporus

Leucoagaricus bisporus showing dark umbo, scaly upper cap surface and free lamellae.

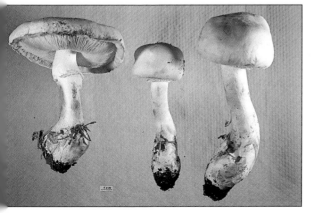

Leucoagaricus leucothites
Smooth Lepiota Fruit-bodies showing smooth, chamois leather-like cap surface, prominent membranous ring and white to pinkish lamellae.

Poisonous

Fruit-bodies with club-shaped stipes

Edibility unknown

27. Leucocoprinus birnbaumii (Corda) Singer   *Lemon Yellow Lepiota*

Formerly known as *Lepiota lutea*, this species has been recorded in southern Africa once before – in Pretoria on old tea leaves. Recently it was found on decaying woody debris on or below the soil in the eastern and northeastern Transvaal during early summer and autumn. It may be more widely distributed but does not appear to be common. It seems to prefer wet, humid conditions for growth.

L. birnbaumii occurs on decaying woody materials in which it apparently causes decay. Its small, bright lemon-yellow fruit-bodies are quite conspicuous and readily recognizable by their uniform colour and the powdery surfaces of the caps and stipes. The fruit-bodies are poisonous.

Fruit-bodies single, grouped or clustered in soil or on woody debris.
Cap: 15-40 mm diam., thin, fleshy, bell-shaped becoming conical to nearly flat with a central rounded umbo; margin even, somewhat incurved at first and deeply grooved, later turning upwards. Upper surface bright lemon-yellow fading to pale yellow in age, powdery or covered with numerous, small lemon-yellow scales, later turning brownish yellow towards the centre. *Stipe:* Central, club-shaped, 20-60 x 2-4 mm widening to 6-10 mm diam. over the widest lower part; covered with yellow powder or fine granules; fleshy-tough, solid; often joined with others below ground level. Ring membranous, lemon-yellow, movable, often disappearing. *Lamellae:* Free, crowded, full and intermediate lengths, narrow, edges finely hairy; lemon-yellow, fading yellowish white. *Flesh:* Very thin, lemon-yellow; without distinctive odour.
Spore print: White to pale yellowish. *Spores:* Hyaline, ellipsoidal, smooth, with thickened wall and apical germ pore, dextrinoid; 8-13 x 5-8 μm.

28. Macrolepiota procera (Scop.:Fr.) Sing.   *Parasol Mushroom*

Macrolepiota procera appears in grassy fields, often near broad-leafed woods in summer and autumn after good rains. It seems to be widely distributed in southern Africa, occurring in the Transvaal, Natal, and in the eastern and southern Cape. It can be distinguished from the closely related *M. zeyheri* by the dark brown scales on the cap and the parallel bands of brown scales on the stipe which is much longer and more slender than that of *M. zeyheri*.

The species illustrated and described here may represent a new species but until this is confirmed the name *M. procera* applies to southern African specimens. The European *M. procera* is edible and tasty but the edibility of the southern African fungus is unknown. (*Afrikaans:* Bruin Sambreelsampioen)

Fruit-bodies single or scattered in soil in pastures or open places near tree
Cap: 100-200 mm diam., thick, fleshy, at first acorn-shaped but expanding to broadly convex with a circular depression around a central umbo; margin regular, striate and splitting. Surface creamy to pale beige, dry, scaly, with pale beige to amber-brown scales in more or less concentric circles but with an unbroken, amber-brown layer over the umbo. *Stipe:* Central, long-cylindrical with a bulbous base, 200-300 x 10-20 mm, white, smooth above ring, smooth brownish below; sometimes with parallel, transverse bands of brownish scales in some parts, and occasionally powdery above the basal bulb; firm, tough, almost woody, solid at first, later hollow. Ring persistent, fixed at first, later free, membranous, white above, brownish below, attached high up on stipe. *Lamellae:* Free, crowded, full and intermediate lengths, thin, fragile, edges entire but crenulate towards the margin; white but later pale beige and drying pale tan. *Flesh:* White, thin, unchanging; odourless or faintly mushroomy. *Spore print:* White to faintly pinkish. *Spores:* Hyaline, ovoid to broadly ellipsoidal, apiculate, smooth, thin-walled, with apical germ pore, dextrinoid; 13-19 x 8-11 μm.

Leucocoprinus birnbaumii
mon Yellow Lepiota

acrolepiota procera
asol Mushroom

Leucocoprinus birnbaumii
showing scaly, lemon-yellow
cap and club-shaped stipe.

Macrolepiota procera
showing brown scales over
white cap, white lamellae,
and tall, slender, greyish-
brown stipe with prominent
ring and bulbous base.

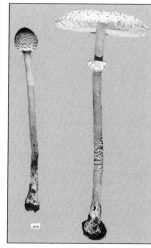

Edible

29. Macrolepiota rhacodes (Vitt.) Sing.　　　*Shaggy Parasol*

Macrolepiota rhacodes has been reported from the south-western Cape where it grows in association with gum trees. The specimens described here were found growing in Pretoria in a kikuyu lawn in late summer. This species appears to be rare in southern Africa.

M. rhacodes differs from the other species of *Macrolepiota* described here by its smooth stipe, the more reddish colour of the scales over the cap surface and the flesh which discolours reddish when cut.

The species is edible with good flavour, but has been reported to cause stomach upsets on occasion. (*Afrikaans:* Oranje Melksambreel.)

Fruit-bodies scattered on ground in lawns or pastures. *Cap:* 50-120 mm diam., fleshy, subglobose at first, expanding to convex without an umbo, finally almost plane; margin regular, downturned, overhanging the lamellae frayed. Surface smooth at first, soon breaking up into large, coarse, greyish to pinkish-brown or cinnamon scales which are arranged in concentric circles over the whitish flesh beneath. *Stipe:* Central, 70-180 x 8-20 mm, cylindrical or widening downwards to a bulbous base, smooth, white with pinkish-brown tints; fleshy-tough, hollow, stuffed with a loose, pith-like substance; turning pinkish brown when cut. Ring prominent, movable, double-edged, attached to upper part of stipe. *Lamellae:* Free, close, full and intermediate lengths, broad, thin, edges entire; white at first turning pinkish cream and darkening to buff. *Flesh:* Thick, white, turning orange to reddish where cut; with pleasant odour and flavour. *Spore print:* White. *Spores:* Hyaline, short ellipsoidal, smooth, thin-walled, with apical germ pore, dextrinoid; 6-10 x 5-7 µm.

Edible

30. Macrolepiota zeyheri (Berk.) Sing.　　　*Parasol Mushroom*

Macrolepiota zeyheri is fairly common in southern Africa, occurring in the south-western and eastern Cape, Natal, and the Transvaal Highveld and also further northwards into tropical Africa. The characteristic large, white fruit-bodies appear after good rains in open, grassy pastures in late summer and autumn to early winter.

M. zeyheri is edible but the flavour is variable. To avoid confusion with the poisonous and very similar *Chlorophyllum molybdites* (p. 44), specimens with lamellae showing a greenish tint should be discarded. The collections should be carefully studied and compared with their descriptions before cooking. (*Afrikaans:* Sambreelsampioen.)

Fruit-bodies scattered in pastures and grassy places. *Cap:* 100-250 mm diam., thick, fleshy, at first acorn-shaped, becoming hemispherical to convex and finally more or less flattened with a slight umbo, often depressed around the umbo; margin even, smooth, often fringed by remnants of veil. Upper surface scaly, white, with a pale brownish skin in the young stage which breaks up into pale brown, easily detached scales except over the umbo where it remains intact; mature surface covered by loose, soft, white and pale brown scales, arranged in concentric circles. *Stipe:* Central, 100-200 x 10-20 mm, slender, cylindrical with a bulbous base, firm; smooth or with loose, white scales above the ring, somewhat striate below it; white turning brownish with handling; fleshy-tough, hollow. Ring large, double, with upper part membranous and shaggy; white or creamy white; movable, persistent. *Lamellae:* Free, crowded, separated from the stipe by a collar, full and intermediate lengths, thin, soft, fragile, with edges fimbriate; white drying to pale tan. *Flesh:* Thin, white but turning pinkish with age, soft; with a faint mushroomy odour. *Spore print:* White with a pinkish tint. *Spores:* Hyaline, broadly ellipsoidal, smooth, with granular contents, and with a germ pore, dextrinoid; 15-17 x 10-12 µm.

Cap margin appendiculate (with adhering veil fragments)

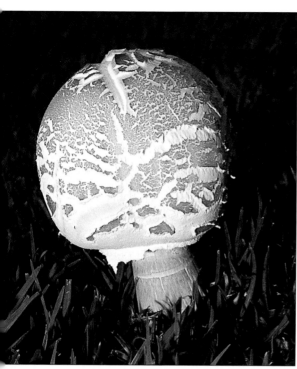

Macrolepiota rhacodes
Shaggy Parasol Young fruit-body showing irregular, reddish-brown scales over white cap.

Macrolepiota zeyheri
Parasol Mushroom Fruit-bodies showing small, pale brown scales over white cap, fringed margin, pale tan lamellae, and white stipe with bulbous base and prominent, white ring.

Inedible

Fruit-bodies with cylindrical stipes

31. Marasmius androsaceus (L.:Fr.) Fr.   *Horse-hair Fungus*

Marasmius androsaceus occurs in the south-western, southern and eastern Cape where the fruit-bodies appear in summer and autumn. Very few records of its occurrence in the region exist and it does not appear to be common, but the fruit-bodies are tiny and may easily be overlooked. It occurs mostly in large groups under pine trees, and the stipes arise from dead pine needles which are invaded and decomposed to compost. A net work of black, shiny, tough strands, resembling the hair of a horse's tail, develop around the needles, binding them into a loose bundle of litter under the troop of fruit-bodies – hence the common name of this species.

The caps appear very fragile and wilt and shrivel rapidly under dry conditions, but revive when wet. The species is considered to be inedible because the fruit-bodies are too small. (*Afrikaans:* Haarsteelswam.)

Fruit-bodies in groups on pine-needles or other litter. *Cap:* 5-10 mm diam., thin, membranous, convex at first, later flattened, often with centre depressed; margin slightly lobed. Surface radially wrinkled, pale pinkish brown but darker reddish brown in central depression. *Stipe:* Central, tall, slender, black, 20-60 x 1 mm, often bent and twisted; stiff, tough-fibrous, solid; without ring; often connected by similar black, tough strands to other stipes and pieces of substrate. *Lamellae:* Adnate, distant, narrow, thin, co colorous with cap or lighter. *Flesh:* Very thin, whitish in cap, dark in stipe, unchanging; no distinctive odour. *Spore print:* White. *Spores:* Hyaline, ovoid, apiculate or pip-shaped, smooth, thin-walled; 6-9 x 3-4 µm.

Edible

Fruit-bodies with stipes off-centre (excentric)

32. Pleurotus ostreatus (Jacq.: Fr.) Kummer   *Oyster Mushroom*

Pleurotus ostreatus is known from the south-western Cape where it occasionally occurs on dead stumps and logs of broad-leafed trees in late winter. It has also been reported from the south-eastern Cape Province and Natal. It is better known as an edible mushroom cultivated commercially o straw bales (see photograph) in small quantities for local markets. A relate species, *P. pulmonarius*, is also being cultivated commercially on an increasing scale in South Africa. It differs from *P. ostreatus* by having fruit bodies with pale cream caps, very short stipes, a mealy odour and a whit spore print. *P. pulmonarius* is better suited for local cultivation because it requires higher temperatures for growth. Both species have an excellent flavour and firm texture. (*Afrikaans:* Oestersampioen.)

Fruit-bodies attached laterally in dense, overlapping clusters to dead woo *Cap:* 50-120 mm wide, fleshy, oyster-shaped, semi-circular to elongate f shaped to partly or unequally shallow funnel-shaped; margin smooth, thir wavy, lobed, incurved and splitting in age. Surface smooth, dry, matt; da beige to flesh-brown with a purplish tinge, or blue-grey changing to grey brown. *Stipe:* Absent or short, lateral to markedly excentric, cylindrical to bent, 10-60 x 5-10 mm, whitish, hairy; fleshy-tough, solid; without ring. *Lamellae:* Close, decurrent on stipe or thickened attachment, full and intermediate lengths, thin, up to 6 mm wide, edges entire; white, changin to cream. *Flesh:* Thick, firm, white, unchanging; with pleasant odour and taste. *Spore print:* Pale lilac. *Spores:* Hyaline, subcylindrical, smooth; 7,5-11 x 3-4 µm.

Marasmius androsaceus
Horse-hair Fungus

10 mm

Marasmius androsaceus
showing distant lamellae in
thin, radially wrinkled caps
and black, hair-like stipes.

Pleurotus ostreatus
Oyster Mushroom

10 mm

Pleurotus ostreatus showing flesh-coloured
fruit-bodies with short lateral stipe, and
decurrent, cream-coloured lamellae.

Inedible

33. Russula caerulea Pers.: Fr. *Violet Russula*

Russula caerulea is known only from fruit-bodies found in a pine plantation near Sedgefield, southern Cape in April 1984. It forms mycorrhizae with pine trees. This species is characterized by a blunt umbo which is almost invariably present on the purplish caps, a very rare feature in *Russula* species. This, together with the tall, slender, white stipe and pale yellow lamellae, should facilitate identification.

Because of the acrid flavour of the flesh which remains tough even after prolonged cooking, the species is inedible. The cuticle of the cap is unpleasantly bitter. (*Afrikaans:* Skildknoprooimus.)

Fruit-bodies in small groups under pine trees. *Cap:* 40-80 mm diam., fleshy almost conical at first, then expanding to flattish with a blunt umbo or somewhat depressed around the umbo; margin thin, even, downturned and with short grooves at maturity. Surface smooth, slightly sticky in humid weather, deep violet to bluish purple or brownish purple. *Stipe:* Central, slender, 60-90 x 8-15 mm, more or less club-shaped, smooth, white or with greyish or brownish areas in age; firm, solid; without ring. *Lamellae:* Adnexed, close, narrow towards the stipe, edges entire, brittle; pale yellowish white, darkening at maturity. *Flesh:* Thick, firm, white; with faint odour and mildly acrid flavour. *Spore print:* Pale yellow. *Spores:* Ovoid, with warts 1-1,2 μm high, single or joined by fine lines forming a scanty network, amyloid; 8-10 x 7-9 μm.

Edible

34. Russula capensis Pearson *Cape Russula*

Russula capensis was first described from the south-western Cape where i is very common in pine plantations. It has since been found in the southern and eastern Cape Province as far as the Hogsback. It appears from April to August in the south-western and southern Cape but was found in late January at Hogsback. It occurs under pine trees of various species with which i forms mycorrhizae.

The fruit-bodies are mostly medium-sized and have pine needles and so adhering to the shiny, sticky, reddish caps. This, together with the white stipe and lamellae which turn yellow to ochre as the spores mature, facilita recognition of the species. The fruit-bodies are edible but should be cooke when fresh and young. The taste varies from slightly peppery to rather tast less. (*Afrikaans:* Kaapse Rooimus.)

Fruit-bodies with deeply depressed caps

Fruit-bodies scattered or grouped under pines. *Cap:* 50-90 mm diam., fleshy, shallow convex at first expanding with a marked depression at the centre; margin smooth, even, finally somewhat upturned so that cap appears shallow funnel-shaped. Surface shiny, viscid, minutely granular; colours varying from dingy pink to vermilion or brownish red, often with pine needles and other debris adhering to the surface. *Stipe:* Central or occasionally excentric, 40-60 x 10-20 mm, even, or with slightly swollen, rounded base, or wider in upper part; straight or slightly curved; white, fair ly striate, spongy, fragile; without ring. *Lamellae:* Adnexed, crowded at firs but subdistant when mature, often forked near the stipe, entire, brittle; whi at first, then creamy and finally deep ochre and powdery. *Flesh:* White, thin; without odour. *Spore print:* Deep ochre. *Spores:* Broadly ovoid or subglobose, surface ornamented with warts and fine network of thin lines, amyloid; 8-10 x 6,5-8 μm.

Russula caerulea **Violet Russula**
Fruit-bodies with umbonate caps.

Russula capensis **Cape Russula**

Russula capensis showing sticky, red cap
urface, yellowish lamellae and short, white stipe.

35. Russula sardonia Fr.

Inedible

Russula sardonia – known earlier as *R. drimeia* – is common in the south-western and southern Cape Province and has also been found in the Midlands of Natal recently. It occurs from April to September, and grows under pines only with which it forms mycorrhizae.

The fruit-bodies may be recognized by the purplish colours of the stipe and by the deep greyish-purplish colours of the cap which often appears faded due to rain washing. This species varies somewhat in appearance but can be identified by taste, a small piece of its flesh placed on the tongue imparting a hot, acrid taste.

R. sardonia resembles another species, *R. quéletii* which has a deep wine-red cap and stipe, and white to cream-coloured lamellae; it seems to be rare in the region. *R. sardonia* is inedible because of the hot, acrid taste of the flesh which persists after cooking, but is not poisonous. (*Afrikaans:* Perssteelrooimus.)

Fruit-bodies scattered or grouped under pine trees. *Cap:* 40-120 mm diam., fleshy, thick, at first convex with margin wavy, faintly striate and somewhat incurved, later flat or somewhat depressed with margin upturned and split-ting in age. Surface smooth, matt, dry or slightly sticky when wet; deep rose pink, greyish magenta to greyish ruby or blackish purple, but colours washing out in rain. *Stipe:* Central, 60-90 x 12-20 mm, expanding at the apex and occasionally towards the rounded base, flattened and elliptical in cross section; white, flushed with pale purplish magenta or entirely pale lilac to greyish rose or light reddish purple; smooth, or slightly powdery in the lower parts; firm, brittle, solid; without ring. *Lamellae:* Close, adnate and slightly decurrent, forked near the stipe, brittle, edges thin, entire; whitish to pale yellow, finally golden yellow. *Flesh:* Thick, firm, creamy white with a faint greenish tinge, unchanging; odourless or with a faint, fruity odour and hot, acrid taste. *Spore print:* Pale cream. *Spores:* Pale ochreous cream, ovoid, covered with warts and a fine network of lines, amyloid; 6,5-8,5 x 6-7,5 µm.

36. Russula sororia (Fr.) Romell

Inedible

Russula sororia has been found under oaks in the Cape Peninsula, eastern Cape and in the eastern Transvaal. It occurs during summer and autumn. It has also been reported growing under conifers in the Cape Peninsula, and forms mycorrhizae with these trees. It does not appear to be common even though it seems to be widely distributed.

The smoky, brownish-yellow colours of the cap, the grooved margin which remains strongly downturned over the pale, brittle lamellae, and the short stipe aid recognition of this inconspicuous mushroom. *R. sororia* is inedible because its unpleasant flavours persist even after cooking.

Fruit-bodies scattered under oak trees. *Cap:* 30-60 mm diam., fleshy, con-vex at first, later expanding and developing a depressed centre; margin even, downturned, striate. Surface smooth, slightly sticky when moist, dull smoky brown but paler towards the margin. *Stipe:* Central, more or less cylindrical or tapering slightly downwards, 30-40 x 10-20 mm; white at first, becoming brownish especially towards the apex; smooth, firm, brittle, solid at first later partly hollow; without ring. *Lamellae:* Close, adnexed, edges entire, brittle, pale creamy white darkening to dirty white. *Flesh:* Thin, white discolouring to pale reddish brown with age; with rancid odour and unpleas-ant, hot, oily taste. *Spore print:* Pale cream. *Spores:* Hyaline, ovoid, with conical, obtuse or truncate warts, amyloid; 6,5-8,5 x 5-7 µm.

Russula sardonia
Purple-stemmed Russula

Russula sororia showing brownish cap with down-turned,striate margin.

Russula sardonia Fruit-bodies with purplish stipes.

Russula sororia

Edible

Fruit-bodies overlapping on substrate (imbricate)

Inedible

37. Schizophyllum commune Fr. *Splitgill*

Schizophyllum commune is common and widely distributed throughout southern Africa. It grows on dead stumps and logs, mostly of broad-leafed trees, particularly *Acacia* species and is very common throughout the summer. It is a wood-decaying species, causing a brown rot of minor importance in dead wood.

The small, hairy, silvery white to grey, bracket-like fruit-bodies with pinkish lamellae split along the edges are distinctive features. *S. commune* is eaten in central and east Africa and throughout south-eastern Asia and the adjoining islands. The fruit-bodies are tough and tasteless. (*Afrikaans:* Waaiertjie.)

Fruit-bodies grouped, clustered and overlapping on dead wood of mostly broad-leafed trees. *Cap:* 10-40 mm wide, sessile, fan-shaped, often fused with adjacent caps, leathery; margin wavy, lobed, commonly split or incised, inrolled. Upper surface densely covered with greyish hairs often with purplish tinges. *Stipe:* Absent, cap laterally attached to the substrate by a reduced base. *Lamellae:* Radiating from the point of attachment of the cap, narrow, pale pinkish tan, split longitudinally along the edge and in dry weather rolling inwards to protect the hymenium. *Flesh:* Very thin, pale greyish, tough; without distinctive odour or flavour. *Spore print:* White. *Spores:* Hyaline, cylindrical, smooth, thin-walled; 6 x 3 µm.

38. Tricholoma albobrunneum (Pers.:Fr.) Kummer *Brown Knightly Mushroom*

Tricholoma albobrunneum grows under pines in the south-western Cape Province where the fruit-bodies can be quite common during late autumn and early winter. Its growth under pines suggests a mycorrhizal association with these trees.

The tall stipe with the ring zone separating two differently coloured parts, and the reddish-brown, depressed, viscid, shiny cap with white lamellae, distinguish this species. A closely related species, *T. ustale*, also occurs in this region but is associated with broad-leafed trees. It has a chestnut-brown cap surface which is lighter at the margin and blackens with age, and a short, reddish-brown stipe becoming gradually lighter towards the apex. *T. albobrunneum* is edible but is unpalatable because of its bitter taste. (*Afrikaans:* Denneridderswam.)

Fruit-bodies grouped and clustered on soil under pines. *Cap:* 40-120 mm diam., fleshy, conical-convex becoming depressed and with a low umbo; margin wavy, smooth, incurved but later striate and turning upwards. Surface smooth, viscid, shiny when wet; rust-brown to reddish brown, covered with fine innate, radiating fibrils, darker towards the centre. *Stipe:* Central, cylindrical but tapering near the base, 40-100 x 15-20 mm, smooth; upper part creamy white with a finely scaly surface and separated from lower part by a reddish-brown, ring-like zone from which reddish-brown streaks colour the lower two-thirds of the stipe; firm, fleshy-fibrous, solid at first, becoming hollow. *Lamellae:* Adnexed, crowded, full and intermediate lengths, sinuate, broad, thin, edges entire; white at first becoming pinkish buff and rust-brown at the edges. *Flesh:* Firm, white tinged with reddish brown below cap cuticle and in base of stipe; faintly mealy odour. *Spore print:* White. *Spores:* Hyaline, broadly ellipsoidal, smooth; 5 x 3 µm.

Schizophyllum commune
Splitgill

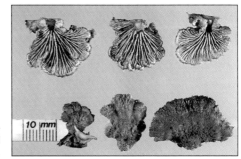

Schizophyllum commune showing fan-shaped, hairy, grey fruit-bodies with lobed margins and lamellae split along their edges.

Tricholoma albobrunneum Brown Knightly Mushroom

Tricholoma albobrunneum showing dark reddish-brown cap surface, white lamellae, and two-coloured stipe.

Cap with broad umbo

39. Tricholoma saponaceum (Fr.) Kummer *Soapy Toadstool*

Tricholoma saponaceum appears in the south-western Cape under *Pinus* species in autumn after good rains. It is very variable in appearance displaying colours from grey to brownish grey to grey-brown with rusty tints; the stipe has reddish tints towards the base. This species may be recognized by its odour and taste of old-fashioned soap. Its constant association with pines indicates a mycorrhizal association with these trees.

   T. saponaceum is edible but the soapy flavour makes it rather unpalatable. (*Afrikaans:* Seepswam.)

Fruit-bodies single or grouped on ground under pine trees. *Cap:* 40-80 mm diam., fleshy, convex then flattening, later with a broad, low umbo; margin even, smooth, incurved at first. Surface dry, or moist in damp weather, not sticky; smooth or cracking into scales; grey-brown or darker when young, often with olive tints, but lighter in age and often somewhat creamy at the margin. *Stipe:* Central, slender barrel-shaped, narrowing below and with a short rooting base, 50-80 x 15-20 mm, white but reddish towards the base; smooth or minutely scaly; fleshy-tough, solid; without ring. *Lamellae:* Adnate or notched, distant, full and intermediate lengths, thick, somewhat wavy, up to 8 mm broad, edges entire; cream to pale greenish, developing reddish spots. *Flesh:* Fairly thick, white, staining pinkish; with soapy or mealy-soapy odour and taste. *Spore print:* White. *Spores:* Hyaline, ellipsoidal, smooth, thin-walled; 5-6 x 3,5-4 µm.

Fruit-bodies with funnel-shaped caps (infundibuliform)

40. Trogia cantharelloides (Mont.) Pat.

The only record of this species in southern Africa is of the small, cream-coloured, funnel-shaped fruit-bodies found growing on a decaying log of an indigenous broad-leafed tree in the Tsitsikamma Forest National Park during early summer. They were possibly associated with a white rot in the wood.

   The shape and consistency of the fruit-bodies and their habitat on dead wood aid recognition of this species which seems to be rare in the region. The fruit-bodies resemble those of some smaller species of *Lentinus* but are light-coloured, without matted hairs or scales on the surface and have broader lamellae which do not have toothed edges. Because of their tough texture they are inedible.

Fruit-bodies grouped on dead wood. *Cap:* Up to 20 mm diam. and 30 mm in height, tough, leathery, funnel-shaped; margin slightly wavy, smooth, incurved at first, later turning up. Upper surface smooth, semi-matt, dry, cream to straw coloured. *Stipe:* Central, cylindrical or tapering somewhat downwards, 10-15 x 2-4 mm, pale tan, appearing waxy when dry; tough-cartilaginous, solid; without ring. *Lamellae:* Close, decurrent on stipe and occasionally forked near the base, full and intermediate lengths, thin, up to 2 mm, edges entire; pale cream. *Flesh:* White, tough, thin, up to 1 mm thick; no odour. *Spore print:* White. *Spores:* Hyaline, ovoid to broadly ellipsoidal, smooth, thin-walled, non-amyloid; 4-7 x 3-4,2 µm.

Tricholoma saponaceum
Soapy Toadstool

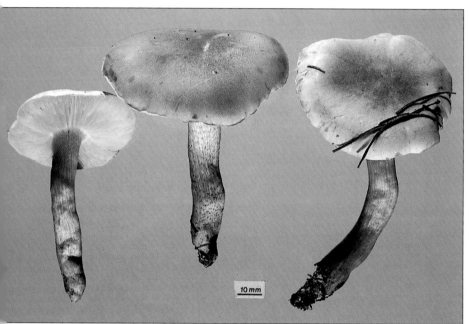

Tricholoma saponaceum showing
greyish-brown cap surface and barrel-
shaped stipe with short, rooting base.

Trogia cantharelloides Funnel-shaped,
stipitate fruit-bodies on dead wood.

Edible

41. Clitopilus prunulus (Scop.:Fr.) Kummer   *The Miller*

Clitopilus prunulus is known from collections around Pretoria, southern Natal and the eastern Transvaal, growing in soil under pines. It is likely that it is more widely distributed.

The species is distinguished by its white, irregular fruit-bodies with short, excentric stipes, pinkish, decurrent lamellae, and strong odour of new meal which is given off, especially when the fruit-body is damaged. It appears in late summer to autumn.

C. prunulus appears to be one of the many species that forms mycorrhizae with pines. It is edible with a good flavour but should be carefully examined for pinkish colours in the lamellae to avoid confusion with similar-looking species that are poisonous. (*Afrikaans:* Meulenaar.)

Fruit-bodies single or scattered on the ground under pine trees or in pastures. *Cap:* 30-80 mm diam., fleshy, convex at first, later depressed, irregular; margin somewhat wavy, incurved at first, later lobed. Upper surface dry but slightly slimy when wet, felt-like, smooth, white to ashy grey. *Stipe:* Often excentric, usually short, cylindrical but often tapering downwards, 25-80 x 5-15 mm, greyish white, downy or smooth, often striate; fleshy-tough, solid; without ring. *Lamellae:* Deeply decurrent on stipe, crowded, full and intermediate lengths, narrow, thin, margins entire; white at first, becoming pale pink. *Flesh:* Firm, thick, white, unchanging; with strong mealy odour and flavour. *Spore print:* Salmon pink. *Spores:* Hyaline, ellipsoidal to fusiform, with fine longitudinal ridges, thin-walled; 10-12 x 5-7 µm.

Fruit-bodies with decurrent lamellae (running down stipe)

Edible

42. Pluteus salicinus (Pers.:Fr.) Kummer

Pluteus salicinus is known in southern Africa only from this one collection which appeared on a piece of hardwood log in an orchid house in Pretoria. It is one of the *Pluteus* species which grows on dead hardwood logs. Another lignicolous species, *P. cervinus*, which has been recorded in southern Africa before, is usually larger and has a dark brown, fibrillar-scaly cap surface. Another species with a white cap surface, *P. semibulbous* has been recorded on dead wood, mostly poplar, from the south-western Cape Province. Species of this genus comprising mushrooms with pink spores are rather rare in the region. *P. salicinus* is reported to be edible.

Fruit-bodies grouped and clustered on dead wood. *Cap:* 25-70 mm diam., fleshy, thin, conical expanding to bell-shaped, sometimes with a broad, rounded umbo; margin even, downturned, striate. Surface dull greenish, bluish or olive-grey, paler towards margin which acquires fawnish tints as spores mature; smooth at first but soon minutely scaly over umbo and with minute, dark, radiating fibrils towards margin. *Stipe:* Central, long, cylindrical with slightly bulbous base, 55-90 x 4-8 mm, creamy white, faintly striate, with fine blackish fibrils on the lower parts; firm, solid; without ring. *Lamellae:* Free, close, full and intermediate lengths, thin, edges entire, broad; creamy white at first changing to brownish pink or salmon. *Flesh:* Creamy white, greyish under cap cuticle, floccose, thin, 1 mm over lamellae to 5 mm under umbo; with faint, mushroomy odour. *Spore print:* Pale brownish pink. *Spores:* Faintly pinkish, broadly ovoid to ellipsoidal, smooth, thin-walled, non-amyloid; 6,2-8 x 4,8-6,9 µm.

Cap with broad umbo

Clitopilus prunulus
The Miller showing smooth, white cap with somewhat irregular margin and pinkish, decurrent lamellae.

Pluteus salicinus

Pluteus salicinus showing greyish, umbonate cap surface, free, mature, salmon-coloured lamellae and white stipe.

43. Termitomyces clypeatus Heim

Edible

Termitomyces clypeatus is known in southern Africa only from occasional collections around Pretoria and Johannesburg. It is fairly common in more tropical African countries like Zambia, Kenya and Zaire. The fruit-bodies appear in December to January over termite nests with mounds so low that they are easily overlooked.

Fruit-bodies of *T. clypeatus* are readily recognized by the brownish cap with a conspicuously pointed umbo, the cylindrical stipe, and by their densely clustered growth habit. The fruit-bodies are edible and have a delicate flavour but the tough stipes are best removed before cooking.

Fruit-bodies closely grouped, occasionally clustered, over termite nests. *Cap:* 40-85 mm diam., fleshy, thin, at first narrow conical, expanding to broadly bell-shaped with a prominent, sharp-pointed umbo; margin inturned, irregularly lobed, splitting in age. Upper surface fibrillose-silky, dry, smooth; dark brown at first becoming ochreous brown and finally greyish at maturity with the umbo remaining dark brown; cuticle cracking radially in dry weather. *Stipe:* Central, cylindrical, 80-180 x 7-15 mm above ground level, creamy white to pale fawn and longitudinally striate; slightly thickened below ground level, then tapering downwards; single, or occasionally with two or three stipes united to form a single, tapering pseudo-rhiza attached to a fungus comb in the termite nest; tough, solid; without ring. *Lamellae:* Free, crowded, full and intermediate lengths, thin, broad, edges entire; creamy white at first turning pale pinkish brown. *Flesh:* Firm, white, unchanging, thin over the lamellae; without distinctive odour. *Spore print:* Pinkish cream. *Spores:* Hyaline, obovoid to ellipsoidal, thin-walled, smooth, non-amyloid; 4,8-7 x 3,2-4 μm.

Fruit-bodies with prominent umbo

44. Termitomyces microcarpus (Berk. & Br.) Heim

Edible

Termitomyces microcarpus, also called *Podabrella microcarpa*, occurs in the Transvaal, Natal, and in tropical African countries. The small, white fruit-bodies appear in large numbers after rain in summer on fragments of old fungus combs brought to the surface by species of wood-destroying termites. It is associated with three species of wood-destroying termites: *Odontotermes badius*, *O. transvaalensis* and *O. vulgaris*, which are common and widely distributed in southern Africa.

T. microcarpus is readily recognizable by its small, whitish fruit-bodies with prominent, pointed umbos. The fruit-bodies lack the subterranean pseudo-rhiza characteristic of other *Termitomyces* species, but its association with termites and the many micromorphological characters it shares with other *Termitomyces* species has lead most mycologists to classify it as such.

T. microcarpus is edible and has a good flavour but the large numbers of fruit-bodies needed for a meal have to be thoroughly washed to get rid of adhering sand grains.

Fruit-bodies in dense groups and clusters on soil brought to the surface by termites. *Cap:* 6-20 mm diam., occasionally larger, fleshy, convex to bell-shaped at first, flattening later and with a prominent umbo or perforatorium at the centre; margin incurved at first, regular to lobate, finally upturned and splitting. Surface smooth, dry, white to creamy, darkening to ochreous at the centre, occasionally streaked with brown. *Stipe:* Central, cylindrical, 15-45 x 1-5 mm, slender, smooth, with slightly bulbous base, white; fibrous solid; without ring. *Lamellae:* Adnexed to free, somewhat crowded, full and intermediate lengths, appearing thick, edges entire; white at first, turning light pinkish. *Flesh:* White, unchanging, firm, thin; odourless. *Spore print:* Light buffy pink. *Spores:* Hyaline, ovoid to ellipsoidal, thin-walled, smooth, with one or more refractive guttules, non-amyloid; 6-8,5 x 3,7-4,8 μm.

Termitomyces clypeatus

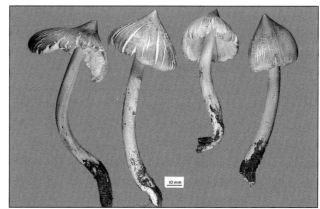

Termitomyces clypeatus
Fruit-bodies showing sharp-
pointed umbo, inturned,
lobate margin and long,
ringless, cylindrical stipe.

:rmitomyces microcarpus

Termitomyces microcarpus showing creamy
white cap with small, pointed umbo, and
slender, white stipe with slightly bulbous base.

45. Termitomyces reticulatus Van der Westhuizen & Eicker

Termitomyces reticulatus is fairly common in the Transvaal and northern Orange Free State. It is associated with the wood-destroying termites, *Odontotermes badius* and *O. transvaalensis*, which are widely distributed throughout southern Africa. The fruit-bodies appear from November to the end of January.

T. reticulatus is easily recognized by the large, striking fruit-bodies with distinctive cap markings and the long, tough, whitish pseudorhiza. It is edible and very tasty.

Fruit-bodies grouped in soil over termite nests. *Cap:* 60-180 mm diam., fleshy, at first egg-shaped but expanding to convex or almost flat and with a low, rounded umbo; margin even, smooth, downturned, occasionally with adhering fragments of veil-like tissue. Surface white, smooth, with small brown, wart-like patches with grit and sand adhering to them, arranged in a more or less concentric pattern; umbo covered with a smooth, dark brown membrane. *Stipe:* Central, cylindrical, 15-40 mm diam., 30-80 mm tall above ground level, white, often veil-like remnants suspended from its apex below ground level 300-900 mm long, greyish, cylindrical, attached to the fungus comb by a narrow, branching base; ring a fixed, white ridge often with a grey to brown margin; tough, solid at first, later hollowed out by the termites. *Lamellae:* Free or slightly adnexed, crowded, full and intermediate lengths, thin, fragile, edges irregularly crenate becoming laciniate, up to 12 mm broad; creamy white at first maturing pale brownish pink. *Flesh:* Firm, white, thin, 2-5 mm over the lamellae but up to 15 mm under the umbo unchanging; with a faint, mushroomy odour. *Spore print:* Brownish pink. *Basidiospores:* Hyaline, broadly ellipsoidal, smooth, thin-walled, non-amyloid; 6,1-8,3 x 4,3-5,6 μm.

Stipe with rooting base

46. Termitomyces sagittiformis (Kalchbr. & Cke.) Reid

Termitomyces sagittiformis was originally collected from Natal in 1880 but has not been reported since. The specimens illustrated here were found above a nest of the wood-destroying termite, *Odontotermes latericius*, in Pretoria after good rains in mid-November. This species resembles another in the genus, *T. clypeatus*, but can be distinguished by having a less sharply pointed umbo, a stout stipe with a swollen base, and a blackish pseudorhiza. The edibility of this rare species is unknown although all the other species of *Termitomyces* are edible.

Fruit-bodies grouped on soil over termite nests. *Cap:* 25-65 mm diam., fleshy, conical to bell-shaped with an acute, conical, almost spine-like umbo; margin uneven to almost lobate, incurved, smooth, splitting in age. Surface grey-brown to greyish umber, darker over the umbo, paler towards the margin; smooth, slightly shiny, dry, cracking radially and concentrically the cuticle sometimes curling into large scales exposing the pale cream flesh. *Stipe:* Central, long-fusiform, white above soil level, longitudinally striate, 25-60 x 6-12 mm, widening downwards to 10-30 mm diam. just below soil level, then tapering downwards into a blackish-brown pseudorhiza 65-160 mm long; tough, fibrous, solid; without ring. *Lamellae:* Free or slightly adnexed, crowded, full and intermediate lengths, thin, edges entire at first, later somewhat crenate to laciniate; creamy white at first changing to ochreous pink to pale pinkish buff. *Flesh:* Creamy white, unchanging, firm, thin; with faint mushroomy odour. *Spore print:* Ochreous pink to pinkish buff. *Spores:* Hyaline, ellipsoidal, apiculate, smooth, thin-walled, non-amyloid; 7,4-10,1 x 5,8-6,4 μm.

Termitomyces reticulatus

Termitomyces reticulatus showing low, rounded, brown umbo, concentric rings of scales on cap surface, pinkish lamellae and long, even pseudorhiza.

Termitomyces sagittiformis

Termitomyces sagittiformis showing prominent, conical umbo, greyish-brown cap surface, stipe with bulbous underground swelling, and tapering pseudorhiza.

47. Termitomyces schimperi (Pat.) Heim

Edible

Termitomyces schimperi is known in South Africa from the north-western Transvaal but is common in northern Namibia and is widely distributed throughout tropical Africa where it grows on termite nests.

The thick, brownish, irregularly cracked scales resembling sun-dried mud which cover most of the upper surface of the cap, and the long, narrow pseudorhiza characterize this species. It is edible and much prized as food in tropical African countries. In Namibia it is known as the 'Omajowa' and 'Termitenpilz'.

Fruit-bodies grouped on or around termite nests. *Cap:* 60-250 mm diam., fleshy, at first subglobose expanding to shallow convex, without a conspicuous umbo; margin even, smooth, straight. Surface white, smooth, covered by a persistent, thick, light to dark brown layer, continuous over the centre but breaking up into thick, flat, irregular, ochreous-brown to rust-brown scales, arranged in concentric circles towards the margin, scales sticky when moist. *Stipe:* Central, tall, cylindrical, 80-125 x 10-25 mm, white, swollen at the base to 40 mm diam. before tapering abruptly into a narrow pseudorhiza up to 400 mm long below soil level; covered with large, thick, brownish scales (the remains of the veil); fibrous, tough, solid; without ring. *Lamellae:* Free, crowded, full and intermediate lengths, thin, up to 14 mm broad, edges entire; creamy white at first, changing to pinkish cream. *Flesh:* White, firm, up to 20 mm thick, unchanging. *Spore print:* Pinkish cream. *Basidiospores:* Hyaline, broadly ellipsoidal, apiculate, smooth, thin walled, non-amyloid; 6-8,5 x 3,6-4,9 µm.

48. Termitomyces umkowaani (Cooke & Mass.) Reid.   *l'Kowe*

Edible

Termitomyces umkowaani occurs in the Transvaal, Natal and eastern Cape Province. It is associated with the wood-destroying termite *Odontotermes badius* which is widely distributed throughout southern Africa. The fruit-bodies appear after good rains from mid-November until the end of January and occasionally until March.

T. umkowaani is readily recognizable by its large, tough fruit-bodies with brown cap, white to pinkish lamellae and black pseudorhiza. The fruit-bodies are edible and tasty. (*Afrikaans:* l'Kowa.)

Fruit-bodies single or scattered over termite nests. *Cap:* Up to 250 mm diam., large, fleshy, at first conical expanding to bell-shaped, finally shallow convex with a broadly conical umbo; margin incurved, uneven to somewhat lobate, striate and splitting with age. Surface smooth and slightly radially striate, viscid when wet, dull greyish brown when young, lighter towards the margin with increasing expansion; cuticle occasionally cracking radially and concentrically and forming large, loose scales. *Stipe:* Central, smooth, creamy white, 70-150 x 10-20 mm at the cap widening downwards to a bulbous base (up to 80 mm diam.) below soil level, and then tapering downwards to a narrow, blackish, striate pseudorhiza up to 10 mm diam. and up to 500 mm long; tough-fibrous, solid; without ring. *Lamellae:* Free, crowded, full and intermediate lengths, thin, edges entire to somewhat uneven, laciniate in age, creamy white at first becoming brownish pink in age. *Flesh:* Thick but thin over the lamellae, firm, creamy white, unchanging; with faint pleasant odour and taste. *Spore print:* Yellowish pink to pale pinkish brown. *Basiodiospores:* Broadly ovoid, ellipsoidal, obliquely apiculate, smooth, thin-walled, non-amyloid; 6,1-11,3 x 4,3-5,6 µm.

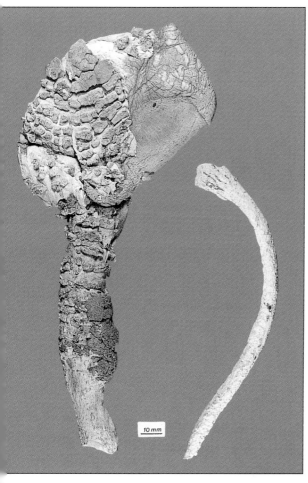

10 mm

Termitomyces umkowaani showing brown cap surface, conical umbo, swollen stipe and blackish pseudorhiza.

rmitomyces schimperi Fruit-body with thick, cked scales on upper surface and stipe, d portion of narrow, white pseudorhiza.

Termitomyces umkowaani I'Kowe

Edibility suspect

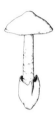

*Stipe with
sac-like volva*

49. Volvariella speciosa (Fr.) Sing. *Rose-gilled Grisette*

Volvariella speciosa appears to be common in the south-western Cape where it occurs in late autumn to early winter. It also appears occasionally in the Transvaal in late summer to early autumn. It grows in well-composted garden soil or on rotting compost which it decomposes to humus.

V. speciosa is recognizable by the white, slimy cap with pink lamellae, and the sac-like volva around the slightly bulbous base of the ringless stipe. The fungus is usually larger and more robust than the specimens illustrated here. Some mycologists regard the form with a striate margin, illustrated here, as a separate species, *V. gloiocephala*, which is poisonous. For this reason this species is best not eaten. (*Afrikaans:* Skynamaniet.)

Fruit-bodies scattered or grouped in well-composted soil or on compost. *Cap:* 30-100 mm diam., fleshy, egg-shaped at first expanding to convex or flat with a slight umbo; margin even, smooth or striate. Surface smooth, sticky, shiny when wet; white to pale greyish, creamy over the centre. *Stipe:* Central, tall, slender, narrowing upwards, 50-150 x 7-20 mm, with a slightly bulbous base enclosed in a white membranous volva with a lobed margin; surface smooth, dry, white; fleshy-tough, solid; without ring. *Lamellae:* Free crowded, full and intermediate lengths, thin, up to 8 mm broad, edges entire; white at first, changing to a rosy flesh colour. *Flesh:* White, soft, thin; with an unpleasant odour. *Spore print:* Salmon to brownish pink. *Spores:* Faintly pinkish, broadly ellipsoidal to obovoid, smooth; 10-12,8 x 6,8-7,9 μm

50. Agrocybe semiorbicularis (Bull.:St. Amans) Fayod

The small fruit-bodies of this species appear in groups in lawns and other grassy places from early summer to autumn, in the summer rainfall regions. It is fairly common in the Transvaal around Pretoria and is widely distributed throughout southern Africa.

Agrocybe semiorbicularis is reported to be edible but the quality of the fruit-bodies is unknown. However, because of the danger of confusing it with other small brown mushrooms, some of which are poisonous, this species is not recommended for eating.

Fruit-bodies scattered or grouped among grass. *Cap:* 10-25 mm diam., thin-fleshy, hemispherical becoming convex; margin even, downturned. Surface smooth, yellowish to ochreous to tan, darker at the centre. *Stipe:* Central, slender, cylindrical, 25-75 x 2-3 mm, smooth, shiny,concolorous with cap or paler; tough, stuffed to hollow in age; without ring. *Lamellae:* Adnate, close, full and intermediate length, edges entire, broad; pale ochreous turning to dark cinnamon. *Flesh:* Thin, yellowish, darkening to tan towards the stipe base; with a mealy odour. *Spore print:* Cigar-brown. *Spores:* Pale yellow-brown, ovoid, smooth; 11-13 x 7-8 μm.

Edible

*Fruit-bodies with
hemispherical caps*

Volvariella speciosa **Rose-gilled Grisette**

Volvariella speciosa showing white cap with striate margin, pink lamellae and ngless stipe with slight basal bulb nclosed in membranous volva.

Agrocybe semiorbicularis

Inedible

51. Bolbitius vitellinus (Pers.:Fr.) Fr.

Bolbitius vitellinus is common and widely distributed throughout southern Africa. The fruit-bodies appear in early summer to autumn, among grass in well composted lawns, on manure pats, and in other places where plant remains are present. The strongly grooved, shiny, yellow caps which fade to pale brownish grey from the margins inwards, and the dark, rust-coloured lamellae distinguish this species.

B. vitellinus is another of the saprophytic species which decompose organic material. It is inedible because the small fruit-bodies are slimy and lack flesh. They may also be slightly poisonous.

Fruit-bodies scattered to grouped or clustered in well-composted soil or dung. *Cap:* 20-60 mm diam., fleshy, at first egg-shaped then conical to bell-shaped expanding to almost flat; margin regularly grooved, the grooves extending almost to the centre. Surface lemon-yellow to egg-yolk yellow, slightly viscid, later dry and shiny and fading to brownish grey at the margin. *Stipe:* Central, slender, cylindrical or slightly tapered upwards, 30-100 x 2-5 mm, pale yellow, with a finely powdery surface; fragile, soft and hollow; without ring. *Lamellae:* Adnexed, crowded, thin, edges entire; pale yellow, darkening to cinnamon or rust colour. *Flesh:* Thin, membranous, translucent over the lamellae; without odour but with a very faint taste. *Spore print:* Dark rust-brown. *Spores:* Rusty brown, almond-shaped, smooth, with apical germ pore; 12-15 x 6-9 µm.

Inedible

52. Conocybe tenera (Schaeff.:Fr.) Fayod   *Dunce Cap*

Conocybe tenera grows in humus-rich soil in gardens and lawns during autumn. It is widely distributed, occurring in the south-western, southern and eastern Cape Province, Natal and Transvaal. It is one of a group of small mushrooms with conical caps, slender stipes and brownish lamellae which require microscopic examination in order to determine the species. A closely related species, *C. lactea*, with a more pronounced conical cap and creamy-white colour, has been seen in lawns in Pretoria; it appears overnight after good autumn rains but has usually shrivelled and gone by the afternoon.

Conocybe species assist in the breakdown of organic materials to humus but are of no value as food. Some are considered to be poisonous. (*Afrikaans:* Kaneelkappie.)

Fruit-bodies grouped on the ground among grass. *Cap:* 10-40 mm diam., thin, fleshy, bluntly conical but expanding to bell-shaped; margin regular, smooth and slightly incurved. Surface smooth, dull, dry, hygrophanous; ochreous to pale rust-coloured when wet, fading to pale brownish yellow or almost white when dry. *Stipe:* Central, slender, cylindrical with a small basal bulb, 55-100 x 1-5 mm, concolorous with cap and with a finely powdery appearance, often somewhat striate; fragile and hollow; without ring. *Lamellae:* Crowded, adnate, full and intermediate lengths, thin, edges entire; at first whitish, darkening to cinnamon. *Flesh:* Thin, concolorous with the surface, unchanging; with a mushroomy odour. *Spore print:* Bright yellow-brown or pale rust colour. *Spores:* Pale yellow-brown, ovoid, smooth; 8,5-1 x 5-8 µm.

Bolbitius vitellinus

Bolbitius vitellinus showing yellow, grooved caps and slender, yellow stipes with white bases.

10 mm

Conocybe tenera
Dunce Cap Fruit-bodies with dry, faded, whitish caps and cinnamon lamellae.

Edible

Fruit-bodies
bracket-shaped

Inedible

53. Crepidotus mollis (Schaeff.:Fr.) Kummer   *Jelly Shell Fan*

Crepidotus mollis has been recorded on decaying hardwood logs in the south-western, southern and eastern Cape Province as well as in Transvaal. It appears to be widely distributed but is not very common, and would seem to require cool, wet conditions for growth.

This species is edible but may be confused with a number of other small species of *Crepidotus*, some of which may be poisonous; it is therefore best avoided. (*Afrikaans:* Jellieskulpieswam.)

Fruit-bodies grouped on decaying wood. *Cap:* 10-60 mm wide, sessile, fleshy, soft, bracket- or fan-shaped, convex; margin even to somewhat undulate, striate, downturned and with a water-soaked appearance. Surface smooth and covered with fine, yellowish hairs, occasionally with large appressed scales; whitish at first behind the greyish, water-soaked margin, then yellowish to ochre-brown in age. *Stipe:* Absent, or rudimentary as a lateral, stout attachment, densely covered with long hairs; without ring. *Lamellae:* Crowded, full and intermediate lengths, decurrent, thin, margins entire; white at first becoming light brown. *Flesh:* White, soft with a gelatinous layer beneath the surface covering; without odour and with a sweetish flavour. *Spore print:* Snuff-brown. *Spores:* Brownish, ellipsoidal, smooth, without a germ pore; 7-11 x 4,5-6,5 µm.

54. Crepidotus variabilis (Pers.:Fr.) Kummer

Crepidotus variabilis was recently found on fallen twigs and thin branches of indigenous hardwood trees near George. It was previously reported last century from near Somerset East in the eastern Cape.

This species can be distinguished from *C. mollis* by the small fruit-bodies with lobate margins which grow on thin, dead branches, and the pinkish-brown spores. Like *C. mollis* and other *Crepidotus* species with small fruit-bodies which grow on wood, *C. variabilis* also assists in the degradation of woody material to compost and humus. Although some *Crepidotus* species are edible, they are best avoided as some can only be distinguished after microscopic examination. They may be poisonous.

Fruit-bodies grouped or clustered on dead twigs and thin branches. *Cap:* 5-20 mm wide, sessile, thin, fleshy, fan- to kidney-shaped; margin often lobed, inturned. Surface finely felt-like, hairy, white. *Stipe:* Absent or rudimentary and lateral; without ring. *Lamellae:* Crowded, full and intermediate lengths; white, becoming yellowish flesh-coloured. *Flesh:* Very thin, whitish; odourless. *Spore print:* Pinkish pale brown. *Spores:* Pale brownish, ellipsoidal, minutely verrucose; 5-7 x 3-3,5 µm.

Crepidotus mollis showing
sessile, water-soaked caps.

Crepidotus mollis
Jelly Shell Fan

Crepidotus variabilis

*Fruit-bodies
with clustered
growth habit*

55. Gymnopilus junonius (Fr.) Orton   Orange Tuft

Previously known as *Pholiota spectabilis*, this species is found in dense clusters at the bases of unhealthy hardwood and coniferous trees in late autumn. It occurs in the south-western, southern and eastern Cape and also in southern Natal.

    G. junonius is quite distinctive with its brightly coloured fruit-bodies with characteristically swollen stipes arising at the bases of trees or stumps. It causes brown rot in dead and dying coniferous and hardwood trees. This species is inedible because of its bitter taste, and is also reported to have a slightly hallucinogenic effect when eaten. (*Afrikaans:* Pragbondelswam.)

Fruit-bodies tufted at the base of trees or stumps. *Cap:* 50-150 mm diam., fleshy, semiglobose at first expanding to convex or almost flat or depressed, and with a slight, broadly rounded umbo; margin even to slightly undulate, smooth, inrolled at first and downturned at maturity. Surface smooth, dry, golden tawny to golden yellow darkening with age; covered with small, appressed, orange-yellow, fibrillar scales. *Stipe:* Central, 50-200 x 15-40 mm, sturdy, often swollen in the lower part but narrowing towards the base, smooth or fibrillose or scaly; tawny yellow to ochre with tawny-orange fibrils, becoming rusty with spores; tough, fibrous, solid. Ring membranous, on upper part of stipe. *Lamellae:* Adnexed, crowded, full and intermediate lengths, broad, thin, margins entire; yellow, turning rusty brown. *Flesh:* Thick, firm, yellowish to ochre, turning faintly reddish when touched; almost odourless but with a bitter taste. *Spore print:* Rust-coloured. *Spores:* Pale rusty brown, ellipsoidal to almond-shaped, finely roughened; 8-10 x 5-6 μm.

56. Gymnopilus penetrans (Fr.:Fr.) Murr.   Small Pine Cap

Gymnopilus penetrans is common in the south-western Cape but also occurs in the southern Cape and eastern Transvaal. The fruit-bodies occur in groups on decaying pine logs and cause a brown rot. It fruits in autumn.

    G. penetrans is one of three species of *Gymnopilus* with small fruit-bodies occurring in southern Africa. One of the others, *G. hybridus*, has an ochre-ous-yellow cap (the surface of which tends to crack) with a pale-coloured stipe, and a sweetly perfumed odour. It is common in the south-western Cape. The other species, *G. sapinea*, closely resembles *G. hybridus* and is probably a variety of this species.

    The three species are regarded as inedible because of their bitter taste. (*Afrikaans:* Gladde Dennevlam.)

Fruit-bodies scattered to grouped on pine logs. *Cap:* 20-70 mm diam., fleshy, somewhat bell-shaped expanding to convex or flat and with a slight umbo at the centre; margin regular, later somewhat undulate, smooth, thin, downturned. Surface smooth, dry, velvety to finely scaly with fine, radiating fibrils, brownish orange to brownish yellow with lighter margin, finally tawny *Stipe:* Central, cylindrical, or widening towards the base, 25-70 x 3-10 mm pale yellowish brown above but darkening to medium brown below and attached to the substrate by a white, hairy base; surface streaked longitud-inally with white fibrils; tough-fibrous, hollow; without ring. *Lamellae:* Close, adnate, full and intermediate lengths, 2-5 mm broad, thin, edges entire; yellowish at first darkening to spotted tawny. *Flesh:* Maize-yellow, darker in stipe, soft, 0,5-6 mm thick, unchanging; without distinctive odour but with a bitter taste. *Spore print:* Orange-brown to rust-coloured. *Spores:* Pale yellow-brown, almond-shaped, finely warty; 8-9 x 4-5 μm.

Gymnopilus junonius
Orange Tuft

Gymnopilus penetrans **Small Pine Cap**

Gymnopilus junonius showing orange-
brown fruit-bodies with rust-brown
lamellae and spindle-shaped stipe.

Gymnopilus penetrans showing
brown, slightly umbonate
cap, brown lamellae and
hairy, white-base of stipe.

57. Hebeloma crustuliniforme (Bull.:St. Amans) Quél.   *Poison Pie*

Hebeloma crustuliniforme is known only from the south-western Cape where it occurs in pine plantations and under broad-leafed trees. It forms mychorrizae with these trees but occurs sporadically and does not seem to be at all common. *Hebeloma* species are readily recognized by their smooth, pale-coloured, sticky caps, pale lamellae, flaky upper stipes and their radishy odour, but can be identified to species level only by examination with a high-powered microscope.

H. *crustuliniforme* is poisonous and because *Hebeloma* species are not well known, all should be avoided. (*Afrikaans:* Radysswam.)

Fruit-bodies scattered to grouped on soil under trees. *Cap:* 20-90 mm diam., fleshy, convex expanding to flat often with an obtuse umbo; margin inrolled and regular at first, smooth, finally slightly lobate and turning upwards. Surface smooth, typically sticky with debris or pine needles adhering to it, appearing varnished when dry; pale beige, darkening to brownish or reddish brownish, slightly darker over the disc. *Stipe:* Central, cylindrical or somewhat flattened or narrowing slightly upwards, 35-70 x 8-20 mm, greyish straw-yellow, darkening to brownish towards the base, finely roughened, appearing mealy over upper part, silky smooth and finely striate over lower part; tough fibrous, solid; without ring. *Lamellae:* Adnate, close to crowded, full and intermediate lengths, thin, up to 5 mm broad, margin entire; exuding watery droplets in moist conditions when young; white at first but soon pale brownish ochre, finally rust-coloured. *Flesh:* Translucent yellowish to pale brownish, up to 5 mm thick; with bitter taste and radish-like odour. *Spore print:* Rust-coloured. *Spores:* Pale rusty brown, ellipsoidal, finely roughened; 8-10,5 x 5-6 µm.

58. Hebeloma cylindrosporum Romag.

Hebeloma cylindrosporum is known from only one collection in southern Africa, that being from the Cape Peninsula. The small fruit-bodies with depressed caps were covered with a conspicuous layer of clear, sticky fluid. This characteristic, together with its lighter cap colours and smaller spores distinguish it from *H. crustuliniforme.*

Like most species of *Hebeloma*, this species is probably poisonous.

Fruit-bodies grouped on ground under pine trees. *Cap:* 25-35 mm diam., fleshy, convex at first, later expanded and depressed to shallow funnel-shaped; margin regular, incurved, faintly striate. Surface pale cream at margin, darkening towards the centre to light brown or cinnamon, smooth, polished, shiny, covered with thick, clear, glutinous fluid with debris and needles adhering to it. *Stipe:* Central, long-cylindrical and bent at the base 30-45 x 3-5 mm, attached to white mycelium in the soil, cream above, darkening to pale brown at the base, with small granular scales over the upper part, smooth or faintly longitudinally striate towards the base; fibrous, hollow without ring or volva. *Lamellae:* Adnate to slightly decurrent at first, later separating from stipe, close, full and intermediate lengths, thin, edges entire, up to 3 mm broad; pale beige. *Flesh:* Pale beige, soft, 1-3 mm thick *Spore print:* Clay-brown. *Spores:* Golden brown, fusiform to ellipsoidal, wall thickened and finely verrucose, with apical germ-pore; 7,6-8,3 x 3,8-4,9 µm

☠ *Hebeloma crustuliniforme*
Poison Pie

Hebeloma crustuliniforme
showing smooth, sticky cap
surface and brownish, ringless
stipe with mealy upper part.

☠ *Hebeloma cylindrosporum*

Hebeloma cylindrosporum
showing shiny, depressed,
sticky caps, and stipe granular
on upper part but smooth and
darker towards the base.

59. Inocybe eutheles (Berk.& Br.) Quél.   *Umbo Toadstool*

Inocybe eutheles is known only from the south-western Cape where it grows under pine trees during autumn to early winter. Most species in this large genus have small fruit-bodies with a prominent umbo, dull colouring, and a more or less scaly, fibrillose surface. *I. eutheles* may be identified by its growth habit among pine needles, the scaly surface of its pale buff to ochreous cap, and its brown spore print. It is possibly a mycorrhizal symbiont of pines. A related species, *I. lanuginella*, known to form mycorrhizae with pines, has been reported from the south-western Cape.

    I. eutheles is considered to be poisonous like many other species of *Inocybe*. (*Afrikaans:* Skildknopswam.)

Fruit-bodies scattered under pines. *Cap:* 15-50 mm diam., fleshy, conical expanding to bell-shaped with a prominent rounded umbo; margin regular to undulate, incurved, striate, splitting later. Surface finely fibrillose but breaking up into coarse fibrous scales, almost smooth over the umbo; yellowish grey to pale buff and darker to ochreous or orange-brown over the umbo. *Stipe:* Central, cylindrical, 30-75 x 2-7 mm, straight or curved with a slightly bulbous base; surface mealy, pale straw-yellow above, darkening to brownish buff towards the base; fibrous and solid; without ring. *Lamellae:* Free, crowded, full and intermediate lengths, thin, edges entire, broad;concolorous with cap to clay colour, but white along the edges. *Flesh:* Creamy, 1-4 mm thick, firm; with mild flavour and earthy odour. *Spore print:* Snuff-brown. *Spores:* Pale brown, ellipsoidal to almond-shaped, smooth; 8,5-10 x 4-5 µm.

Fruit-bodies with prominent umbo

60. Lepista caffrorum (Kalchbr. & MacOwan) Singer   *Deceptive Mushroom*

Lepista caffrorum was first reported from the eastern Cape as *Tricholoma caffrorum* in the previous century. It is fairly common around Pretoria during late summer in seasons of good rains. It may thus be more widely distributed than records indicate.

    L. caffrorum may be mistaken for the Field Mushroom, *Agaricus campestris*, hence its common name. However it is readily distinguishable from this species by the absence of a ring on the stipe, its strongly incurved margin and its white lamellae which gradually turn pale tan or fawn. The edibility of the species is suspect. Some people have reported eating it with impunity whereas others have suffered headaches, giddiness and colic about
24 hours after eating it: symptoms which indicate poisoning. It is thus best avoided. (*Afrikaans:* Skelmsampioen.)

Fruit-bodies grouped, sometimes forming fairy rings in lawns and other grassy places. *Cap:* 50-220 mm diam., thick, fleshy, at first hemispherical but expanding to shallow convex; margin strongly incurved but eventually turning outward and becoming undulate or somewhat lobate. Surface pure white, smooth and silky, later developing tinges of pale tan; cuticle cracking irregularly. *Stipe:* Central, straight, cylindrical or slightly swollen towards the base, 50-120 x 20-50 mm, white but turning yellowish when bruised, smooth or slightly ridged; solid, firm, cheesy; without ring. *Lamellae:* Crowded, adnate, notched, thin, edges entire, 5-10 mm broad, easily breaking away from the cap; white, gradually turning pale tan to pale fawn. *Flesh:* Up to 20 mm thick in cap, white, firm, unchanging when cut; with a slight, pleasant odour which later turns acrid. *Spore print:* Fawn to clay coloured. *Spores:* Pale pinkish, ellipsoidal, wall slightly thickened, coarsely verrucose; 5,5-6,7 x 3,7-4,5 µm.

? ☠ *Inocybe eutheles* **Umbo Toadstool** (above left and right) showing umbonate, fibrous, scaly cap surface.

☠ *Lepista caffrorum*
Deceptive Mushroom

Lepista caffrorum showing thick, fleshy, smooth, white cap and white lamellae notched at thick, ringless, white stipe.

Edible

61. Lepista sordida (Fr.) Kummer

Lepista sordida is known only from collections around Pretoria. A related species, *L. nuda*, which has larger fruit-bodies and lamellae which fade to buff in age, has been recorded in the vicinity of Pretoria. The lilac to brownish fruit-bodies of *L. sordida* appear in densely packed groups in lawns and well-composted flower beds in late summer after good rains, but this fungus is not at all common and little is known about it in the region. *L. sordida* is said to be edible but caution should be exercised as some *Lepista* species are poisonous.

Fruit-bodies closely grouped and clustered among grass. *Cap:* 15-70 mm diam., fleshy, convex becoming flattened to depressed or slightly umbonate and often wavy; margin regular or wavy, smooth, slightly viscid, incurved, splitting in age. Surface smooth, matt, hygrophanous, lilac-mauve at first changing to lilac-brownish and fading to dark biscuit. *Stipe:* Central, cylindrical or thickening slightly towards the base, 20-60 x 3-8 mm, occasionally bent, smooth, silky, pale-coloured towards the apex, otherwiseconcolorous with cap and finely streaked with darker lilac; fleshy-tough, fibrous, stuffed in the centre; without ring. *Lamellae:* Close, notched with a decurrent tooth, in age tearing free, full and intermediate lengths, thin, edges entire, up to 6 mm broad; lilac fading to lilac-brown in age. *Flesh:* Pale lilac, soft cheesy, changing to brownish, 1-2 mm thick. *Spore print:* Pale greyish lilac. *Spores:* Faintly brownish, ellipsoidal, minutely roughened; 6-8 x 3-4 µm.

Poisonous

62. Paxillus involutus (Bat.:Fr.) Fr.   *Brown Roll-rim*

Paxillus involutus occurs sporadically in woods of broad-leafed trees and pines in the south-western, southern and eastern Cape and in the Transvaal, but it is not common. The species is known to form mycorrhizae with both pines and broad-leafed trees but does not appear to be important in this respect because of the comparative rarity of its fruit-bodies in the region. The fruit-bodies form during summer and autumn.

  P. involutus is readily recognized by the dull brownish colours of its somewhat hollow cap, the strongly inrolled margin and the brownish, decurrent lamellae. It is poisonous when eaten raw although it is reportedly rendered harmless with cooking. However, the coarse, tasteless or somewhat sour, acidic flesh is not particularly palatable. It is also reported to cause a gradually acquired hypersensitivity that leads to kidney failure. (*Afrikaans:* Gesteelde Krulsoom.)

Fruit-bodies single or scattered under broad-leafed trees, particularly oaks. *Cap:* 40-120 mm diam., fleshy, convex at first then flat and becoming depressed; margin strongly and persistently inrolled, downy. Upper surface smooth and shiny when dry, slimy in centre when wet, ochreous to tawny yellow at first, becoming snuff-brown with hazel blotches. *Stipe:* Central, occasionally excentric, cylindrical or widening upwards, 40-100 x 8-20 mm, dry, smooth, hairless, cap colour or lighter, streaked or spotted darker brown especially when handled; fleshy-tough, solid; without ring. *Lamellae* Crowded, decurrent on stipe, branching and anastomosing at top of stipe, thin, edges entire, narrow; yellowish, darkening to yellowish olive, bruising brown. *Flesh:* Thick, firm, pale ochre in cap, tawny yellow in stipe, darkening to brown when cut or bruised; with a fungusy odour and acrid flavour. *Spore print:* Sienna. *Spores:* Ellipsoidal, smooth, pale brownish, thin-walled; 8-10 x 5-6 µm.

Lepista sordida

Lepista sordida showing hygrophanous cap with wavy margin and notched attachment of lamellae.

10 mm

☠ *Paxillus involutus*
Brown Roll-rim Fruit-bodies showing inrolled margin and brown, decurrent lamellae.

10 mm

Inedible

Fruit bodies
petal -shaped

Inedible

63. Paxillus panuoides (Fr.) Fr. *Stalkless Roll-rim*

Paxillus panuoides is known from the south-western, southern and eastern Cape and eastern Transvaal. It grows on dead pine wood, especially on pine stumps, in which it causes a decay which discolours the wood a bright yellow colour. It can be quite common in some areas and appears in early summer to late autumn.

The species is readily recognized by the sessile, dark yellow, overlapping fruit-bodies with hairy, lilac-coloured bases and radiating, branching lamellae. It is not edible. (*Afrikaans:* Steellose Krulsoom.)

Fruit-bodies sessile, clustered and overlapping on dead logs and stumps. *Cap:* 10-80 mm wide and 20-100 mm long, fleshy, petal-shaped to fan-shaped and laterally attached; margin thin, wavy and strongly incurved. Surface dry, smooth, finely velvety and buffy yellow, olive-yellow to yellow-brown with darker tinges in older parts; with a lilac to mauve somewhat hairy area near the attachment. *Stipe:* Absent, rudimentary or lateral,concolorous with cap, up to 10 mm long; tough, solid; without ring. *Lamellae:* Close, decurrent on rudimentary stipe, forked and radiating from attachment, often anastomosing or branching laterally near the base, thin, edges entire, narrow; yellow to yellowish buff, bruising darker; separating easily from the cap. *Flesh:* Thin, soft, creamy yellow to pale ochre, unchanging; without distinctive odour or taste. *Spore print:* Rusty yellow. *Spores:* Subhyaline, ellipsoidal, smooth, some dextrinoid; 4-6 x 3-4 µm.

64. Tubaria furfuracea (Pers.:Fr.) Gill.

Tubaria furfuracea is known from the south-western Cape Province and eastern Transvaal. Its fruit-bodies appear after rains in late summer and autumn on dead twigs and woody debris from broad-leafed trees. It does not appear to be common.

This small brown mushroom can be recognized by its brownish lamellae which briefly descend the stipe and by the white, woolly mass of threads around the base of the stipe where it emerges from the substrate. It is a wood-decaying species. It is inedible and may be poisonous.

Fruit-bodies grouped or scattered on wood. *Cap:* 10-30 mm diam., fleshy, convex at first expanding to flat often with a central depression; margin even, downturned, turning upwards later. Surface smooth, matt when wet, finely striate from margin inwards; cinnamon to tan, drying to buff or pinkish buff; slightly scaly, usually with minute whitish fibres and small white patches on the cap margin. *Stipe:* Central, cylindrical, 20-45 x 1-4 mm, widening towards the base which is densely covered with white, cottony threads; smooth, silky,concolorous with cap and finely striate with dark-coloured fibrils; fibrous, hollow. Ring membranous, disappearing. *Lamellae:* Close, broadly adnate to briefly decurrent, full and intermediate lengths, broad, edges entire; pale dull yellow at first, darkening to tawny. *Flesh:* Creamy beige or darker, soft fibrous, thin; without distinctive odour or taste. *Spore print:* Ochre to ochreous brown. *Spores:* Pale brown, ellipsoidal, smooth, without germ pore, very thin-walled, collapsing at maturity; 6-8,5 x 4-6 µm.

Paxillus panuoides
Stalkless Roll-rim

Paxillus panuoides showing
curved margin, rudimentary
pe and forked, radiating lamellae.

Tubaria furfuracea

Tubaria furfuracea showing
brown cap and lamellae,
and white, cottony threads
at stipe base.

65. Agaricus augustus Fr.   *The Prince*

Edible

Agaricus augustus grows under coniferous and broad-leafed trees in late summer and autumn. It is rare in southern Africa but can be found in the south-western and eastern Cape Province, and apparently more commonly in the Transvaal.

This species may be recognized by the large creamy cap copiously covered with brownish, fibrillose scales, by the scales on the stipe below the ring, and the lamellae that slowly change colour from whitish to creamy brown to dark reddish brown. It is edible and very tasty.

Fruit-bodies single or scattered in ground under trees. *Cap:* 100-200 mm diam., fleshy, at first broad ovoid, expanding to convex with a central depression; margin even and somewhat incurved. Surface yellowish brown and covered with numerous dark, reddish-brown, fibrous scales merged into a continuous disc at the centre. *Stipe:* Central, long-cylindrical or widening downwards to a bulbous base, 100-200 x 20-40 mm, whitish, with small brown scales below the ring, bruising yellowish; fleshy-tough, solid. Ring large, membranous, pendulous, white at first later brownish. *Lamellae:* Free, crowded, full and intermediate lengths, thin, edges entire; whitish for a long time then darkening to creamy buff and finally reddish brown, lighter along the edges. *Flesh:* Thick, firm, white at first becoming reddish with age, unchanging when cut; with a mushroomy taste and odour of almonds. *Spore print:* Purplish brown to chocolate-brown. *Spores:* Ovoid to ellipsoidal, brownish black, smooth, thick-walled, without a germ pore; 6,3-8,7 x 4,5-5,5 μm.

66. Agaricus bisporus (Lange) Imbach   *Cultivated Mushroom*

Edible

Agaricus bisporus is the most common commercially cultivated mushroom species, different strains of the species being used for this purpose. In the natural state it grows on compost and manure heaps, rotting garden waste and heavily composted open soil, but not among grass. It is not abundant but can appear throughout summer and autumn after good rains.

The species is best distinguished by examining the lamellae microscopically. It has only two spores per basidium instead of the usual four. It is edible, with a good flavour. (*Afrikaans:* Gekweekte Sampioen.)

Fruit-bodies scattered singly or grouped on compost. *Cap:* 40-100 mm diam., fleshy, hemispherical at first expanding to broadly convex; margin regular and projecting slightly beyond the lamellae. Surface finely scaly with brown, radiating fibrils uniting into small scales, these arranged concentrically around the centre but larger and more irregularly placed towards the margin; cuticle dry and peeling easily. *Stipe:* Central, cylindrical, with rhizoids attached to the base, 30-65 x 12-18 mm; white at first, darkening later and turning pale yellow-brown when handled; fleshy-tough, solid at first, later hollow. Ring membranous, persistent, narrow, with a double margin. *Lamellae:* Free, crowded, full and intermediate lengths, thin, edges entire; dirty pinkish, darkening to pinkish beige, finally purplish brown. *Flesh:* Firm, thick, white turning faint pinkish brown on bruising; with mushroomy odour. *Spore print:* Dark blackish brown. *Spores:* Cocoa to violet-brown, ovoid to subglobose, smooth; 4-7,5 x 4-5,5 μm.

Agaricus augustus showing reddish-brown scales on upper surface, dark brown lamellae and stipe bruising yellow.

Agaricus augustus
The Prince

Agaricus bisporus Cultivated Mushroom showing brown, fibrillar scales on cap, purplish-brown lamellae, cylindrical stipe, and ring with double margin.

Edible

Fruit-bodies with flat caps

Edible

Stipe with double ring

67. Agaricus arvensis Schaeff.:Fr.   *Horse Mushroom*

Agaricus arvensis appears in grassy, well-composted pastures, lawns and similar places after good rains in autumn. It occurs throughout southern Africa. The fruit-bodies are similar to those of the Field Mushroom, *Agaricus campestris*, but are larger and more robust. The cogwheel ridges on the expanding ring and veil are characteristic of this species, and its lamellae never display the bright rose-pink colours of those of the Field Mushroom. *A. arvensis* is edible, with an excellent flavour. (*Afrikaans:* Perdesampioen.)

Fruit-bodies single or scattered, occasionally in rings in grassy pastures. *Cap:* Up to 200 mm diam., ovoid at first expanding to convex, finally almost flat; margin even. Surface silky smooth, creamy white, yellowing slightly with age or on bruising. *Stipe:* Central, long-cylindrical or widening slightly towards a bulbous base, 80-120 x 12-20 mm; smooth, white but very pale beige towards the base; solid at first, later hollow. Ring double, large, pendulous, membranous, with thickened, radiating ridges resembling a cogwheel on the underside in young stage. *Lamellae:* Free, crowded, full and intermediate lengths, thin, edges entire; white at first then brownish and finally purplish brown. *Flesh:* White, firm, thick in cap, unchanging; with aniseed odour. *Spore print:* Dark, purplish brown. *Spores:* Blackish brown, ovoid, smooth; 5-6,5 x 3,5-5 µm.

68. Agaricus bitorquis (Quél.) Sacc.

Agaricus bitorquis is known only from around Pretoria at present, where it occurred in late spring to early summer in a public park and in one other grassy area. In Europe it is known as the Pavement Mushroom because of its ability to grow through hard-packed soil, even asphalt pavements. The white, thick, fleshy cap with its strongly inrolled margin and the two rings on the short stipe distinguish it. This species is edible with tough, strongly but pleasantly flavoured flesh. It is cultivated commercially on occasion.

Fruit-bodies scattered to grouped in a lawn. *Cap:* 45-110 mm diam., thick, fleshy, convex but soon flattened or slightly depressed; margin consistently and persistently inrolled, even, smooth with ragged veil remnants. Surface silky, smooth, white with small, pale brownish scales over the centre. *Stipe:* Central, short, stout, widening slightly downwards, tapering below ground level, 25-65 mm tall and 15-25 mm thick, white, silky, with two separate rings, the lower one narrower and just above soil level and resembling the edge of a volva; fleshy-tough, solid. *Lamellae:* Free, crowded, full and intermediate lengths, narrow, thin, edges entire; pale greyish pink at first but gradually darkening to brownish black with whitish edges. *Flesh:* Firm, white, faintly pinkish after cutting, thick, 8-15 mm; with a pleasant mushroomy odour. *Spore print:* Dark chocolate-brown. *Spores:* Dark brown, subglobose; 4-7 x 4-5 µm.

Agaricus arvensis
Horse Mushroom

Agaricus arvensis showing
yellow-bruising, white cap,
mature, purplish-brown
lamellae, and remains of ring.

Agaricus bitorquis showing
inrolled margin and thick flesh.

Edible

69. Agaricus campestris L.:Fr. *Field Mushroom*

The fruit-bodies of this species appear singly or in groups, sometimes in fairy rings in open grassy places soon after the first spring rains and during late autumn rains. It is widely distributed throughout southern Africa in areas of relatively high rainfall.

A. campestris is readily recognized by its smooth, silky, white fruit-bodies with bright, rosy pink lamellae which soon darken to brown, and by the ring on its white stipe. It is edible, soft and tasty. (*Afrikaans:* Veldsampioen; Kampernoelie.)

Fruit-bodies single or grouped in grassy pastures and lawns. *Cap:* Up to 120 mm diam., fleshy, spherical when young, then convex, later plane; margin even, usually projecting beyond the lamellae. Surface white to pearl-grey or beige, sometimes reddish brown; dry, smooth, silky or covered with fine scales. *Stipe:* Central, cylindrical, 30-100 x 10-25 mm, white, firm, more or less even or swollen at the base. Ring white, membranous, halfway up or above middle of stipe, sometimes disappearing partly or entirely in older fruit-bodies. *Lamellae:* Free, crowded, full and intermediate lengths, edges entire, thin; white at first, very soon rosy pink, darkening to chocolate-brown, finally almost black. *Flesh:* Thick, soft, white, turning brownish when bruised; with a sweetish mushroom odour. *Spore print:* Chocolate-brown. *Spores:* Dark brown, ovoid, smooth; 7-8 x 4-5 µm.

Suspected poisonous

70. Agaricus placomyces Peck

Agaricus placomyces occurs in both coniferous and broad-leafed woods but is rather rare in southern Africa. It has been recorded during summer and autumn in the south-western, southern and eastern Cape Province and in the Transvaal.

Distinguishing characteristics of this species include the blackish scales over the ivory-white cap surface, lamellae that remain greyish pink before finally turning blackish brown, and a stipe which bruises yellow. The edibility of *A. placomyces* is unknown but is strongly suspect like other species of *Agaricus* that stain yellow and have a strong, unpleasant odour.

Fruit-bodies scattered or single in ground under trees. *Cap:* 50-95 mm diam., fleshy, ovoid at first expanding to convex and finally almost flat with a depressed centre; margin even, slightly incurved at first. Surface ivory-white underneath a covering of blackish-brown, fibrillose scales which form an unbroken disc at the centre. *Stipe:* Central, long-cylindrical or widening towards the somewhat bulbous base, greyish white, glabrous, staining yellowish; fleshy-tough, stuffed, becoming hollow. Ring large, membranous, high up on stipe, upper surface whitish, under surface brownish. *Lamellae:* Free, crowded, full and intermediate lengths, thin, edges entire; at first white, then greyish pink for long time, finally blackish brown. *Flesh:* Thin, firm, white, staining yellowish when cut, finally pale brownish; with a strong, unpleasant odour. *Spore print:* Chocolate-brown. *Spores:* Dark brown, ellipsoidal, smooth; 5-6 x 3,5-4 µm.

Agaricus campestris
Field Mushroom

Agaricus placomyces

Agaricus placomyces
wing blackish scales on white
ap, pale greyish-pink lamellae
and large membranous ring.

Poisonous

71. Agaricus semotus Fr.

Agaricus semotus occurs in grassy places or clearings on the edges of broad-leafed and coniferous woods during summer and autumn. It is known to occur in the south-western and eastern Cape and in southern Transvaal, but is rarely seen.

The egg-shaped, flat-topped fruit-bodies of the button stage are distinctive. The small fruit-bodies of *A. semotus* are poisonous for some people.

Fruit-bodies single or grouped in woodland or in grass under trees. *Cap:* Up to 50 mm diam., small, fleshy, ovoid at first with flattened top, expanding to convex, finally almost flat with flattened central part; margin even. Surface smooth, white with fine, vinaceous fibrils radiating from the tawny-reddish centre, later yellowing and becoming dirty brownish; with occasional small, flaky scales. *Stipe:* Central, long-cylindrical, 22-60 x 4-8 mm, with a slightly bulbous base; silky white, darkening to yellow brownish and yellowing in the bulbous base; fleshy-tough, hollow. Ring double, thin, white, membranous and pendulous. *Lamellae:* Free, close, full and intermediate lengths, thin, edges entire; pale pinkish cream, later pinkish grey and finally greyish brown. *Flesh:* Firm, thin, white turning yellow in stem base, without distinctive odour. *Spore print:* Dark greyish brown. *Spores:* Dark brown, ellipsoidal, smooth; 4,5-5 x 2,5-3 µm.

72. Agaricus diminutivus Peck

Edible

Agaricus diminutivus grows in lawns and among grass in autumn. It is known only from Pretoria. The species is readily recognizable as a small *Agaricus* species by its purplish-brown lamellae and spores, whitish cap, and stipe with a persistent ring. It is one of a number of small and inconspicuous species of *Agaricus* which are neither common nor well known.

A. diminutivus is edible but not worthwhile because of its small size.

Fruit-bodies scattered or in groups among grass. *Cap:* 15-30 mm diam., fleshy, fragile, convex expanding to flat; margin even, smooth. Surface silky fibrillose, the fibrils reddish to reddish brown on a white to greyish surface but with a brownish disc; surface later darkened by spores. *Stipe:* Central, cylindrical occasionally with slight basal bulb, 20-50 x 3-5 mm, smooth or somewhat fibrillose, white; fleshy-tough, stuffed, becoming hollow. Ring delicate, membranous, persistent, white. *Lamellae:* Crowded, full and intermediate lengths, moderately broad, thin, edges entire; at first whitish, soon deep pink, finally dark purplish brown. *Flesh:* Thin, whitish; with a mild odour and taste. *Spore print:* Purplish brown. *Spores:* Purple-brown, ellipsoidal, smooth; 5-6 x 3-3,5 µm.

☠ *Agaricus semotus*

Agaricus semotus showing radiating, vinaceous fibrils on cap, greyish-brown lamellae, and large, membranous ring.

10 mm

Agaricus diminutivus

Edible

73. Agaricus sylvaticus Schaeff.:Secr.   *Scaly Forest Mushroom*

Agaricus sylvaticus grows in coniferous woods in the south-western Cape, the eastern Cape and Natal. It has also been found in indigenous broad-leafed forests in the Tsitsikamma Coastal National Park in soil richly composted with leaf-litter during early summer. This particular collection may in fact be the very similar species *A. haemorrhoidarius* which grows in deciduous woods, but is unknown in southern Africa.

A fairly rare species in the region, *A. sylvaticus* is characterized by an orange-brown, scaly cap and flesh that turns red when cut. It is edible and tasty but rather tough. (*Afrikaans:* Skubbige Bossampioen.)

Fruit-bodies grouped in soil with abundant leaf-litter under broad-leafed and coniferous trees. *Cap:* 50-100 mm diam., fleshy, conical to convex with flattened top, expanding to almost plane with a slight, flat, central umbo and regular margin. Surface densely covered with brownish-orange to caramel-brown fibrillar scales over a slightly lighter coloured base. *Stipe:* Central, slender, long-cylindrical with a slightly bulbous base, 45-80 x 6-12 mm; smooth or mostly scaly, white to pale brownish; fleshy-tough, solid at first, later hollow. Ring white to pale brown, membranous, pendulous. *Lamellae:* Free, crowded, full and intermediate lengths, thin, edges entire; pale greyish pink, darkening to dark purplish brown. *Flesh:* Firm, white, medium to thick, turning reddish when cut, later brownish; without distinctive odour. *Spore print:* Purplish brown. *Spores:* Dark brown, ovoid, smooth; 4,5-6 x 3-3,5 µm.

Edibility unknown

74. Agaricus trisulphuratus Berk.

Agaricus trisulphuratus is known from Pretoria and the north-eastern Transvaal Lowveld where it grows on compost or among grass in compost-rich soil. It also occurs throughout tropical Africa where it is believed to be the most widespread of the *Agaricus* species. However, it is not common in southern Africa.

This species is most conspicuous and easily recognized by its bright orange, scaly cap and stipe, and its lamellae which turn dark reddish brown as the spores ripen. It is probably involved in the decomposition of plant remains to humus. The edibility of *A. trisulphuratus* is not known but its scarcity prevents one from collecting enough for a meal.

Fruit-bodies scattered to grouped in soil or among grass. *Cap:* 20-50 mm diam., subglobose at first expanding to convex and finally flat or with a low umbo at the centre; margin slightly wavy, inturned at first with many adhering veil remnants. Surface covered by numerous, small, felt-like, apricot-orange to pinkish-orange scales, overlapping and fading to pale reddish buff. *Stipe:* Central, cylindrical, 25-50 x 4-7 mm, smooth, whitish or with pale orange tints above the ring but scaly and concolorous with the cap surface below it; fleshy-tough, solid becoming hollow. Ring thin, membranous but disappearing; set high up on stipe. *Lamellae:* Free, crowded, full and intermediate lengths, thin, margins entire, up to 6 mm broad; pale pinkish at first changing to dark reddish brown. *Flesh:* Pinkish to pale wine-red, thin, up to 3 mm over the stipe, unchanging when cut; without distinctive odour. *Spore print:* Cinnamon-brown. *Spores:* Ovoid to ellipsoidal, often depressed on adaxial surface, smooth, thick-walled with endospore thickened at the apex; 4,8-6,5 x 3,2-4,5 µm.

garicus sylvaticus
caly Forest Mushroom

Agaricus sylvaticus showing
cap with caramel-brown scales,
pale greyish-pink lamellae, and
pale brown, membranous ring.

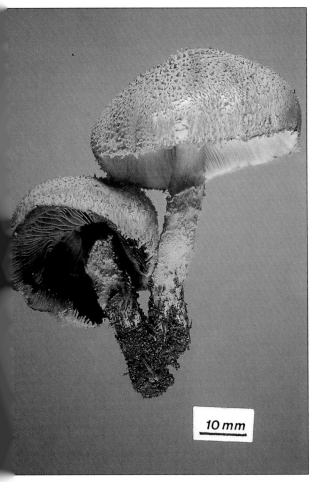

10 mm

Agaricus trisulphuratus with
apricot-orange scales over cap
and lower stipe, immature, pale
pink lamellae and mature, dark
purplish-brown lamellae.

Poisonous

Stipe with
bulbous base

Edible

75. Agaricus xanthodermus Genevier *Yellow-staining Mushroom*

Agaricus xanthodermus grows in groups in grassy places or open woodland near various species of trees (e.g. Acacias). It appears in the Transvaal from March to April and in the south-western Cape from May to July.

The whitish forms of this species may be mistaken for the edible Horse Mushroom, *A. arvensis*, but can be distinguished by the slender stipe with a bulbous base and the yellow-staining flesh with an odour of carbolic acid. Both the whitish and grey varieties of *A. xanthodermus* are poisonous, causing nausea, vomiting, headaches, profuse sweating and diarrhoea two to four hours after eating. (*Afrikaans:* Geelvleksampioen.)

Fruit-bodies grouped among grass or open woodland. *Cap:* 70-130 mm diam., fleshy, bell-shaped at first and flattened on top, later expanding to convex, sometimes with a slight central depression; margin even and inturned. Surface smooth, silky and creamy at first, later turning pale tan or greyish and cracking radially into small, dark grey, fibrillose scales, often imparting a sooty appearance to the cap; staining chrome-yellow when bruised but fading quickly. *Stipe:* Central, cylindrical, 60-120 x 8-15 mm, widening abruptly into a basal bulb 15-30 mm diam., silky striate, creamy white turning bright yellow when bruised or cut; solid, hard, later hollow. Double ring on upper part of stipe. *Lamellae:* Free, crowded, full and intermediate lengths, fragile, edges entire; whitish, turning greyish pink and finally blackish brown. *Flesh:* Firm, white turning yellow when bruised; with pleasant flavour but odour of carbolic acid. *Spore print:* Blackish brown. *Spores:* Dark brown, ellipsoidal, smooth; 5-6,5 x 3-4 μm.

76. Coprinus comatus (Müller:Fr.) S.F. Gray *Shaggy Ink Cap*

Coprinus comatus is widely distributed throughout southern Africa, its fruit-bodies appearing after good rains in summer and autumn. The unusual shape of the fruit-bodies and their characteristic deliquescence into a black liquid which often stains other plants nearby make this species easy to recognize. The fluid was used in the past as ink for writing. This fungus is one of the many species which assist in the conversion of plant debris to compost and humus.

C. comatus is edible and tasty but only young specimens in which deliquescence has not started should be eaten. (*Afrikaans:* Wolhaarinkmus.)

Fruit-bodies grouped or clustered on well-composted lawns, open grassy places or in flower gardens. *Cap:* 35-50 mm diam. and 70-150 mm tall, fleshy, long-ellipsoidal to almost cylindrical at first with the margin closely connected to the stipe by a ring, expanding to barrel-shaped then narrowly bell-shaped, the surface breaking up into broad appressed scales, white to creamy white at first, later pale ochreous and with pale yellowish-brown tips; apical disc smooth and pale ochreous to light brown; margin of expanding cap pinkish turning to dark grey and finally deliquescing into a black fluid until only the disc remains. *Stipe:* Central, up to 220 x 20 mm, tapering upwards from a bulbous base, white, silky; tough, hollow; with a movable, white ring which often disappears. *Lamellae:* Free or narrowly attached, crowded, broad, thin, margins entire; white, turning pinkish then grey, finally deliquescing black. *Flesh:* Thin, soft, white, turning pinkish and deliquescing black. *Spore print:* Black. *Spores:* Ellipsoidal, black, smooth 10-13 x 6,5-8 μm.

☠ *Agaricus xanthodermus*
Yellow-staining Mushroom
Fruit-bodies showing smooth white cap, greyish-pink lamellae turning blackish brown, and yellow-staining stipe with abruptly bulbous base.

Coprinus comatus
Shaggy Ink Cap

Coprinus comatus showing white, scaly, barrel-shaped caps, one starting to deliquesce at margin.

77. Coprinus disseminatus (Pers.:Fr.) S.F. Gray   *Fairies' Bonnets*

Coprinus disseminatus has been reported from the south-western Cape, Natal and Transvaal but may be more widely distributed and common than records indicate because the fruit-bodies are very short-lived and may thus escape notice.

This species plays a role in the decomposition of dead stumps of broad-leafed trees to compost and humus. A network of tough strands of brown-ish-red mycelium is formed by which the fungus spreads from the wood onto the adjoining soil where large clusters of tiny fruit-bodies are produced after good rains. These seldom last for longer than one day however. The growth habit of this species is characteristic, the small fruit-bodies appearing clustered in very large groups.

C. disseminatus is edible, with a mild taste but the fruit-bodies virtually disappear during cooking. (*Afrikaans:* Bondelinkmus.)

Fruit-bodies with grouped growth habit

Fruit-bodies in large groups, often hundreds, on stumps of broad-leafed trees or nearby soil. *Cap:* Up to 10 mm diam., 5-10 mm high, small, fleshy, ovoid at first expanding to hemispherical; margin even. Surface grooved almost as far as centre, yellowish or whitish becoming pale buff to greyish brown, fragile. *Stipe:* Central, short, slender, cylindrical, 20-40 x 0,5-2 mm, white, smooth or minutely hairy and darker towards the base; hollow, fragile without ring. *Lamellae:* Adnate, distant, thin, broad; white, turning grey to black, not deliquescing. *Flesh:* Very thin, membranous; without distinctive odour. *Spore print:* Umber to blackish brown. *Spores:* Dark brown, ellipsoidal, smooth, with apical germ pore; 7-9 x 4-5 µm.

78. Coprinus micaceus (Bull.:Fr.) Fr.   *Glistening Ink Cap*

Coprinus micaceus is common throughout southern Africa, appearing soon after rain from spring to late autumn. The clustered fruit-bodies are usually attached to buried, decaying wood, or to tree roots.

C. micaceus can be recognized by the glistening mica-like particles on the small, brownish, young caps. However, a number of other species are very similar and are mostly distinguishable according to microscopic characters only.

The species is edible but rather tasteless and should be eaten fresh before the lamellae start to decay. It is advisable to always cook these mushrooms as mild poisoning is known to occur when eaten raw. (*Afrikaans:* Glinsterinkmus.)

Fruit-bodies in clusters on the ground, at the bases of tree trunks or stumps and on decaying wood. *Cap:* 10-35 mm diam. and 25-35 mm high, fleshy, conical to bell-shaped; margin striate, uneven and somewhat inturned, fragile, splitting easily. Surface smooth or slightly pleated or striate, rusty yellow at first with a darker centre, darkening to date-brown; covered in the young stages with glistening mica-like particles which soon disappear. *Stipe:* Central, cylindrical, often curved, 20-50 x 3-6 mm, white to pale brownish yellow, smooth, silky but slightly downy around the base; soft fleshy and hollow; without ring. *Lamellae:* Free but touching the stipe, close, thin, fragile, margins entire; white at first, changing to biscuit then lead-coloured and finally decaying into a soft, dark, brownish-black, semi-fluid mass, especially in wet weather. *Flesh:* Thin, soft, pale yellowish; with a mushroomy odour. *Spore print:* Brownish black. *Spores:* Ovoid to ellipsoidal, dark brown to black, smooth; 7-10 x 4,5-6 µm.

Coprinus disseminatus
Fairies' Bonnets

Coprinus micaceus
Glistening Ink Cap

Coprinus micaceus showing
conical, striate cap with
glistening, mica-like particles.

10 mm

Edible

Fruit-bodies with
conical caps

Edible

79. Coprinus lagopus (Fr.) Fr.

Coprinus lagopus occurs mostly in shaded places among leaf-litter or the woody debris of broad-leafed trees. It is known from the south-western and eastern Cape and the Transvaal and appears to be widely distributed but rare. The species is edible but not worth considering because it is rare and its fruit-bodies short-lived.

Fruit-bodies solitary or in small groups on the ground in compost-rich soil or leaf-litter. *Cap:* 20-40 mm diam., fleshy, cylindrical-ovoid or conical at first expanding to almost flat. Surface greyish and covered with greyish-white scales at first, later darker with the margin splitting and turning upwards, then rolling inwards as the spores mature. *Stipe:* Central, tall, 50-110 x 2-4 mm, tapering upwards from a slightly swollen base, white, covered in fine down at first, later smooth; hairy at the base; fleshy-tough, hollow; without ring. *Lamellae:* Free, crowded, narrow; white at first, soon brownish and finally violaceous black, not deliquescing but producing an inky fluid and drying later. *Flesh:* Thin, delicate, white; odourless. *Spore print:* Black. *Spores:* Ellipsoidal, black, smooth; 11-14 x 6-7 µm.

80. Coprinus plicatilis (Curt.:Fr.) Fr. *Japanese Umbrella*

Coprinus plicatilis occurs in open grassy places and lawns in the Transvaal, Natal and Cape Province but is not as common as other ink caps. The tiny fruit-bodies appear after summer rains and are readily identified by their characteristic pleated, umbrella-like caps. They are short-lived, and although edible are not worthwhile. (*Afrikaans:* Geriffelde Inkmus.)

Fruit-bodies scattered to grouped in well-manured grassy places. *Cap:* 5-25 mm diam., egg-shaped at first expanding to shallow convex with a depressed centre, thin, membranous, almost translucent; margin even, thin or slightly lobed. Surface radially grooved and appearing pleated, buff to yellowish ochre in the centre, greying from the margin inwards. *Stipe:* Central, tall, slender with a slight basal bulb, 30-70 x 1-2 mm, white at first, becoming buff from the base upwards; without ring. *Lamellae:* Free distant, thin, narrow; clay-pink at first darkening to grey and finally black, withering away. *Flesh:* Membranous, fragile, same colour as cap; odourless. *Spore print:* Black. *Spores:* Ovoid-rhomboidal, smoky black, smooth; 11,5-16,5 x 8,5-10,5 µm.

Coprinus lagopus showing conical cap covered with greyish-white scales in young stage, and smaller older cap with margin turning black and inky.

Coprinus plicatilis
Japanese Umbrella

Coprinus plicatilis showing fragile, strongly pleated caps.

81. Hymenagaricus luteolosporus Heinem.

Edibility unknown

This species is known from one collection only which was found growing in soil under *Eucalyptus cloeziana* near Sabie, eastern Transvaal in late summer. It is one of three species of the genus *Hymenagaricus* which was described from tropical Africa in 1981. No information on its occurrence in southern Africa is available. It does not seem to be mycorrhizal but appears to be associated with the decay of woody litter.

H. luteolosporus is readily recognized by the striking appearance of the densely clustered fruit-bodies, the yellow caps covered with dark brown, wart-like scales, and the pinkish-grey lamellae that later turn black. Its edibility is unknown.

Fruit-bodies in dense clusters in soil under *Eucalyptus* spp. *Cap:* 20-45 mm diam., fleshy, bell-shaped at first, flattening later to convex-umbonate; margin regular, slightly incurved with adhering remnants of veil, smooth. Surface dry, dull yellow darkening towards the centre, with numerous, small, clay-brown to dark brown, wart-like scales, scattered but becoming more numerous towards the centre; umbo covered by an unbroken, dark brown disc. *Stipe:* Central, long-cylindrical, 40-140 x 3-7 mm, slender, curved or sinuous, fibrous; pale greyish yellow, silky over upper part, slightly scaly below the ring, the scales minute, brownish. Ring membranous, persistent, high up on stipe. *Lamellae:* Free, close, full and intermediate lengths, thin, edges entire, up to 6 mm broad; pinkish grey at first changing to purplish brown. *Flesh:* Pale greyish yellow changing to pale brownish in the stipe, 1-4 mm thick. *Spore print:* Black. *Spores:* Mid-brown, ellipsoidal, with smooth, slightly thickened wall and a single guttule; 4,2-5,5 x 3,7-3,9 μm.

82. Hypholoma fasciculare (Huds.:Fr.) Kummer   *Sulphur Tuf*

Poisonous

Hypholoma fasciculare is quite common in the south-western, southern and eastern Cape and has also been found in the eastern and north-eastern Transvaal. The fruit-bodies commonly occur on decaying stumps of broad-leafed trees from summer to autumn. The species may be recognized by the large clusters of smallish fruit-bodies with their distinctive sulphur-yellow colours, and lamellae that turn to dark brown.

H. fasciculare is a wood-rotting fungus which helps in the breakdown of dead wood, especially hardwood stumps. It causes a white rot. It is inedible, has an unpleasant flavour and is believed to be poisonous. (*Afrikaans:* Swawelkop.)

Fruit-bodies in dense clusters on dead hardwood. *Cap:* 10-70 mm diam., fleshy, convex, occasionally slightly umbonate, expanding to plane; margin smooth, wavy, downturned, sometimes ragged with adhering remnants of veil. Surface smooth, dry, bright sulphur-yellow but darkening to orange-tan over the centre. *Stipe:* Central, widening slightly towards the base, 50-200 x 2-10 mm, often curved or bent, joined at the base to other stipes; sulphur-yellow and smooth over the upper part, darkening to brownish and fibrillose towards the base; with a faint ring zone, often darkened by trapped purplish-brown spores; firm, solid at first, later hollow. *Lamellae:* Adnexed, crowded, full and intermediate lengths, up to 9 mm broad, thin; sulphur-yellow at first then pale greenish yellow to greyish brown to chocolate when mature. *Flesh:* Thin, firm, yellow but darker in stipe, unchanging when cut; with bitter taste and mushroomy odour. *Spore print:* Purplish brown. *Spores:* Smoky yellow-brown, ellipsoidal, smooth, with apical germ pore; 6-8 x 4-5 μm.

Fruit-bodies with clustered growth habit

Hymenagaricus luteolosporus

Hymenagaricus luteolosporus
showing dull yellow cap surface
with numerous dark brown, wart-
like scales, pinkish-grey lamellae
and slender stipe with ring.

Hypholoma fasciculare
Sulphur Tuft

Hypholoma fasciculare
showing yellow caps,
greenish-brown lamellae
and stipes joined at base.

Inedible

83. Panaeolus papilionaceus (Bull.:Fr.) Quél. *Cracked Mottle Gill*

Panaeolus papilionaceus occurs in the south-western, southern and eastern Cape Province, Natal and eastern Transvaal but does not appear to be common. It is one of a group of related species that grow on dung or soil of well-manured pastures. *Panaeolus* species are characterized by small caps, tall stipes and lamellae on which the dark-coloured spores mature in patches, imparting a mottled appearance before the lamellae turn uniformly black. This species is not easily distinguished from other *Panaeolus* species but has greyish, instead of brownish caps and the stipes are tall and do not have a ring.

Panaeolus species are not edible, and some are known to be poisonous. (*Afrikaans:* Barsvleklamel.)

Fruit-bodies grouped on dung. *Cap:* 15-35 mm diam., fleshy, delicate, conical to conical bell-shaped; margin regular, slightly incurved, projecting beyond lamellae. Surface smooth, dark grey and slightly sticky when wet, drying to ashy white, occasionally pale ochreous over the centre and cracking in dry weather. *Stipe:* Central, tall, slender, cylindrical with a slight basal bulb, 60-110 x 2-3 mm; greyish white, finely striate and powdery over upper part, darker towards the base; brittle, solid; without ring. *Lamellae:* Adnate, close, full and intermediate lengths, thin, broad, ventricose, edges entire; greyish at first, soon mottled with patches of mature spores, finally black but edges remaining white. *Flesh:* Very thin, fragile, greyish; with faint odour of burnt sugar when cut. *Spore print:* Black. *Spores:* Dark smoky brown, lemon-shaped, smooth; 11-16 x 9-12 μm.

Edibility unknown

84. Psathyrella candolleana (Fr.) Maire *Two-tone Veil Cap*

Psathyrella candolleana has been reported from the south-western and eastern Cape Province but is probably much more widely distributed. The fruit-bodies are formed from early summer to autumn, and require wet conditions for growth.

This species is very variable in colour and appearance but may be distinguished by the brittle, bell-shaped cap with thin flesh, the purplish colours of the lamellae, and the silvery white stipe which is slender, brittle and fibrous. Fruit-bodies grow in groups or clusters on or near old stumps or on the trunks of broad-leafed trees or dead logs. This species probably assists in the breakdown of dead wood to humus. The edibility of *P. candolleana* is unknown. (*Afrikaans:* Bleekbruin Sluierhoed.)

Fruit-bodies grouped and clustered in humus-rich soil or on dead wood. *Cap:* 20-60 mm diam., fleshy, rounded-conical at first, expanding to bell-shaped and then almost plane; margin somewhat wavy, downturned when young, appearing toothed with adhering remnants of veil which later disappear. Surface smooth or finely radially wrinkled, pale ochreous brown when moist, almost white when dry, often pale beige to buff-yellow over the centre; finally tinged dark purple near the margin from maturing spores. *Stipe:* Central, cylindrical or widening slightly downwards, 40-80 x 2-6 mm, smooth, fragile, silky, silvery white; fibrous, hollow; without ring. *Lamellae:* Adnate, crowded, full and intermediate lengths, narrow, thin, edges entire; whitish at first but soon greyish lilac and darkening to purplish brown with edges white. *Flesh:* White, soft, very thin; without distinctive odour or flavour. *Spore print:* Purplish brown. *Spores:* Dark brown, ellipsoidal, smooth, with apical germ pore; 7-10 x 4-5 μm.

Panaeolus papilionaceus
Cracked Mottle Gill

Panaeolus papilionaceus Fruit-bodies with ashy grey caps, black lamellae with white edges, and tall, slender, ringless stipes.

10 mm

10 mm

Psathyrella candolleana Two-tone Veil Cap (left and above) showing whitish, wrinkled cap surface, crowded, purplish-brown lamellae and slender, ringless, silky stipe.

Suspected
poisonous

85. Psilocybe coprophila (Bull.:Fr.) Kummer

This species is known in southern Africa from only one collection found on cow dung near Grahamstown in late summer. It is one of the many species of small, short-lived mushrooms that grow on dung. It also occurs in tropical Africa. It is rather inconspicuous but may be recognized by its smooth, shiny, brownish cap, its dark, brownish lamellae and its spores which have a violet tint.

P. coprophila is inedible and is probably poisonous. It has been reported to be hallucinogenic.

Fruit-bodies grouped to clustered on dung. *Cap:* 5-25 mm diam., thin, fleshy, hemispherical to broadly bell-shaped, often umbonate; margin even, smooth, slightly inturned. Surface smooth, shiny, viscid, tan to pale reddish brown; cuticle peeling easily. *Stipe:* Central, cylindrical, 25-40 x 1-3 mm, often bent near the base, smooth, pale, flushed with cap colour, covered with fine, cottony tufts near the base; fragile and brittle; without ring. *Lamellae:* Adnexed, crowded, full and intermediate lengths, broad, thin, edges entire; pale grey brown at first, darkening to dark brown. *Flesh:* Very thin, concolorous with cap; with a faint, mealy odour and taste. *Spore print:* Violaceous brown. *Spores:* Dark brown, ellipsoidal, smooth, with apical germ pore; 11-14 x 7-8,5 μm.

Suspected
poisonous

86. Stropharia aurantiaca (Cke.) Orton

Stropharia aurantiaca occurs sporadically in the south-western Cape Province but has been recorded from the eastern Transvaal as well. It appears in autumn to late winter and grows on sawdust and other forms of woody debris under broad-leafed trees, assisting in the decomposition of these materials. The fruit-bodies are attached to the substrate by means of yellowish mycelial threads.

The species can be recognized by its brightly coloured caps with drab lamellae, the tall, slender stipes and its growth on woody debris under trees. The edibility of *S. aurantiaca* is unknown but it is probably poisonous.

Fruit-bodies scattered or grouped in litter under broad-leafed trees. *Cap:* 10-50 mm diam., fleshy, semiglobose at first, expanding to bell-shaped or convex and with a slight umbo; margin even, somewhat incurved, smooth, often with adhering whitish veil remnants in the young stages. Surface smooth, dry, shiny, viscid when wet, orange-red to reddish brown, lighter in age. *Stipe:* Central, long-cylindrical, often bent and widening towards the base, 50-100 x 2-6 mm, smooth, cream-coloured at the top but streaked reddish brown towards the base; hollow, fibrous; ring disappearing or leaving remnants on the stipe. *Lamellae:* Adnate often with slightly decurrent teeth, close, full and intermediate lengths, thin, up to 4 mm wide, edges entire; creamy white at first, changing to dark olivaceous yellow to greyish brown. *Flesh:* Pale buff to orange-red, firm, thin, 1-3 mm in cap; without distinctive odour or taste. *Spore print:* Dark purplish brown. *Spores:* Dark brown, ellipsoidal, smooth, with apical germ pore; 11-13 x 6-8 μm.

10 mm

? ☠ *Psilocybe coprophila*

Psilocybe coprophila showing hemispherical, shiny, brown caps, and dark brown lamellae.

☠ *Stropharia aurantiaca*

10 mm

Stropharia aurantiaca showing shiny, reddish-brown caps, greyish-brown lamellae and tall, cylindrical stipes.

Suspected poisonous

Fruit-bodies with hemispherical caps

Edible

Stipe surface net-like (reticulate)

87. Stropharia semiglobata (Batsch.:Fr.) Quél.   *Dung Roundhead*

Stropharia semiglobata is known from collections in the south-western and eastern Cape and the north-eastern Orange Free State but may be much more widely distributed. It grows on horse and cattle dung during summer and autumn, assisting in its decomposition to humus.

It is one of a number of small, dark-spored mushrooms that grow on dung and some confusion may therefore arise about its identity. This species has bright, shiny, light yellow, hemispherical fruit-bodies which are quite conspicuous on dung. It is not edible and is probably poisonous. (*Afrikaans:* Koepelmisswam.)

Fruit-bodies grouped to clustered on dung. *Cap:* 10-50 mm diam., fleshy, hemispherical; margin even and somewhat incurved at first. Surface shiny, smooth, viscid, light yellow. *Stipe:* Central, long-cylindrical, 50-120 x 2-5 mm or thickening slightly towards the base, smooth, pale-coloured above the ring but covered by a glutinous, transparent layer beneath it; fibrous, hollow. Ring mostly thin, incomplete, often present as blackish fibrils. *Lamellae:* Adnate, close, full and intermediate lengths, broad, thin, edges entire; dark greyish yellow becoming purplish brown with blackish spots. *Flesh:* Pale yellow, thin; with mealy odour and sweetish flavour. *Spore print:* Purplish brown. *Spores:* Dark brown, ellipsoidal, smooth with apical germ pore; 15-19 x 7,5-10 µm.

88. Boletus aestivalis Paulet:Fr.   *Oak Bolete*

Boletus aestivalis is known only from the eastern Cape. The fruit-bodies grow singly or in groups under oaks with which it forms mycorrhizae. It can also form mycorrhizae with pines, but oaks are the preferred hosts. The fruit-bodies appear from early summer to autumn.

This species may be distinguished from *B. edulis* by the pale cap colours, the less massive appearance of the stipe in relation to cap size, and the brownish stipe which is covered for most of its height by a pale brownish network of threads. In *B. edulis* white threads form a network over the upper part of the stipe only.

B. aestivalis is edible and very tasty but tubes showing greenish colours should be removed and discarded before cooking. (*Afrikaans:* Eike Boleet.)

Fruit-bodies scattered or grouped under oak trees. *Cap:* 70-200 mm diam., thick, fleshy, almost hemispherical expanding to convex; margin even, downturned, smooth. Surface straw-coloured to pale snuff-brown, smooth, matt to finely velvety, often cracking in age at the centre. *Stipe:* Central, thick, robust, 60-160 x 20-60 mm, usually wider towards the base which tapers rapidly to a rounded point; uniformly pale brownish and covered by a network of raised threads – at first whitish later pale brownish – over the upper three quarters or more of its height; hard, solid; without ring. *Tubes:* Free, depressed around stipe, creamy white becoming greenish yellow, finally greenish ochreous-brown; pores small, 2-3 per mm; mouths circular, up to 20 mm deep. *Flesh:* Firm, white, thick; with strong nutty, mushroomy odour and taste. *Spore print:* Olivaceous snuff-brown. *Spores:* Brownish yellow, fusiform to elongate-ovoid, smooth; 14-16 x 4-5 µm.

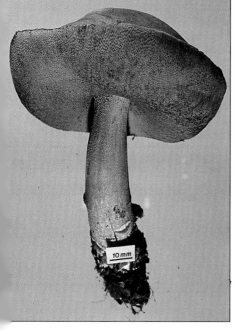

? ☠ *Stropharia semiglobata* **Dung Roundhead** (top and above) showing smooth, shiny, yellow, hemispherical cap, mature, purplish-brown lamellae, and long, cylindrical stipe.

oletus aestivalis Fruit-bodies owing smooth, pale brown ap, free, depressed tubes d stout stipe.

Boletus aestivalis
Oak Bolete

89. Boletus edulis Bull.:Fr. *Cep*

Edible

Boletus edulis forms mycorrhizae with pines and oaks and is distributed throughout southern Africa wherever these trees are grown in plantations. The fruit-bodies appear in late autumn to early winter in the south-western and southern Cape but in summer-rainfall areas appear from early summer to late autumn. In some areas they are harvested commercially for export.

This species can be recognized by the massive appearance of the fruit-bodies. The smooth, dark-coloured cap surface and large, pale stipe with a network of white threads over its upper part only are also quite distinctive. *B. edulis* is edible and very tasty but the tubes should be removed before cooking if they appear greenish. (*Afrikaans:* Eetbare Boleet, Sep.)

Fruit-bodies single or scattered under pines and oaks. *Cap:* 80-200 mm diam., fleshy, thick, hemispherical at first expanding to shallow convex; margin smooth and projecting slightly beyond the tubes. Surface smooth, dry, glossy, buffy brown to reddish brown or chestnut-brown, often paler towards the margin. *Stipe:* Central, swollen, barrel-shaped or club-shaped or more or less cylindrical, up to 120 x 60 mm, mostly thickened towards the base, at first appearing massive in comparison to cap; whitish to fawny brown, the upper half covered with a network of raised, white threads, the base smooth; hard, firm, solid, becoming spongy with age; without ring. *Tubes:* Almost free, depressed around stipe, at first white and stuffed with fungus tissue, up to 25 mm deep; pore mouths small, 2-3 per mm, circular to angular, turning creamy yellow to brownish green, resembling fine sponge rubber. *Flesh:* Thick, white, firm, becoming spongy and reddish in age; with fruity odour and nutty taste. *Spore print:* Olive-brown. *Spores:* Pale olive-brown, fusiform, smooth; 15-17 x 4-5 µm.

90. Chalciporus piperatus (Bull.:Fr.) Sing. *Peppery Bolete*

Edible

Chalciporus piperatus is known mainly from the south-western Cape Province where it occurs under pines during early winter. It was collected recently in the eastern Transvaal under pines in late summer. This fungus forms mycorrhizae with pines but can also associate with oak, beech and birch trees.

C. piperatus is readily recognized by the small fruit-bodies with reddish-cinnamon tubes, and the lemon-chrome colour at the base of the stipe. It is edible and has a good peppery flavour.

Fruit-bodies scattered on the ground under pines. *Cap:* 15-55 mm diam., fleshy, hemispherical at first, expanding to thick convex; margin regular or slightly wavy, somewhat incurved, smooth. Surface smooth, slightly slimy when wet, shiny when dry, occasionally cracking over the centre, ochre-brown to cinnamon or sienna. *Stipe:* Central, tall, slender, tapering towards the base; 20-60 x 3-15 mm, concolorous with cap surface but frequently lemon-chrome at the base and faintly longitudinally striate; fleshy-tough, solid; without ring. *Tubes:* Attached to stipe and slightly decurrent, more or less concolorous with cap but rust-coloured at maturity, up to 20 mm deep; pore mouths circular, simple, with reddish tinge, no colour change on bruising. *Flesh:* Deep straw-yellow, flushed reddish under the cuticle and deep lemon-chrome in base of stipe; cheesy, thick; odour faint but with peppery taste. *Spore print:* Ochreous cinnamon to snuff-brown. *Spores:* Light yellowish brown, oblong-ellipsoidal, smooth; 8-12 x 3-3,5 µm

Boletus edulis Cep

Boletus edulis showing brown cap and massive stipe with network of white threads covering upper half.

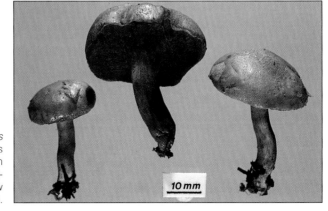

Chalciporus piperatus
Peppery Bolete Fruit-bodies showing shiny, dark brown cap surface, decurrent rust-coloured tubes, and yellow colour at base of stipe.

Edible

91.Gyroporus castaneus (Bull.:Fr.) Quél.   *Chestnut Bolete*
Gyroporus castaneus is known from the south-eastern Cape Province where
it was found fruiting under oaks from early December to late January. This
species forms mycorrhizae with oaks.

The common name refers to the distinctive colours of the cap and stipe
rather than to any association with a host species. These colours, together
with the pale-coloured pores, distinguish the species. *G. castaneus* is
edible and said to have an excellent flavour.

Fruit-bodies scattered under oak trees. *Cap:* 35-90 mm diam., thick, fleshy,
broadly convex to flat; margin even to undulate, downturned at first, finally
turning upwards. Surface smooth, dry, uniformly tawny orange to cinnamon,
rusty tawny to chestnut-brown. *Stipe:* Central, cylindrical or tapering
towards the base, often laterally flattened and bent near the base which
is narrowly rounded, sometimes bulbous, 25-70 x 6-15 mm or up to 30 mm
at the base; smooth, unmarked, concolorous with cap surface or slightly
lighter; fleshy-tough, firm, loosely stuffed, becoming hollow; without ring.
Tubes: Depressed around the stipe, white to cream to pale lemon-yellow,
5-10 mm deep; pore mouths small, 3-4 per mm, angular, single. *Flesh:*
White, unchanging, firm, 3-15 mm thick; with faint, pleasant odour and
sweet, nutty taste. *Spore print:* Pale straw-yellow. *Spores:* Subhyaline,
ellipsoidal-fusiform, smooth; 7-10 x 4,5-6 μm.

Edible

92. Leccinum duriusculum (Kalchbr. & Schulz *apud* Fr.) Singer *Poplar Bolete*
Leccinum duriusculum, formerly known as *Boletus duriusculus*, grows in
association with poplars – especially *Populus canescens* – with which it
forms mycorrhizae. It is distributed throughout southern Africa wherever
poplars grow in groups. The fruit-bodies appear in winter in the south-
western Cape and in late summer to autumn in summer-rainfall areas.

L. duriusculum is edible, with a pleasant flavour but is rather tough.
(*Afrikaans:* Populierboleet.)

Fruit-bodies single or scattered on ground under poplars. *Cap:* 30-90 mm
diam., fleshy, thick, convex; margin regular to vaguely undulate, slightly
overhanging the tubes. Surface somewhat downy, often stippled at first,
later smoother, viscid when wet; sepia-grey to blackish yellow-brown or
dark brownish grey. *Stipe:* Widening towards the base and tapering near
the base to a narrowly rounded point, 60-150 x 15-30 mm; whitish, with
dense vertical striations and minute black dots in lines which coalesce
to form small scales or a network of lines; often with greenish to bluish tints
near the base; firm, fleshy-tough, solid; without ring. *Tubes:* Depressed,
free around the stipe, deep; pore mouths small, single, circular; white at
first, soon beige, bruising olive-brown. *Flesh:* White, firm, thick, turning
slightly reddish and finally vinaceous grey in the cap and stipe apex, but
with tinges of blue-green which fade to brownish at the base of the stipe
when exposed to air; without distinctive odour and taste. *Spore print:* Blac
ish brown. *Spores:* Dark brown, subfusiform, smooth; 14,5-16 x 4,5-6 μm.

*Stipe surface
scaly (scabrous)*

Gyroporus castaneus
Chestnut Bolete

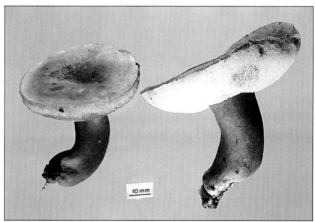

Gyroporus castaneus
showing uniformly brown
cap surface and stipe,
and creamy white tubes.

10 mm

10 mm

Leccinum duriusculum Poplar Bolete

cinum duriusculum showing smooth,
surface, depressed whitish tubes, black
tions on stipe, and blue-staining flesh.

93. Phlebopus sudanicus (Har. & Pat.) Heinemann   *Bushveld Bolete*

Phlebopus sudanicus, formerly known as *Boletus sudanicus*, is known from the central, north-eastern and eastern Transvaal. It is widely distributed throughout tropical Africa but is not common. It is found in late summer, usually among grass, and has also been reported in the vicinity of indigenous broad-leafed trees.

   P. sudanicus may be recognized by its large *Boletus*-type fruit-bodies with brownish colours, its blue-staining flesh and its short, thick, bulbous, excentric stipe. The edibility of this species is unknown but it has been reported to cause intoxication among the indigenous people of tropical Africa. (*Afrikaans:* Bosveld-boleet.)

Fruit-bodies single in open grassland. *Cap:* 80-570 mm diam., thick, fleshy, convex at first becoming plane and centrally depressed, often unequally expanded and saddle-shaped at maturity; margin thin, smooth, wavy, remaining inturned until maturity. Surface dry, smooth or becoming irregularly cracked, olive-brown at the centre and paling to ochreous buff towards the margin or speckled ochreous yellow in the olive-brown cuticle. *Stipe:* Mostly excentric, 60-270 x 40-90 mm, inflated at the base to up to 220 mm diam., smooth, dark yellowish but darkening from the base upwards to become concolorous with the cap surface, darker and longitudinally grooved over lower part, with basal tuft of brownish-olive mycelium, fleshy-tough, solid; without ring. *Tubes:* Adnexed, later free; 9-30 mm deep but shorter towards the margin; greenish yellow at first darkening to yellowish olive, ochreous behind margin; pore mouths angular and edges ragged, small, 2-3 per mm, concolorous with tubes. *Flesh:* White at first, soon yellow then brownish beige, 20-40 mm thick, soft to firm, changing to bluish green when cut; with pleasant odour and taste. *Spore print:* Olivaceous brown. *Spores:* Broadly ellipsoidal to subglobose, pale brownish, smooth, wall slightly thickened, non-amyloid; 6,2-9,3 x 4,8-7,2 µm.

Fruit-bodies with stipes off-centre (excentric)

94. Suillus bellinii (Inz.) Watling   *Pine Bolete*

Suillus bellinii is fairly common in the south-western Cape during the rainy winter season. It is always associated with pines with which it forms mycorrhizae. This species can be recognized by the cap surface which has ivory colours surrounding a darker brown central area, and by the short, downward-tapering stipe with the dark granules on its upper part.

   S. bellinii is edible but not as tasty as *B. edulis*. The sticky skin over the upper surface and the soft tubes should be removed before cooking. The fruit-bodies are sometimes attacked by a yellowish parasitic fungus. Such specimens should not be eaten. (*Afrikaans:* Denne Boleet.)

Fruit-bodies single to scattered under pines. *Cap:* Up to 120 mm diam., fleshy, convex when young but flattening out later and finally with margin upturned and cap bowl-shaped. Surface smooth, shiny, sticky when young, ivory at first, soon darkening to honey-brown with an ivory margin, finally deep leather-brown. *Stipe:* Central, short, 35-60 x 10-20 mm, tapering downwards towards a somewhat pointed base, pale yellow with deep red to chocolate-coloured granules or spots towards the apex; firm, solid; without ring. *Tubes:* Decurrent on stipe, up to 10 mm deep; pores small, 2-3 per mm, cream with an orange tinge at first, changing to greenish yellow, later yellowish olive with orange tints. *Flesh:* Thick, white with a lemon yellow tint; with a pleasant odour and mild taste. *Spore print:* Clay-colour. *Spores:* Pale yellow, subfusiform to cylindrical, slightly oblique at the distal end, smooth, thin-walled; 8-10 x 3-3,5 µm.

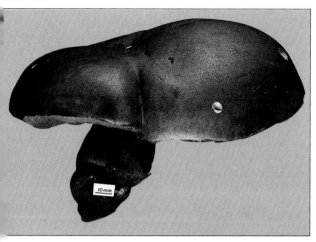

Phlebopus sudanicus
Bushveld Bolete

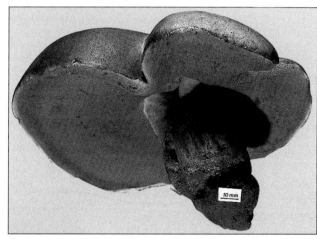

Phlebopus sudanicus showing fleshy, saddle-shaped cap, excentric stipe and yellowish-olive pore mouths.

illus bellinii Pine Bolete

Suillus bellinii showing sticky cap surface, decurrent tubes and short, tapering stipe with chocolate-coloured spots.

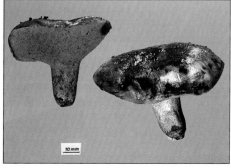

Edible

95. Suillus bovinus (L.:Fr.) O. Kuntze   *Cow Bolete*

Suillus bovinus grows under pines in the south-western, southern and east-ern Cape Province, appearing in late autumn to late winter in the winter-rainfall regions and during summer to autumn elsewhere. It is one of the species that forms mycorrhizae with pines and at times is fairly abundant.

This species may be recognized by its cushion-shaped cap with rather dull colours and by the large, compound pore mouths of the lower surface. It is edible but rather tasteless. The sticky skin over the upper surface and soft, ageing tubes should be removed from the fruit-body before cooking. (*Afrikaans:* Koeiboleet.)

Fruit-bodies single or scattered under pine trees. *Cap:* 30-100 mm diam., fleshy, convex at first and round cushion-shaped, later expanding to plane; margin even or slightly wavy. Surface smooth, sticky, deep warm buff to ochreous, often with pinkish tints and darker towards the centre, margin pale almost whitish. *Stipe:* Central, cylindrical, 40-80 x 6-12 mm, occasion-ally slightly swollen towards the base, smooth, concolorous with the cap or more reddish; firm, fleshy-tough, solid; without ring. *Tubes:* Adnate and slightly decurrent on stipe, up to 10 mm deep; pore mouths large, angular, edges thin, somewhat toothed, compound with several tubes opening into each pore; ochreous to ochreous orange to clay-buff. *Flesh:* Firm, thin, pale yellow, turning clay-pink in cap, yellowish rusty in stipe; with sweet, pleasant odour and fruity flavour. *Spore print:* Olive-brown. *Spores:* Dark brown, ellipsoidal to subfusiform, smooth; 8-10 x 3-4 μm.

Edible

96. Suillus granulatus (Linn.:Fr.) O. Kuntze   *Granular Stalk Bolete*

Suillus granulatus usually forms dense groups of fruit-bodies under pine trees in plantations and has also been seen growing under groups of orna-mental pines. It occurs in the south-western, southern and eastern Cape Province, Natal and Transvaal and is very common after good summer and autumn rains. It is important as a mycorrhizal fungus of many pine species.

This bolete is readily recognized by its yellow pores which ooze a milky white latex when young, the brownish granules on the upper part of the stipe, and the smooth, yellowish to reddish orange-tan surface of the cap.

S. granulatus is edible and has a good flavour but the cuticle should be removed from the cap before cooking. (*Afrikaans:* Melkboleet.)

Fruit-bodies in groups under pine trees. *Cap:* 30-90 mm diam., fleshy, hemispherical at first, expanding to convex, finally almost plane; margin regular or slightly undulate. Surface smooth, shiny when dry, viscid in wet weather, yellow tinged with brown or red, to entirely brownish red; cuticle peeling easily and entirely. *Stipe:* Central, cylindrical or slightly tapered downwards, often curved, 35-100 x 7-20 mm, light yellow but later marked with brown; upper part covered with small, reddish-brown marks or granules (dried droplets of white latex secreted in the young stage), reddish towards the base; fleshy-tough, firm, solid; without ring. *Tubes:* Adnate; pore mouths small, 3-4 per mm, angular, pale yellow to yellowish buff, exuding pale, milky droplets when young; tubes up to 8 mm deep and concolorous with the pores. *Flesh:* Firm, thick in cap, pale lemon-yellow, lemon-chrome in the stipe, unchanging, soft, spongy in age; with pleasant, slightly acid, fruity odour and sweetish flavour. *Spore print:* Ochreous sienna. *Spores:* Pale reddish brown, subfusiform to ellipsoidal, smooth; 8-10 x 2,5-3,5 μm.

Stipe surface granular

Suillus bovinus **Cow Bolete** (left and below left) showing warm buff-coloured cap, and large, compound pore mouths.

Suillus granulatus **Granular Stalk Bolete** (below) showing granules on stipe; in the field (bottom).

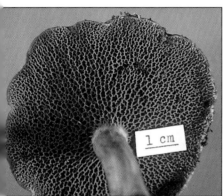

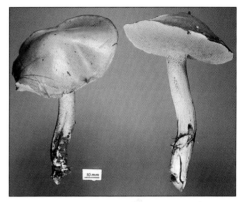

Edible

97. Suillus luteus (L.:Fr.) S.F. Gray   *Slippery Jack*

Suillus luteus has been recorded from Bloemfontein, Johannesburg and the Royal Natal National Park where it was found under pines during early autumn. It is not common in southern Africa but is always associated with pine trees with which it forms mycorrhizae. It appears to prefer certain species of pines.

S. luteus is the only bolete species with a ring on the stipe known in southern Africa at present. This character, together with the dark-coloured, sticky, smooth cap surface and pale-coloured pores distinguish it. It is edible but the sticky cuticle of the cap and any ageing tubes should be removed before cooking. (*Afrikaans:* Goudgeel Boleet.)

Fruit-bodies in groups under pines. *Cap:* 40-100 mm diam., fleshy, hemi-spherical at first becoming convex, sometimes with a slight umbo; margin even, occasionally with adhering veil remnants. Surface smooth, shiny, viscid in wet weather, chestnut-brown to sepia with violet tints when wet, fading, lighter coloured in dry weather, cuticle detachable. *Stipe:* Central, cylindrical, 50-100 x 10-20 mm, upper part white to pale yellow roughened with pale yellow dots which darken to reddish brown, below ring smooth, white to vinaceous; soft, solid. Ring large, membranous, white to cream darkening to sepia. *Tubes:* Adnate and briefly decurrent on stipe; pore mouths minute, circular, becoming polygonal with age, sulphur-yellow at first changing to pale greenish to pale olivaceous yellow. *Flesh:* Tender, thick, whitish but vinaceous in stipe, unchanging; with indistinct odour and sweetish flavour. *Spore print:* Clay-colour to ochreous. *Spores:* Subfusiform to elongate-ellipsoidal, pale yellow-brown, smooth; 7-10 x 3-3,5 µm.

Edibility unknown

98. Fistulina africana Van der Bijl

Fistulina africana was originally reported from Knysna on the trunk of living *Platylophus trifoliatus* but has been reported two or three times from the southern Cape since. It was also found by the authors on the dead trunk of an indigenous, broad-leafed tree at Mariepskop, eastern Transvaal. The species may be widely distributed but occurs very rarely.

A related European species, the Ox-tongue or Beefsteak fungus, *Fistulina hepatica*, is parasitic on chestnut and oak trees, causing brown trunk rot. *F. africana* causes a brown rot in wood of indigenous broad-leafed trees but unlike the European species does not have reddish flesh or blood red sap, and its tubes turn chocolate brown. The edibility of *F. africana* is unknown although the European species is edible.

Fruit-bodies single on living or dead trunks of indigenous broad-leafed trees. *Cap:* 50-120 mm radius, 30-110 mm wide and up to 35 mm thick; fleshy, bracket-shaped to fan-shaped with a short lateral stipe, margin somewhat uneven, downturned. Upper surface convex, dark brownish red to maroon, with a horny crust and roughened by darker coloured, raised pustules. *Stipe:* Lateral, short, cylindrical, 8-40 x 10-25 mm, with longi-tudinal grooves, deep rosy pink to vermilion and rough with numerous, raised pustules, many with brownish points; solid, fleshy; without ring. *Hymenial surface:* Formed by numerous, short, separate tubes, 1-2 mm long, pore mouths circular, deep ochreous at first, darkening to chocolate-brown. *Flesh:* Up to 30 mm thick, soft, somewhat gelatinous under the crust, colourless to ashy grey, drying brownish. *Spore print:* Yellowish brown. *Spores:* Ovoid to ellipsoidal, smooth, light yellow, thin-walled with large central guttule; 5-6 x 4-4,5 µm.

Fruit-bodies with lateral stipes

Suillus luteus **Slippery Jack**
Fruit-bodies showing ring
and veil remnants.

Fistulina africana (right and
below) showing upper
surface (right), and stipe
and pore surface (below).

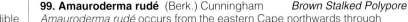

99. Amauroderma rudé (Berk.) Cunningham *Brown Stalked Polypore*

Amauroderma rudé occurs from the eastern Cape northwards through Natal and the eastern Transvaal and is usually associated with *Acacia mearnsii* (black wattle). The fruit-bodies appear from summer to autumn, usually after good rains. The fungus is not common however. It grows on dead, mostly buried wood, and is frequently found attached to the roots of the black wattle. It apparently does not cause root-rot or serious damage to the trees, but as yet little is known about its biology.

This fungus is easily recognized by the stipitate, brown, woody fruit-bodies with white pore surfaces which instantly turn red on bruising, and by their usual association with wattle trees. The tough fruit-bodies are probably inedible. (*Afrikaans:* Bruinsteel Porieswam.)

Fruit-bodies single or grouped under wattle trees. *Cap:* 20-80 mm diam., hard, corky to woody, convex to flat to broadly inverted conical and depressed; margin thick, rounded, even. Upper surface finely velvety, smooth or more frequently radially and concentrically grooved and ridged, chestnut-brown to umber, zonate. *Stipe:* Central or excentric, more or less cylindrical, 50-150 x 5-15 mm, straight or flexuous, occasionally branched; surface smooth, or irregularly knobbly, dull umber or snuff-brown, matt; tough, fibrous, solid, without ring; occasionally attached to a root. *Hymenial surface:* White to silvery white turning red on bruising, later dark blackish brown; with small circular pores, 3 per mm, partitions thick, even; tubes depressed, free or attached to stipe, up to 4 mm deep, concolorous with pores. *Flesh:* Creamy brown, turning red on cutting, fibrous, thick. *Spore print:* Dark brown. *Spores:* Subglobose to ellipsoidal, golden yellow, faintly punctate to verrucose, double-walled; 7-10 x 6-8 µm.

100. Ganoderma applanatum (Pers.:Wallr.) Pat. *Artist's Palette*

Ganoderma applanatum is distributed throughout the south-western, southern and eastern Cape, Natal, Transvaal and Zimbabwe and is fairly common on broad-leafed trees in indigenous forests. The fruit-bodies are perennial and may be found all year round, but in dry or unfavourable conditions do not show the white pore surface indicative of active growth. *G. applanatum* is an important pathogen of indigenous broad-leafed trees in which it causes severe and extensive white trunk rot.

The species can be recognized by the large fruit-bodies with a dull brown, horny surface. Recent studies suggest the existence of a *Ganoderma applanatum* complex of closely similar species which may be distinguished only on microscopic characters.

The hard, woody fruit-bodies are inedible. However, in her book *Gorillas in the Mist*, Dian Fossey reports that the fruit-bodies of this species are a favourite food of the mountain gorillas of Ruanda, Uganda and Zaire. (*Afrikaans:* Paletswam.)

Fruit-bodies bracket-shaped

Fruit-bodies single, scattered or occasionally compound on the trunks of broad-leafed trees; sessile, perennial. *Cap:* Up to 600 mm wide, 300 mm long and up to 100 mm thick; hard, woody, bracket-shaped to semicircular, widely attached, large; margin acute. Surface more or less flat, concentrically grooved, occasionally knobbly, covered with a hard, hairless, greyish-brown to umber crust. *Hymenial surface:* White, bruising brown; with small circular pores, 4-5 per mm; tubes layered, 7-25 mm deep each season. *Flesh:* Brown, felt-like, thinner than the tube layer; with mushroomy odour and bitter taste. *Spore print:* Brown. *Spores:* Ovoid-ellipsoidal and truncate at one end, yellow-brown, roughened, double-walled, the outer wall thin and suspended on the apices of the echinulae of the thick, inner wall; 6,5-9,5 x 5-7 µm.

Amauroderma rudé
Brown Stalked Polypore

Amauroderma rudé showing dark
brown cap surface and stipe, and
white hymenial surface bruising red.

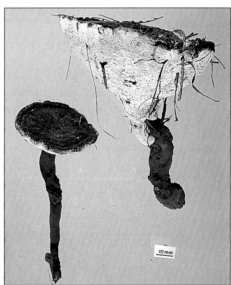

Ganoderma applanatum
Artist's Palette

Ganoderma applanatum
showing dull brown, grooved
and cracked upper surface,
white to yellowish pore surface
and brown tubes and flesh.

Inedible

101. Ganoderma lucidum (Leyss.:Fr.) Karst. *Orange-brown Lacquered Bracket*
Ganoderma lucidum occurs in the south-western, southern and eastern
Cape Province, Natal, Transvaal, Mozambique and Zimbabwe, and is quite
common in all of these areas during summer and autumn. The shiny, varnished upper surface is the most distinctive feature of the fruit-bodies,
although a number of similar species share this feature.

These fungi are important pathogens of broad-leafed trees. Some develop on the trunks of living trees, and stipitate forms attached to roots
appear to grow in the soil.

The woody fruit-bodies are inedible, although in the Far East they are
sliced and dried and used to prepare a tea-like decoction which is highly
valued as a health drink. It is believed to possess anti-carcinogenic properties. (*Afrikaans:* Oranjebruin vernisswam)

Fruit-bodies single or compound on or near trunks of broad-leafed trees;
sessile or stipitate. *Cap:* Up to 500 mm wide and long, and 10-50 mm thick;
large, circular to bracket-shaped or kidney-shaped, often grown together
laterally or arranged in overlapping tiers, corky when fresh, drying to woody;
margin thin, entire to somewhat wavy. Upper surface flat, occasionally concentrically grooved; covered with a thin, shiny, lacquer-like crust, yellow to
red to dark chestnut-brown, usually extending downwards and covering the
stipe as well. *Stipe:* Absent or lateral to excentric, more or less cylindrical,
up to 80 mm long and varnished like the cap surface. *Hymenial surface:*
White changing to brown on bruising or ageing, with small, circular to angular pores, 3-4 per mm, tubes 3-15 mm deep, brown within, in one layer.
Flesh: Whitish in upper layers to brown above the tubes or evenly brownish
throughout, soft, fibrous in upper part, firm corky in lower part, concentrically zoned. *Spore print:* Rust-brown. *Spores:* Yellowish brown, ovoid, truncate, roughened, with thin, outer wall suspended over the ends of the
echinulae of the thick inner wall; 9-11 x 5-7,5 µm.

Inedible

102. Coltricia perennis (L.:Fr.) Murr.
Coltricia perennis has been recorded once before in southern Africa. The
specimens illustrated here were collected in the eastern Transvaal, from soil
among charred wood under young pine trees. The fruit-bodies are rather
inconspicuous and may be overlooked, but the species does seem to be
quite rare in the region. *C. perennis* resembles *Polyporus arcularius*, a
wood-inhabiting species that has large, white, radially elongated pores
(see page 152). It is regarded as inedible.

Fruit-bodies scattered, grouped to clustered on ground among burnt wood.
Cap: 15-80 mm diam., thin, leathery, circular, depressed in centre or shallow
funnel-shaped, often grown together laterally; margin regular to finely fringed
in younger specimens. Surface dry, pale cigar-brown to rust-brown or pale
coloured, zonate, finely velvety, radially fibrillose. *Stipe:* Central, cylindrical
or slightly irregular, with a swollen to bulbous base, 20-45 x 2-8 mm; uniformly dark yellow-brown to rusty brown, velvety; tough-fibrous, solid; without
ring. *Tubes:* Attached and slightly decurrent on stipe, pale brownish at first,
later dark greyish beige, 1-5 mm deep; pores irregularly angular, 1-3 per
mm, edges thin, even or slightly uneven in parts, concolorous with tubes.
Flesh: Thin, up to 0,5 mm thick, fibrous, leathery, dark yellow-brown to
rust-brown; with a faint mushroomy odour. *Spore print:* Ochreous to light yellowish brown. *Spores:* Oblong to broadly ellipsoidal, pale yellowish brown,
smooth, thin-walled, non-amyloid; 6,5-9 x 4-5 µm.

*Fruit-bodies with
deeply depressed
caps*

134

Ganoderma lucidum
range-brown Lacquered
acket

Ganoderma lucidum showing
rnished, reddish-brown upper
surface, pale brown flesh and
white hymenial surface.

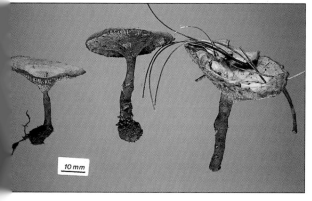

10 mm

Coltricia perennis showing
thin, shallow funnel-shaped,
cigar-brown cap and greyish-
beige tubes decurrent on
stipe with bulbous base.

103. Phellinus gilvus (Schw.) Pat. *Golden Bracket*

Phellinus gilvus, formerly known as *Polyporus gilvus*, occurs in the southern and eastern Cape Province, Natal, Transvaal and Zimbabwe. The fruit-bodies appear in summer and can survive for more than one season. This species is fairly common in some areas, growing on dead wood of broad-leafed trees in which it causes a white rot.

P. gilvus is very variable in form and appearance and not easily recognizable. The surface may vary from smooth to very rough although the colour is less variable. Identity should always be confirmed by microscopic observations. The fruit-bodies are inedible. (*Afrikaans:* Geelbruin Rakswam.)

Fruit-bodies sessile, grouped or compound on dead wood of broad-leafed trees. *Cap:* 2,5-150 mm wide, 20-60 mm radius and 2-20 mm thick; corky, tough, bracket-shaped to semicircular, often in overlapping tiers; margin entire, thin, rounded. Upper surface convex, yellowish brown to reddish brown, darker in the older parts, often more or less zoned; finely velvety at the margin, becoming hairless or rough with stiff projecting hairs. *Hymenial surface:* Pores minute, circular, reddish brown or darker, 5-8 per mm; tubes concolorous with pores, 1-5 mm deep, occasionally in layers. *Flesh:* Yellowish brown, corky to woody, tough, occasionally zoned, often darker brown in lower part over tubes, 1-15 mm thick; without distinctive odour. *Spore print:* White. *Spores:* Hyaline, oblong to ellipsoidal, smooth, thin-walled; 5-7 x 2,5-3,5 μm. Hymenial setae dark rust-coloured, ventricose to subulate, acute, thick-walled, 20-45 x 6-11 μm.

104. Phellinus rimosus (Berk.) Pilat *Cracked Bracket*

Phellinus rimosus is better known as *Fomes rimosus* Berk. This name is incorrect as it was originally applied to another species. However, it was used by Van der Bijl (1922) for the fungus described here. Until a thorough study has been made to establish the correct name for this fungus, both names can be used to indicate this fungus in the region.

P. rimosus occurs in the southern and eastern Cape, Natal, Transvaal and Zimbabwe, where it may be found on indigenous broad-leafed trees. It is an important pathogen, causing a brown heart-rot which gradually weakens and finally kills the tree. It is one of the common large, pore fungi in southern Africa, and its fruit-bodies are present all year round.

P. rimosus is one of a number of species with hard, cracking fruit-bodies. It may be confused with the related and very similar *P. robustus* Karst. However, the latter is known only from the eastern Cape and Natal. It causes a white rot and can be distinguished from *P. rimosus* by its hyaline, subglobose, smooth, thick-walled spores (6-8,5 x 5,5-7,5 μm) which give a whitish spore print.

The fruit-bodies of both species are inedible. (*Afrikaans:* Barsrakswam.)

Fruit-bodies sessile, solitary on trunks of living broad-leafed trees. *Cap:* 30-730 mm wide, 30-360 mm radius and 15-280 mm thick; hard, woody, bracket-shaped to hoof-shaped; margin yellowish brown, velvety, thick, rounded, even, merging into the upper surface. Surface grey to almost black, hairless, concentrically grooved, radially and concentrically cracked, and breaking up. *Hymenial surface:* Yellowish brown to dark brown, with minute circular pores, 3-6 per mm, partitions thick, velvety, yellowish brown to dark brown; tubes concolorous with pores, 2-6 mm deep in indistinct layers. *Flesh:* Yellowish brown to reddish brown, hard, woody, 5-15 mm thick. *Spore print:* Brown. *Spores:* Globose to broadly ovoid, rust brown, smooth, thin-walled; 4,5-6 x 3,5-5 μm.

Fruit-bodies hoof-shaped

Phellinus gilvus
Golden Bracket

Phellinus rimosus showing small pores in brown, velvety hymenial surface.

Phellinus gilvus showing rough upper surface, brown pore surface and brown, zonate flesh.

Phellinus rimosus **Cracked Bracket** Hoof-shaped fruit-body with cracked surface.

105. Coriolopsis polyzona (Pers.) Ryvarden *Leathery-brown Bracket*

Coriolopsis polyzona, previously known as *Polystictus occidentalis*, occurs in the eastern Cape, Natal and eastern Transvaal and further northwards into tropical Africa. It is fairly common on dead trunks, stumps and logs of broad-leafed trees and occurs during late summer and autumn after good rains. It occasionally is found on dead pine wood too.

The fungus is a strong wood-rotting species which causes severe and extensive white rot. The fruit-bodies are fairly drought resistant and can survive repeated dry spells but do not survive from one season to the next. The tough fruit-bodies are inedible. (*Afrikaans:* Leerbruin Rakswam.)

Fruit-bodies single, grouped or compound on dead wood. *Cap:* 60-130 mm wide, 15-80 mm deep and 1-10 mm thick; sessile to effused-reflexed, fan-shaped or kidney-shaped or shelf-like, flat or frequently concave and over-lapping, tough-leathery to firm and rigid; margin thin, acute, wavy. Upper surface hairy, concentrically grooved, olive-brown to buffy brown with zones of ochreous buff to cinnamon-buff or darker brown. *Hymenial surface:* Concolorous with upper surface, pores rounded at first, becoming angular or elongated towards the older parts, 1-3 per mm, light ochreous buff or darker with age, partitions even, thick or thin; tubes 1-3 mm deep, concolorous with pores, decurrent on the base of the cap. *Flesh:* Pale ochreous buff, 0,5-8 mm thick, fibrous, corky to woody, zonate; without distinctive odour. *Spore print:* White. *Spores:* Hyaline, oblong to ellipsoidal, smooth, thin-walled; 4,5-8,5 x 2-3,5 μm.

106. Coriolus hirsutus (Wulf.:Fr.) Quél. *Hairy Bracket*

Coriolus hirsutus is widely distributed in southern Africa, occurring in the south-western, southern and eastern Cape, Natal and Transvaal and further north into tropical East Africa. It grows on dead wood of broad-leafed trees, fruiting on logs and thinner branches during summer and autumn, or in early winter in areas of winter rainfall. It causes a severe white rot of the sapwood.

C. hirsutus is related to *C. versicolor*, a more common species which can be distinguished by the differently coloured zones on the surface of its fruit-bodies. Another very similar species, *C. pubescens* also occurs in southern Africa but its fruit-bodies grow in circular and imbricate clusters. Some mycologists place these species with their thin, leathery fruit-bodies in the genus *Trametes*. Species of this genus have thicker, softer fruit-bodies but there are no clear differences in the micromorphological characters of the fruit-bodies of these two genera.

The fruit-bodies of *C. hirsutus* are inedible. (*Afrikaans:* Harige Rakswam.)

Fruit-bodies sessile or effused-reflexed, solitary or scattered on dead hardwood. *Cap:* 15-100 mm wide, 15-60 mm radius and 1,5-10 mm thick; bracket-shaped to fan-shaped, tough, leathery when fresh, drying rigid. Surface flat, greyish pale cream to greyish pale yellow, same colour throughout but occasionally darker grey or blackish towards the centre; covered with longish hairs which form bristle-shaped bundles towards the older parts, concentrically zoned or furrowed. *Hymenial surface:* White to yellowish; with more or less circular pores, 3-4 per mm, partitions thick, even at first, later becoming thin and dentate; tubes 1-4 mm deep, concolorous with pores, decurrent on the base. *Flesh:* White, firm, unchanging, 1-6 mm thick; with faint mushroomy odour when growing actively.
Spore print: White. *Spores:* Hyaline, cylindrical to allantoid, smooth, thin-walled; 4,5-7 x 2-2,5 μm.

Coriolopsis polyzona
Leathery-brown Bracket

Coriolopsis polyzona showing brownish, hairy, zoned upper surface and ochreous-buff hymenial surface with angular to elongate pore mouths.

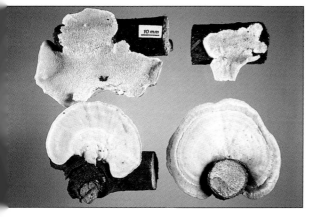

Coriolus hirsutus **Hairy Bracket**
Fruit-bodies showing hairy, greyish-cream upper surface and whitish hymenial surface with circular pores.

Inedible

107. Coriolus versicolor (L.:Fr.) Quél. *Turkey Tail*

Coriolus versicolor, also known as *Trametes versicolor*, is widely distributed throughout southern Africa and is fairly common on dead stumps and logs of broad-leafed trees. It is an important wood-rotting species which causes severe white rot in the wood. The tough fruit-bodies are fairly resistant to drought and often appear in rather exposed situations during the rainy season. They usually revive after a dry spell but do not survive from one season to the next.

The species is easily recognized by the multicoloured, zonate upper surface of the cap which is thin, tough and leathery, and it usually occurs in clusters. The pores in the lower surface distinguish this species from the similar *Stereum ostrea* which has a smooth hymenial surface. The tough fruit-bodies are inedible. (*Afrikaans:* Elwebankie.)

Fruit-bodies overlapping on substrate (imbricate)

Fruit-bodies sessile, grouped or in compound clusters on dead hardwood. *Cap:* Up to 80 mm diam, 50 mm radius, 1-3 mm thick; bracket-shaped or fan-shaped to kidney-shaped or circular, attached by reduced bases, often growing together laterally or arranged in overlapping tiers or forming rosettes; thin, tough-leathery; margin thin, somewhat bayed or lobed or wavy, white to pale yellowish. Upper surface covered with velvety hairs in multicoloured zones ranging from white to yellow-brown, brownish grey, reddish, greenish, bluish to blackish grey. *Hymenial surface:* White to pale cream drying to deep cream or brownish yellow, with small pores, 3-5 per mm, pore mouths angular, dividing walls even, thin; tubes up to 2 mm deep *Flesh:* White to pale cream, tough, cottony, thin 0,5-2,5 mm; with faint, mushroomy odour. *Spore print:* White. *Spores:* Hyaline, long-cylindrical, slightly curved, smooth, thin-walled; 4,5-6,5 x 1,2-2 µm.

108. Daedalea quercina L.:Fr. *Oak Maze Gill*

Inedible

Daedalea quercina is found in the south-western, southern and eastern Cape where it grows on dead logs, mostly oaks. The large fruit-bodies are perennial but seem to grow most actively during cool seasons after periods of good rain. This species causes extensive brown-rot in dead wood.

D. quercina is readily recognized by the bulky appearance of the fruit-bodies and the wide, elongate, labyrinth-like pores. Because of the tough, corky texture of the large fruit-bodies, these were frequently used in the pas to rub down horses. The Afrikaans common name most probably originated from this practice. The species is inedible because of the toughness of the fruit-bodies. (*Afrikaans:* Roskamswam.)

Fruit-bodies single or grouped or compound on dead wood. *Cap:* Up to 200 mm wide, 150 mm long and 80 mm thick at the oldest part; sessile, bracket-shaped, convex to flat, occasionally growing together laterally or overlapping; hard corky to rigid; margin thick, rounded, entire. Surface covered by a thin layer of downy hair at first, later smooth, hairless; uneven or somewhat furrowed; at first whitish to beige, later turning ochreous fawn or pale cinnamon, often zonate, darker in oldest parts, pale at the margin. *Hymenial surface:* Labyrinthiform, pore mouths elongate, occasionally resembling lamellae, 1 mm or wider, partitions thick, even; tubes 5-30 mm deep; white when fresh, later beige to pale fawn. *Flesh:* Whitish to pale brown, 2-15 mm thick, marked with concentric, light and dark zones, tough corky; with faint, pleasant, mushroomy odour when growing actively. *Spore print:* White. *Spores:* Hyaline, smooth, long-ellipsoidal to cylindrical, flattened on one side, thin-walled; 4,8-6,5 x 2,4-3,2 µm.

Coriolus versicolor
Turkey Tail

Coriolus versicolor showing multicoloured, zoned upper surface and white pore surface.

Daedalea quercina
Oak Maze Gill

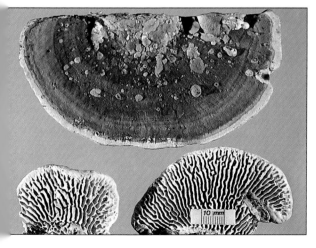

Daedalea quercina showing downy, brown upper surface and whitish hymenial surface with elongate, maze-like pores.

Inedible

109. Favolus spathulatus (Jungh.) Bres. *Stalked-fan Polypore*

Favolus spathulatus is known to occur in the Transvaal, Natal and the eastern and southern Cape. These records indicate a wide distribution but the fungus does not appear to be common. It seems to occur in autumn during prolonged spells of wet weather. This species grows on dead logs of broad-leafed trees in which it causes a decay of unknown character and severity.

The laterally stipitate, cream-coloured fruit-bodies with radially elongated pores are characteristic of this and another similar species, *F. brasilliensis*. However, the latter species has larger pores (2-3 mm long) and brownish spines in its hymenium which are lacking in *F. spathulatus*. The fruit-bodies are tough and probably inedible. (*Afrikaans:* Gesteelde poriewaaier.)

*Fruit-bodies
fan-shaped
(flabellate)*

Fruit-bodies grouped and clustered on dead wood. *Cap:* Up to 65 mm wide, 70 mm long and 1-6 mm thick; leathery, tongue-shaped, fan-shaped to kidney-shaped, mostly depressed but later more applanate; margin even, entire to somewhat lobed, later turning downwards. Upper surface dry, fine downy to smooth hairless, finely radially striate, ivory to cream colour. *Stipe:* Lateral, short-cylindrical, 5-25 x 3-10 mm, broadened at attachment, concolorous with cap, smooth, finely downy; tough-leathery, solid; without ring. *Hymenial surface:* White to cream, with small, angular, radially elongated pores, 0,3-0,6 mm long and 0,2-0,3 mm wide, partitions thin, white to cream; tubes 1-3 mm deep, concolorous with pores, decurrent on stipe. *Flesh:* Thin, white, soft, tough. *Spore print:* White. *Spores:* Hyaline, smooth, ellipsoidal, thin-walled; 4,2-6,2 x 2-2,5 µm.

Inedible

110. Fomitopsis lilacino-gilva (Berk.) Wright & Deschamps

Fomitopsis lilacino-gilva is known from Natal but has recently been collected from the south-western Cape and eastern Transvaal. It is possibly widely distributed but does not appear to be very common. The fruit-bodies seem to form after good rains, having been collected in winter in the south-western Cape and during summer and autumn in regions of summer rainfall. This fungus grows on dead logs and stumps of broad-leafed trees, especially *Eucalyptus* and oaks, in which it causes a brown rot.

F. lilacino-gilva was described from Natal in 1921 by P.A. van der Bijl as *Trametes griseo-lilacina*, but recent studies showed the two to be identical. It was reported prior to this from Australia and has recently been reported from Argentina too. It is one of a group of *Fomitopsis* species with pink to rose-coloured flesh. The fruit-bodies are inedible.

Fruit-bodies sessile, grouped or compound on dead hardwood logs. *Cap:* 30-100 mm wide, 20-40 mm long and 4-8 mm thick; leathery to corky bracket-shaped, flat, often in overlapping tiers; margin acute, even, soft, hairy on upper part. Surface covered with soft, matted hairs, often in sharp pointed bundles in the older parts, uneven, grooved; lilac in young parts becoming greyish fawn, brownish or dark grey in the older parts. *Hymenial surface:* Bright rose to lilac-mauve, with unequal, circular to elongated and angular pores, 2-3 per mm, partitions thick, entire; tubes 0,5-2,5 mm long, often with a cream-coloured layer inside. *Flesh:* Dark rose-pink to lilac-mauve, firm, corky, fibrous, 3-6 mm thick; with faint, pleasant, mushroomy odour. *Spore print:* White. *Spores:* Hyaline, long-ellipsoidal, smooth, thin-walled, non-amyloid; 6,8-8,2 x 3,2-4 µm.

Favolus spathulatus
Stalked-fan Polypore

Fomitopsis lilacino-gilva
showing rough, brownish
upper surface with pinkish
tints and rose to lilac-mauve
hymenial surface with
angular to elongate pores.

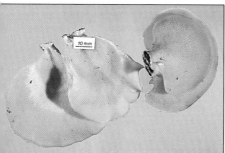

Favolus spathulatus showing
radially striate upper surface
of fruit-body and small, radially
elongated pores.

Fomitopsis lilacino-gilva

111. Funalia protea (Berk.) Reid

Brown Cork Polypore

Inedible

Funalia protea, formerly known as *Trametes proteus* (Berk.) Fr., is widely distributed in southern Africa and is one of the most common species of polypore fungi which grows on the dead wood of broad-leafed trees. It has been recorded in the south-western, southern and eastern Cape, Natal, Transvaal, Botswana, Zimbabwe, and in other tropical African countries. It occurs on logs and other timbers in contact with soil, causing a severe and extensive white rot. The fruit-bodies appear in summer and frequently survive a second season.

This species can be readily identified by the dark brown, hairy surface of the reflexed cap and the greyish colour of the pores in young fruit-bodies. The fruit-bodies are quite variable in form and are easily overlooked because of their inconspicuous colouring. They are tough and thus inedible. (*Afrikaans:* Bruin Kurkporieswam.)

Fruit-bodies sessile, in groups or compound clusters on dead wood of broad-leafed trees. *Cap:* 10-100 mm wide, 5-55 mm long and 2-10 mm thick, tough, leathery, shelf-like, often growing together laterally, mostly very thin, flexible, frequently extended downwards into a thin, wide part, closely appressed to the substrate; margin even, thin, entire, acute. Surface flat, smooth, velvety to hairy with soft, brown hairs, becoming greyish and roughened in age, azonate. *Hymenial surface:* Concolorous with upper surface, pores roundish to angular or elongate, 2-3 per mm, the partitions entire, thin tubes 1-2 mm deep, in one layer, with a greyish to bluish lining in young specimens. *Flesh:* Corky, fibrous, olive-brown, thin, 1-5 mm; with a faint, fungusy odour when fresh. *Spore print:* White. *Spores:* Hyaline, ellipsoidal, smooth, thin-walled; 7,5-9,7 x 2,8-3,2 µm.

112. Funalia trogii (Berk.) Bond. & Sing.

Inedible

Funalia trogii has been collected from the southern and south-eastern Cape, Natal and the Transvaal. It occurs on dead wood of broad-leafed trees, especially willow and poplar, and causes a stringy, white rot. The fruit-bodies develop in early summer but do not survive into a second season. It can be recognized by the reddish-brown, hairy upper surface of the fruit-bodies which are thick and largely resupinate, and by the large, angular pores. They are not very common as they seem to be destroyed by insects soon after they are formed.

A closely related species, *F. gallica* (Fr.) Bond. & Sing. also occurs in southern Africa. Formerly known as *Trametes hispida* Bagl., it differs from *F. trogii* by having more shelf-like fruit-bodies with darker colours, darker, reddish-brown flesh and much larger cylindrical spores measuring 12-15 x 4-5 µm. The tough fruit-bodies of *F. trogii* are inedible.

Fruit-bodies sessile, grouped on dead wood of broad-leafed trees. *Cap:* 40-100 mm wide, up to 40 mm long and up to 10 mm thick; firm to woody; reflexed, descending into a larger part closely appressed to the substrate; often growing together laterally to form a large, compound fruit-body; margin entire, thick, hairy, rounded. Upper surface densely covered with long, tawny to rust-brown hairs which turn grey in age and then disappear leaving the surface hairless and azonate. *Hymenial surface:* Pale brownish cream with a pinkish to lavender tinge, darkening to beige in age; pores angular, 1-2 per mm, the partitions thick, entire, tubes 1-5 mm deep and decurrent on the resupinate part. *Flesh:* Pale cream to wood-brown, 5-7 mm thick, fibrous, corky in lower part, becoming woody, soft in upper part which passes into the hairy surface. *Spore print:* White. *Spores:* Hyaline, long-ellipsoidal to cylindrical, smooth, thin-walled; 7-10 x 3-5 µm.

...nalia protea **Brown Cork**
...lypore (top and above)
...owing dark brown fruit-
...dies with angular pore
...ouths and faintly greyish
...een in some of the tubes.

Funalia trogii Fruit-bodies on
willow log (above right), and
showing hairy, reddish-brown
upper surface and brownish-
cream hymenial surface with
large, angular pores (right).

113. Gloeophyllum sepiarium (Wulf.:Fr.) Karst.

Gloeophyllum sepiarium was found in the eastern Transvaal 30 years ago for the first time in southern Africa, but recently was found to be common in the south-western and southern Cape. The fruit-bodies appear from summer to autumn and grow on dead pine logs and stumps, causing a severe and extensive brown rot of the wood. The tough, hairy fruit-bodies with their distinctive colours and brownish, lamella-like hymenial surface are readily recognized where they grow on dead pine wood.

A related species, *G. trabeum*, which has wider, more evenly coloured, shelf-like fruit-bodies with elongated pores in the hymenial surface, grows on wood of broad-leafed trees. It has been recorded from the south-western Cape, eastern Orange Free State, and southern Transvaal. The tough fruit-bodies of *G. sepiarium* are inedible.

Fruit-bodies sessile, grouped or clustered on dead pine logs. *Cap:* 25-120 mm wide, 20-40 mm long and 5-10 mm thick; tough, leathery, semi-circular to shelf-shaped, sometimes growing together laterally or in overlapping tiers; margin regular to slightly wavy, rounded, downy, brightly coloured. Upper surface slightly convex to plane or slightly depressed, hairy to bristly and concentrically grooved and zoned, reddish to bright yellow-brown at the margin, dark brown to blackish in the older parts. *Hymenial surface:* Tubes elongate with lamella-like partitions radially arranged, crowded and anastomosed, not separable from the cap, brownish ochre, up to 5 mm deep; pores 1-2 per mm, edges at first powdery, whitish, then reddish brown. *Flesh:* Thin, corky, tobacco-brown; lacking a particular odour or flavour. *Spore print:* White. *Spores:* Hyaline, ellipsoidal to cylindrical, smooth, thin-walled; 9-12,5 x 3-4,5 µm.

114. Hexagona tenuis Hkr.:Fr.   *Thin-cap Honeycomb Bracket*

Hexagona tenuis is widely distributed in the south-western, southern and eastern Cape, Natal, central, eastern and northern Transvaal and in Zimbabwe. It is more common in the subtropical and tropical parts of the region where the fruit-bodies occur during summer and autumn. It is usually found on dead wood of broad-leafed trees, on branches about 10-100 mm thick lying on the ground beneath the trees, and causes a white rot in the wood. It seems to be capable of growing under dry conditions and reviving after drought, but does not survive from one season to the next.

This species can be identified by the thin, leathery, brown fruit-bodies and large, honeycomb-like pores of the hymenial surfaces. The tough fruit-bodies are inedible. (*Afrikaans:* Dunhoedheuningkoekswam.)

Fruit-bodies single or grouped on dead wood of broad-leafed trees. *Cap:* 30-70 mm wide, 20-45 mm long and 0,5-2 mm thick; sessile, often narrowly attached, or effused-reflexed, shell-shaped to fan-shaped, free or growing together laterally; thin, leathery, flexible; margin thin, acute, entire to somewhat lobed, often wavy. Surface flat or slightly depressed, hairless, shiny, smooth or grooved, concentrically zoned in snuff-brown, cinnamon to haze or chestnut-brown but often blackish brown around the base. *Hymenial surface:* Tubes 0,5-1 mm deep, greyish inside; pores large and angular 0,5-1 mm diam., partitions thin, dark brown. *Flesh:* Rusty brown, tough-fibrous and up to 1 mm thick. *Spore print:* White. *Spores:* Hyaline, cylindrical, smooth, thin-walled; 10-15 x 4-6 µm.

Gloeophyllum sepiarium showing hairy, yellowish-brown fruit-bodies and brown hymenial surface with elongate pores and lamella-like partitions.

Gloeophyllum sepiarium

Hexagona tenuis showing shiny, dark brown and black upper surface, and large, honeycomb-like pores of hymenial surface.

Hexagona tenuis
Thin-cap Honeycomb Bracket

Edible

Fruit-bodies overlapping on substrate (imbricate)

Inedible

115. Laetiporus sulphureus (Bull.:Fr.) Murr.　　　*Sulphur Shelf*

Laetiporus sulphureus occurs throughout the south-western, southern and eastern Cape, Natal and the eastern and north-eastern Transvaal. The fruit-bodies are formed during late summer and autumn. The fungus is parasitic on living oaks and *Eucalyptus* species in which it causes a brown, cubical heart-rot. It can survive saprophytically on the dead wood and stumps of the trees which it killed, and seems to prefer tree species with high levels of phenolic compounds in the wood. The fruit-bodies are frequently seen on the trunks of the old, dying oaks lining the streets of Stellenbosch.

The large, fleshy, compound, bright yellow to yellow-orange fruit-bodies are very conspicuous and unmistakable. They are edible when young and have a flavour resembling breast of chicken. However, fruit-bodies growing on certain tree hosts, *Eucalyptus* for example, are reported to cause digestive upsets. (*Afrikaans:* Swawel Rakswam.)

Fruit-bodies sessile, in clusters on dead stumps of hardwood trees. *Cap:* 50-300 mm wide, thick, fleshy, fan-shaped to semi-circular, in overlapping tiers; becoming rigid and brittle with age; margin obtuse, rounded, wavy. Upper surface uneven, lumpy, wrinkled, suede-like; sulphur-yellow to yellow-orange and fading to white or straw-colour. *Hymenial surface:* Bright sulphur-yellow fading to whitish; tubes 1-6 mm deep, in single layer; pores angular, 2-4 per mm. *Flesh:* Cheesy, 4-20 mm thick, white to pale yellow or pale salmon, succulent when young and exuding a yellowish juice when squeezed, in age white and crumbly; with strong mushroomy odour and pleasant, sourish flavour. *Spore print:* White. *Spores:* Hyaline, broadly ellipsoidal to almost subglobose, smooth, thin-walled; 5-7 x 3,5-5 μm.

116. Lenzites betulina (L.:Fr.) Fr.

Lenzites betulina occurs in the south-western, southern, and eastern Cape, Natal and Transvaal. Although widely distributed, the fruit-bodies are not common, occurring occasionally during summer and autumn on stumps and dead logs of broad-leafed trees and causing an extensive and severe white rot. It has also been reported on *Podocarpus* species (yellowwood) in the Knysna area, and is seen occasionally on dead branches of living trees but it is not a pathogen of trees.

L. betulina resembles some species of mushrooms with sessile caps, but the hairy cap surface and tough, leathery nature of the branching and anastomosing 'lamellae' distinguish it from the mushrooms.

The fruit-bodies are considered to be inedible because of their leathery consistency but some reports indicate that the young fruit-bodies are edible, having a nutty flavour.

Fruit-bodies sessile, single, grouped or compound on dead wood of broad leafed trees. *Cap:* 15-90 mm wide, 10-60 mm long, 3-12 mm thick and often thicker at attachment; tough, leathery, bracket-shaped to fan-shaped, occasionally grown together laterally, often in overlapping tiers, with thickened attachment; margin acute, entire, velvety, concolorous with upper surface of lighter. Surface flat, densely hairy, slightly furrowed and grooved, with concentric zones of white to greyish, greenish-grey or greyish-brown hairs. *Hymenial surface:* White to cream, slightly darker on drying; tubes elongate branching, up to 5 mm deep, partitions appearing lamellate, anastomosing edges entire. *Flesh:* Tough, fibrous, white, 1-5 mm thick but thicker at attachment, with mushroomy odour when fresh. *Spore print:* White. *Spores:* Hyaline, cylindrical to slightly curved, smooth, thin-walled; 4,5-6 x 2-2,5 μm

Laetiporus sulphureus
Sulphur Shelf

Laetiporus sulphureus showing smooth, creamy upper surface, thick white flesh, and yellow tubes with angular pores.

Lenzites betulina showing hairy, grooved, greyish-brown upper surface and lamella-like pore surface.

117. Lenzites elegans (Spreng.: Fr.) Pat. *Elegant Bracket*

Inedible

Lenzites elegans, also known as *L. palisoti*, has been recorded in the southern and eastern Cape, Natal and the eastern and northern Transvaal, and extends into Zimbabwe and other more northerly tropical African countries. It is also known on other continents. It is fairly common in the eastern and northern Transvaal and Natal.

The fruit-bodies are found in summer and autumn on dead logs of broad-leafed trees and may survive into a second season. *Acacia* and *Eucalyptus* wood seem to be the favourite hosts. *L. elegans* causes a severe white rot of the dead wood. When the fungus is growing actively, the affected wood gives off a characteristic, sweetly fragrant, spicy odour.

L. elegans is a strikingly beautiful fungus, its large, pure white fruit-bodies having a smooth surface and characteristic radiating, elongated pores on the hymenial surface. The tough, hard fruit-bodies are inedible. (*Afrikaans:* Bruidsrakswam.)

Fruit-bodies single or grouped on dead hardwood logs. ***Cap:*** Up to 350 mm wide and 2-15 mm thick, hard-leathery to woody, sessile or narrowly attached laterally or substipitate; fan-shaped to kidney-shaped or circular, often depressed; margin thin, acute, entire or somewhat wavy. Upper surface pure white when fresh, drying cream, hairless, smooth, without zones or sometimes faintly concentrically or radially grooved. ***Hymenial surface:*** With radiating, elongated pores, 0,2-0,5 mm wide, 1-4 mm deep, somewhat labyrinthiform, the partitions branching and anastomosing, leathery, tough, edges thin, white but drying cream. ***Flesh:*** Pure white, tough, fibrous, 1-5 mm thick, occasionally thicker over the attachment; with a strong, fragrant, sweet, fruity-spicy odour. ***Spore print:*** White. ***Spores:*** Hyaline, cylindrical, smooth, thin-walled; 5,5-8,5 x 2-3 µm.

118. Lignosus sacer (Fr.) Ryvarden *Olive-brown Funnel Cap*

Inedible

Lignosus sacer, formerly known as *Polyporus sacer*, occurs in the eastern Cape, Natal and eastern Transvaal, as well as in the tropical African countries. It is not at all common but the fruit-bodies occur in summer and autumn in humus-rich soil. This species is not known to cause decay of wood but may grow on buried decayed wood.

The fungus may be recognized by the unusual combination of characters in its fruit-bodies which have dark, thin, tough, circular caps with whitish pores underneath, and central, woody stipes which arise from a tuber-like sclerotium. The fruit-bodies are too tough for eating. (*Afrikaans:* Olyfbruin Tregterswam.)

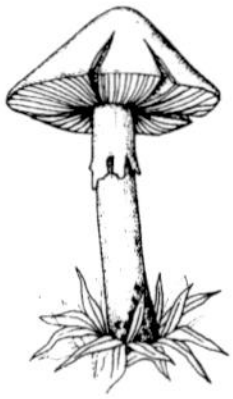

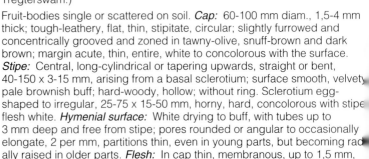

Fruit-bodies attached to substrate by stipe (stipitate)

Fruit-bodies single or scattered on soil. ***Cap:*** 60-100 mm diam., 1,5-4 mm thick; tough-leathery, flat, thin, stipitate, circular; slightly furrowed and concentrically grooved and zoned in tawny-olive, snuff-brown and dark brown; margin acute, thin, entire, white to concolorous with the surface. ***Stipe:*** Central, long-cylindrical or tapering upwards, straight or bent, 40-150 x 3-15 mm, arising from a basal sclerotium; surface smooth, velvety, pale brownish buff; hard-woody, hollow; without ring. Sclerotium egg-shaped to irregular, 25-75 x 15-50 mm, horny, hard, concolorous with stipe, flesh white. ***Hymenial surface:*** White drying to buff, with tubes up to 3 mm deep and free from stipe; pores rounded or angular to occasionally elongate, 2 per mm, partitions thin, even in young parts, but becoming radially raised in older parts. ***Flesh:*** In cap thin, membranous, up to 1,5 mm, white to pale cream, tough, fibrous; no distinctive odour. ***Spore print:*** White. ***Spores:*** Hyaline, ovoid to ellipsoidal, flattened on one side, smooth, thin-walled; 5-7 x 3-4,5 µm.

Lenzites elegans
Elegant Bracket

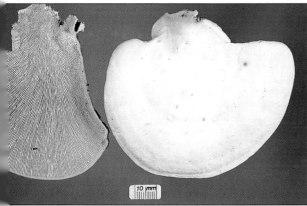

Lenzites elegans Fruit-bodies
showing smooth, white upper
surface, and hymenial surface
with radiating, branching,
elongate pores.

Lignosus sacer Olive-brown Funnelcap
Fruit-bodies with circular cap, white pores
on hymenial surface, and central stipe
arising from egg-shaped sclerotium.

119. Phaeolus schweinitzii (Fr.) Pat. *Dye Polypore*

Phaeolus schweinitzii has been found in pine plantations in the southern, south-western and eastern Cape and in the Transvaal. It is a pathogen of pine trees, causing a severe brown, cubical rot in the roots and lower trunks. In Europe and North America it can cause considerable damage but information available at present indicates that the southern African strains may not be as virulent as the American and European strains.

The fruit-bodies are formed in summer and autumn in areas of summer rainfall, and in autumn to early winter in the winter-rainfall regions. They can be recognized by their bright yellow-brownish colours, greenish-yellow pores and their constant association with pine trees. The young fruit-bodies contain fluids from which dyes of different colours can be extracted.

P. schweinitzii is inedible. (*Afrikaans:* Dennevoetswam.)

Fruit-bodies solitary or scattered on the ground or in compound clusters on pine stumps. ***Cap:*** Up to 260 mm wide, and 6-45 mm thick; soft, corky or spongy when fresh; laterally attached to the stump or base of a pine tree, bracket-shaped, fan-shaped to kidney-shaped and somewhat depressed over the upper surface, thickening towards the attached area; single or in compound structures with caps arranged in overlapping tiers and growing together laterally; or inverted cone-shaped and arising from a stipe; margin even or slightly wavy, rounded and sterile below. Upper surface finely downy and yellow to lemon-yellow at the margin, becoming more velvety to woolly or covered with long, coarse hairs towards the older parts which become wrinkled and roughened, darkening to ochre-yellow, yellowish brown to deep reddish brown. ***Stipe:*** Absent or present, central or excentric, ochre-yellow to rust-brown, hairy, soft, 10-60 mm long and 10-40 mm thick; occasionally fused together with several others and expanding upwards. ***Hymenial surface:*** Greenish yellow when fresh, turning dark reddish brown on bruising or drying; tubes concolorous, in one layer, 1-8 mm deep; pore mouths angular, 1-2 per mm at the margin, larger and irregular to elongated in the oldest parts. ***Flesh:*** Soft corky to spongy when fresh, brittle when dry, yellowish brown to rust-brown, 3-30 mm thick. ***Spore print:*** White to pale ochreous. ***Spores:*** Hyaline, ovoid-ellipsoidal, smooth, thin-walled; 6-8 x 4-5,6 µm.

120. Polyporus arcularius (Batsch.) Fr. *Large-pored Funnel Cap*

Polyporus arcularius is known from the southern and eastern Cape, Natal and Transvaal but is not common. The fruit-bodies are easily overlooked as their dull colours tend to blend with the surroundings. They are annual and appear in spring to early summer on dead wood of broad-leafed trees in contact with soil. This species causes a white rot in wood.

P. arcularius is recognizable by the radially elongated pores of the thin cap, the fringed cap margin, and the tough, central stipe. The tough fruit-bodies are inedible. (*Afrikaans:* Grootporie-tregterswam.)

Fruit-bodies stipitate, grouped on dead hardwood. ***Cap:*** 15-60 mm diam., 1-4 mm thick; fleshy, tough, circular, convex with a central depression or shallow funnel-shaped; margin even, thin, fringed with fine, short hairs, inrolled on drying. Surface dry, scaly, concentrically grooved, golden brown to buff. ***Stipe:*** Central, 15-60 x 0,5-3 mm, cylindrical, yellowish brown to dark brown, hairy to slightly scaly; tough, solid; without ring. ***Hymenial surface:*** White, pore mouths hexagonal to angular, slightly radially elongated, 0,5-3 mm long; tubes up to 2 mm deep, sometimes decurrent on stipe. ***Flesh:*** Thin, 1-2 mm, white, leathery; with mushroomy odour. ***Spore print:*** White. ***Spores:*** Hyaline, cylindrical, smooth, thin-walled; 6-9 x 2-3,5 µm.

Phaeolus schweinitzii
Dye Polypore

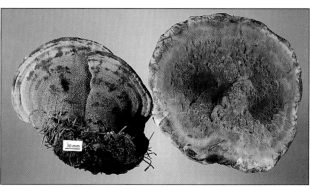

Phaeolus schweinitzii showing pores of hymenial surface, and upper surface of cap with pale margin and roughened darker central area.

Polyporus arcularius
Large-pored Funnelcap

Polyporus arcularius showing cap with fringed margin, central stipe, and white, radially elongated pores.

121. Polyporus dictyopus Mont.

This fungus is another of the stipitate, wood-rotting species of the genus *Polyporus*. It is known from the south-western and eastern Cape Province and Natal. The fruit-bodies are formed in early summer and grow on dead hardwood, causing a white rot. They are probably easily overlooked because of their dark, dull colours.

P. dictyopus is distinguished by the dark colours of the stipe and upper surface of the cap, the lobed margin and the fan-like form of many of its fruit-bodies. A similar fungus has been reported from the south-western Cape as *P. badius*. The tough fruit-bodies of *P. dictyopus* are inedible.

Fruit-bodies solitary or grouped on dead hardwood. *Cap:* 10-40 mm diam., up to 2 mm thick; thin, leathery, circular to fan-shaped, depressed; margin wavy, often lobed, thin, acute. Surface hairless, smooth to uneven, zoned, radially striate, dark reddish brown to black. *Stipe:* Excentric or lateral, partly cylindrical but widening slightly upwards, 5-35 x 2-6 mm, smooth, dull, dark brown to reddish brown and merging with the upper surface of fan-shaped specimens, widening below into a bulbous base; tough fibrous, solid; without ring. *Hymenial surface:* White when fresh, brownish with age; tubes up to 1 mm deep, sometimes decurrent on stipe; pore mouths angular, 4-6 per mm, partitions thin, entire, becoming slightly toothed. *Flesh:* Leathery, thin, up to 0,5 mm, white to yellowish. *Spore print:* White. *Spores:* Hyaline, ellipsoidal, smooth, thin-walled; 7-8 x 3-3,5 μm.

122. Pseudophaeolus baudonii (Pat.) Ryv.   *Orange-yellow Rough Top*

Pseudophaeolus baudonii is known from the southern, south-western and eastern Cape, Natal, Transvaal, Mozambique, Angola and tropical African countries. The fruit-bodies appear from mid-December to mid-January.

P. baudonii was known earlier as *Polyporus baudonii* and has also been referred to, erroneously, as *Ganoderma colossum*. It is pathogenic on broad-leafed trees and shrubs and has caused extensive damage to *Eucalyptus* plantations in the eastern Transvaal and northern Natal. Pines are less severely affected. The fungus has also been collected on clumps of perennial grasses from savannah veld.

The species can be recognized by the large, brightly coloured, spongy, fragile fruit-bodies. These are reported to be eaten by the Bushmen, and also by tortoises, duikers and other small mammals, but no other information on its edibility exists. (*Afrikaans:* Bloekomvoetswam.)

Fruit-bodies single or scattered on ground close to trees or at the base of trunks. *Cap:* 120-400 mm diam., soft spongy, fragile; circular, mostly broadly inverted cone-shaped and attached by a narrow pad or very short stipe, or bracket-shaped to more or less kidney-shaped, up to 480 mm wide and appressed to a tree trunk; single or with tiers of smaller caps grown together laterally, reduced below to a narrow base formed by a pad of tissue attached to a dense conglomerate of mycelium mixed with soil around a root; margin rounded, thick, wavy or lobed. Upper surface flat, uneven with rounded lumps, grooves or short ridges, finely downy to hairless, with bright orange-yellow colours which darken to brownish with ageing and drying. *Hymenial surface:* Bright lemon-yellow to apricot when fresh, drying to brown where bruised; tubes concolorous with surface, 1-4 mm deep, in one layer; pore mouths angular to labyrinthiform, 1-4 per mm, partitions even, thin. *Flesh:* 5-70 mm thick, pale orange-yellow to orange-buff when fresh, drying brownish, soft felty, occasionally with concentric zones; with mushroomy odour. *Spore print:* White. *Spores:* Hyaline, long-ellipsoidal, smooth, thin-walled, non-amyloid; 5-11 x 3-5 μm.

Polyporus dictyopus showing circular to fan-shaped, stipitate fruit-bodies with reddish-brown upper surface, lobed margin, and pale brownish, angular pores of hymenial surface.

10 mm

Pseudophaeolus baudonii
Orange-yellow Rough Top

Pseudophaeolus baudonii showing circular fruit-body on ground and bracket-shaped fruit-bodies at base of *Eucalyptus* trunk.

123. Pycnoporus sanguineus (L.:Fr.) Murr. *Tropical Cinnabar Bracket*

Pycnoporus sanguineus is widely distributed in southern Africa and also in tropical Africa. It is quite common, the conspicuous fruit-bodies appearing on dead wood of broad-leafed and occasionally pine trees during summer and autumn. Often thinnish branches in dry, exposed positions are attacked. Faded fruit-bodies are found at the end of the season. This species causes severe and extensive white rot in the wood on which it grows. Often the decayed wood is coloured bright orange by the mycelium of the fungus.

P. *sanguineus* is easily identified by its thin, bright reddish-orange fruit-bodies with caps that are narrowly attached, and smooth and shiny above. A very similar species, *P. coccineus*, can be distinguished by its thicker, more yellowy-orange, shelf-like and broadly attached fruit-bodies, with even, velvety cap surfaces, and obtuse and rounded margins. *P. cinnabarinus*, another similar species, has also been reported in southern Africa, but this species is restricted to the cool, temperate regions of the Northern Hemisphere. All of these fungi are inedible. (*Afrikaans:* Dunhoedrooirakswam.)

Fruit-bodies single, grouped or clustered on dead wood of broad-leafed and pine trees. *Cap:* 20-75 mm wide, 10-40 mm long and 1-5 mm thick; tough, leathery to rigid, bright reddish orange, fan-shaped to bracket-shaped or kidney-shaped, occasionally circular, often grown together laterally or occasionally in overlapping tiers, always narrowly attached to the substrate, often appearing to have a short stipe; margin thin, acute, even, velvety to touch. Upper surface velvety at first, later smooth, shiny, appearing seared with a hot iron; usually zonate with zones somewhat lighter in colour, fading in age to grey or dirty white. *Hymenial surface:* Concolorous with surface but usually darker; tubes 0,5-2 mm deep; pores minute, 5-6 per mm, mouths circular becoming angular, concolorous with tubes. *Flesh:* Thin, 0,5-2 mm, concolorous with surface, zoned, tough felty; without distinctive odour. *Spore print:* White. *Spores:* Hyaline, short-cylindrical to ovoid, smooth, thin-walled, non-amyloid; 4-5,2 x 2-2,6 µm.

Fruit-bodies with poorly defined stipe (substipitate)

124. Trametes cingulata Berk. *Black Cork Polypore*

Trametes cingulata occurs in the eastern Cape Province, Natal and Transvaal on the dead wood of broad-leafed trees. The fruit-bodies appear in late summer to autumn, often in dry and exposed positions. They are annual but occasionally survive until the following season. The fungus causes a severe and extensive white rot of the sap-wood and is frequently found on dead *Acacia* and *Eucalyptus* species.

The black surface which contrasts strongly with the creamy white margin and pore surface are characteristic of this common wood-rotting fungus. The tough fruit-bodies are inedible. (*Afrikaans:* Witrandkurkporieswam.)

Fruit-bodies sessile, grouped on dead hardwood logs. *Cap:* 30-90 mm wide, 16-50 mm long and 3-10 mm thick; leathery to woody, fan-shaped to kidney shaped or shelf-like, slightly convex to flat, broadly attached or sometimes with a reduced base, occasionally in overlapping tiers, sometimes grown together laterally; margin even, acute, thin or thick and rounded. Upper surface black, concentrically grooved, smooth or rough with rounded tubercles fading to grey or brownish grey in age; margin creamy white, velvety in young actively growing specimens, darkening to yellowish brown on drying. *Hymenial surface:* White when fresh, darkening to yellowish or brownish in age, glistening; tubes concolorous, up to 3 mm deep, in single layer; pores circular, 3-4 per mm. *Flesh:* White to creamy white, fibrous, corky, zoned, 1-4 mm thick; with pleasant, fungusy odour. *Spore print:* White. *Spores:* Hyaline, ovoid to short-cylindrical, smooth, thin-walled; 4-6 x 2,5-3,5 µm.

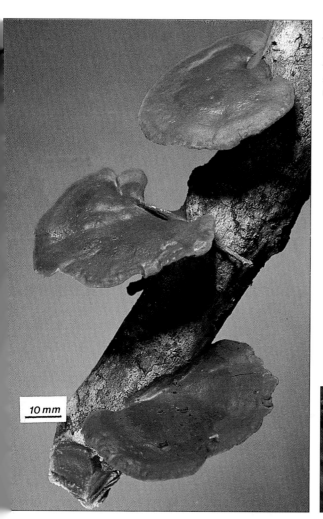

Pycnoporus sanguineus
Tropical Cinnabar Bracket
showing bright orange-red
fruit-bodies with shiny upper
surface, and wood discoloured
red by mycelium.

10 mm

Trametes cingulata
Black Cork Polypore

Trametes cingulata showing
kidney-shaped fruit-bodies
with characteristic black
upper surface, and creamy
margin and pore surface.

10 mm

125. Trametes meyenii (Klotzsch) Lloyd　　　　　*Large Cork Polypore*

Inedible

Trametes meyenii is widely distributed in southern Africa, occurring through-out the south-western, southern and eastern Cape, Natal and Transvaal and further northwards into tropical Africa. It is also known from other continents and is often named *Cerrena meyenii*. The fruit-bodies appear from summer to autumn.

The species is more common in the warmer parts of the region, often growing at the bases of trunks of living *Acacia* species. It also grows on stumps and dead logs of these and other broad-leafed trees. It appears to be pathogenic on living trees but may be a wound pathogen. A severe and extensive white rot is caused in affected wood.

T. meyenii resembles *Lenzites elegans* but can be distinguished by the presence of a hairy upper surface and much narrower, maze-like pores.

The hard, woody fruit-bodies of *T. meyenii* are inedible. (*Afrikaans:* Groot Kurkporieswam.)

Fruit-bodies sessile, solitary or compound on dead stumps and living trunks of broad-leafed trees. *Cap:* 70-300 mm wide, 40-120 mm long, 10-50 mm thick; sessile, hard, woody, bracket-shaped to kidney-shaped, frequently with a thick attachment, or in overlapping tiers, or effused-reflexed; margin obtuse, thick, rounded, entire or somewhat lobed, finely velvety, creamy white. Surface mostly concave but may be flat, densely covered with long, velvety hairs, yellowish buff, greyish to brownish, zoned or azonate, some-times concentrically grooved or knobbly, often coloured bright green by microscopic algae growing among the hairs of the concave surface. *Hymenial surface:* White to creamy, with elongated and sinuous to maze-like pores, 0,2-1 mm wide, white to cream inside; tubes 0,5-2 mm deep. *Flesh:* Creamy white to yellowish white, 10-40 mm thick, hard-woody, fibrous and shiny, zoned or azonate; with faint mushroomy odour. *Spore print:* White. *Spores:* Hyaline, smooth, ellipsoid-cylindrical, thin-walled; 4,5-6 x 2-2,5 μm.

126. Trichaptum byssogenus (Jungh.) Ryv.

Inedible

Trichaptum byssogenus is known from the eastern Transvaal where its fruit-bodies occur on dead hardwood logs from summer to early autumn. This species causes a white rot in the wood. It is known to occur in tropical Africa but has not been recorded in southern Africa previously so little is known about it.

T. byssogenus resembles *Funalia protea* but can be distinguished by the violet colours of the fresh pore surface, the lighter colours of the fruit-body and the dentate partitions between pores in the older parts. Its fruit-bodies are inedible.

Fruit-bodies grouped or compound on dead wood. *Fruit-body:* 15-80 mm wide, 10-20 mm long and up to 5 mm thick; tough, flexuous, sessile, often mostly resupinate, shelf-like or semi-circular and growing together laterally margin thin, acute, entire. Surface densely hairy, especially in older parts, becoming matted, concentrically and radially grooved, yellowish brown or greyish brown to dark grey in older parts. *Hymenial surface:* Pore mouths angular, 1-3 per mm near the margin, becoming radially elongate to almost lamellate in older parts; partitions thin, even at first, becoming dentate late tubes 2-5 mm deep, purplish, lavender or lilac when fresh, drying wood colour to yellowish brown. *Flesh:* Very thin over the tubes and passing into the matted surface hairs; wood-coloured to deep buff. *Spore print:* White. *Spores:* Hyaline, broadly ellipsoidal, smooth, thin-walled, non-amyloid; 5,5-8 x 3,5-4 μm.

Fruit-bodies effused-reflexed

Trametes meyenii showing narrow, maze-like pores of hymenial surface.

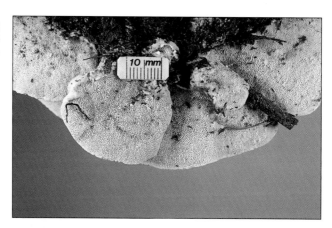

Trametes meyenii
Large Cork Polypore

Trichaptum byssogenus Shelf-like fruit-bodies showing dark brown, tufted upper surface and purplish to lavender hymenial surface with elongate pores.

10 mm

127. Tremella mesenterica Retz.:Fr.   *Jelly Brain Fungus*

Tremella mesenterica has been recorded from the southern and south-western Cape, Natal and the eastern Transvaal. It is probably much more widely distributed and common than these records indicate.

The species grows on dead branches of broad-leafed trees, frequently while the branch is still attached to the tree, and apparently plays some part in the breakdown of the dead wood. The fruit-bodies are only conspicuous, however, during or immediately after rainy weather when they absorb water and swell to their original size. In dry weather they are inconspicuously dark, shrunken, hard and dormant. This is one of a group of fungi which behave in this way. The fruit-bodies do not survive from one season to the next.

This fungus is reported to be edible and may be used in soups. (*Afrikaans:* Geel jellieswam.)

Fruit-bodies single or scattered on dead wood. *Fruit-body:* 10-80 mm diam., jelly-like when wet, consisting of numerous contorted lobes and folds which form a more or less rounded mass; yellow to orange and with a powdered appearance when sporulating, drying dark orange to orange-brown and horny, later brittle, reviving in rain. *Spore print:* White to yellowish. *Spores:* Hyaline, ellipsoidal, smooth; 7-15 x 6-10 μm.

128. Calocera cornea (Batsch:Fr.) Fr.

Calocera cornea is known from the southern and eastern Cape, Natal and eastern Transvaal, but there are very few records of its occurrence in the region. It appears in summer and autumn on dead logs, mostly on hard-wood but occasionally also on pine logs on which it grows saprophytically. It apparently causes an insignificant brownish rot in the underlying wood.

The tiny fruit-bodies are insignificant but may sometimes be present in such large numbers that they appear striking and are then readily recognizable. They are not edible.

Fruit-bodies grouped, occasionally clustered, often in large groups on dead wood. *Fruit-body:* 4-10 mm high, erect, awl-shaped, rarely forked, often two or more fruit-bodies appearing partially joined at their bases, gelatinous-tough; bright orange-yellow, drying brownish orange and horny. *Spore print:* White. *Spores:* Hyaline, sausage-shaped, smooth, thin-walled 7-10 x 3-4 μm.

Tremella mesenterica
Jelly Brain Fungus

Calocera cornea
Orange-yellow, awl-
shaped fruit-bodies
clustered on dead wood.

Calocera cornea

10 mm

Fruit-bodies lying
flat on substrate
(resupinate)

129. Serpula himantioides (Fr.:Fr.) Karst.

Serpula himantioides, formerly known as *Merulius himantioides*, is known to occur in the south-eastern and eastern Transvaal, but seems to be very rare. The fruit-bodies appear in autumn and grow on the underside of dead logs, preferably coniferous wood, in contact with the ground. The species seems to require conditions of high moisture in order to produce fruit-bodies. It is a wood-rotting species which causes a brown rot.

The presence of irregular ridges forming a pore-like pattern over the hymenial surface is characteristic of the genus while the colour of the ridges distinguishes the species. This fungus is inedible.

Fruit-bodies single or scattered on dead logs. *Fruit-body:* Resupinate, spreading over the surface of the wood especially the underside; margin thin, white, in older parts of the fruit-body forming irregular ridges in a net-like to pseudoporoid pattern over which the hymenium forms; lilac at first, soon brownish to dark warm brown in age. *Flesh:* Soft, pale brownish yellow, thin, less than 1 mm. *Spore print:* Yellowish brown. *Spores:* Light yellow, broadly ellipsoidal, with one side flattened, smooth; 8-10 x 5-6,5 µm

130. Clavulina cristata (Fr.) Schroet.   *Crested Coral Fungu.*

Clavulina cristata, formerly known as *Clavaria cristata*, is found in the south-western and eastern Cape and in the eastern Transvaal. The species may be more widely distributed but does not appear to be common. It grows under pines as well as broad-leafed trees in the leaf-litter and woody debris which it helps to decompose to humus.

The fruit-bodies appear from summer to autumn in summer-rainfall regions and in early spring in the south-western Cape. They are quite conspicuous and readily recognizable by their shrub-like, much-branched form. A related species, *C. cinerea*, is very similar but is ash-grey in colour sometimes tinged with purple.

C. cristata is edible while the fruit-bodies are young and fresh. (*Afrikaans* Wit Koraalswam.)

Fruit-bodies single to scattered or grouped under trees. *Fruit-body:* Up to 70 mm high and 35 mm wide, fleshy, shrub-like, consisting of dense tufts cylindrical branches arising from a short stipe, tips of branches becoming flattened and crested; white to pale greyish. *Stipe:* White, fleshy, 5-25 mm tall, branching above and with rhizoids at the base. *Flesh:* Thin, white; without distinctive odour or taste. *Spore print:* White. *Spores:* Hyaline, sub-globose, smooth; 7-11 x 6,5-10 µm.

Serpula himantioides Fruit-body with brown, folded, pore-like hymenial surface.

Clavulina cristata
Crested Coral Fungus

Clavulina cristata showing cylindrical branches of fruit-body arising from central stipe.

131. Ramaria formosa (Fr.) Quél.

Ramaria formosa is known only from the south-western Cape Province where it grows in humus-rich soil or compost under broad-leafed trees. It is often found under *Eucalyptus* species. The fruit-bodies appear in late autumn after the first good rains and during winter, but are not common. They are quite conspicuous because of their bright colours.

R. *formosa* is one of a number of very similar coral fungi which are best identified on microscopic characters. Some are edible but since they also grow in leaf-litter and humus-rich soil under trees, they may be confused with this species which is poisonous, and therefore are best avoided. R. *formosa* causes severe diarrhoea when eaten.

Fruit-bodies single, scattered or grouped on ground under broad-leafed trees. **Fruit-body:** Up to 150 mm high and 120 mm wide, fleshy, shrub-like, consisting of numerous branches; branches crowded, cylindrical, pinkish ochreous to orange-pink with yellowish tips, smooth at first, later becoming powdery with maturing spores. **Stipe:** Fleshy, 20-60 x 10-30 mm, white below, soon orange-pink, branching, smooth. **Flesh:** White or tinged orange-yellow, darkening slowly on exposure to air; odourless but with a slightly bitter taste. **Spore print:** Ochreous. **Spores:** Pale yellow, ellipsoidal, roughened; 8-15 x 4-6 µm.

132. Thelephora terrestris (Ehrh.) Fr. *Earth Fans*

Thelephora terrestris is widely distributed in pine plantations throughout southern Africa. It is quite common in autumn when it fruits among pine needles lying beneath the trees.

T. *terrestris* is an important mycorrhizal symbiont of pines. It is an aggressive early invader of pine seedling roots, and the fruit-bodies may be seen enveloping the young stems in the nursery, especially in sandy, acid soils. It also appears on oaks but at a later stage of the tree's development.

T. *terrestris* is inedible because of its tough texture and unpleasant taste. (*Afrikaans:* Fraiingswam.)

Fruit-bodies growing as multiple fans

Fruit-bodies in clusters on the ground under pines. **Fruit-body:** Leathery, consisting of fan-shaped, overlapping caps in spreading, often rosette-like clusters. **Cap:** 10-60 mm radius, with undulating, somewhat frayed margin sometimes growing together laterally. Surface felt-like, with radiating fibrils, reddish brown to chocolate-brown, almost black in age; pale to almost white at the growing margin, otherwise concolorous with the surface. **Hymenial surface:** Somewhat wrinkled or radially ridged, or papillate; clay-brown to chocolate-brown and with a powdered appearance. **Flesh:** Dark reddish brown, thin, soft, fibrillose and leathery; with odour of damp soil and an astringent taste. **Spore print:** Dark brown. **Spores:** Purplish brown, angularly ellipsoidal and lobed, sparsely spiny; 8-12 x 6-9 µm.

 *Ramaria formosa*

Thelephora terrestris showing the somewhat wrinkled and ridged, chocolate-brown hymenial surface.

...maria formosa showing ...indrical branches of fruit-...dy arising from main ...anch with whitish base.

Thelephora terrestris
Earth Fans

Inedible

133. Laxitextum bicolor (Pers.:Fr.) Lentz   *Light-rimmed Crustɑ*

Laxitextum bicolor, known previously as *Stereum bicolor*, has been reporte on dead wood of broad-leafed trees from the southern and eastern Cape, Natal, and eastern and north-eastern Transvaal. The fruit-bodies appear ir late summer and may survive until the following season. It seems to prefer wood of trees with a high content of phenolic substances, such as wattle, *Eucalyptus* and oak, and causes a white rot.

The fruit-bodies may vary in appearance, the size and shape of the cap depending on the position in which they form on the log. The unique and contrasting colour combination of the hymenium and reflexed part of the fruit-bodies make this species readily recognizable. It is considered to be inedible. (*Afrikaans:* Ligbruin Gerande Kruiphoed.)

Fruit-bodies clustered on dead hardwood logs. *Cap:* 2-3 mm thick, up to 150 mm wide and reflexed part projecting up to 50 mm; soft spongy, mos resupinate-reflexed, sometimes laterally attached, overlapping, and latera grown together; margin thin, rounded, even to somewhat wavy. Surface snuff-brown, cotton wool-like, concentrically furrowed in older parts, smoo and pale towards the margin. *Hymenial surface:* Smooth, velvety, white tc creamy white, not furrowed, sometimes cracking on drying. *Flesh:* Thin, spongy, brownish, with hyaline hymenial layer; faint mushroomy odour wh fresh. *Spore print:* White. *Spores:* Hyaline, ellipsoidal and unilaterally depressed, frequently uniguttulate; 3-4,5 x 2-3 μm.

Inedible

134. Cymatoderma elegans Jungh.

Cymatoderma elegans is widely distributed in tropical Africa and Asia anc is known from indigenous forests in the Transvaal, Natal and the southern Cape Province. It is fairly common in the Tsitsikamma Coastal National Pa where it occurs from November to March on dead logs and thinner brancl es (20-50 mm) of indigenous trees. It seems to be an early invader of dea wood in which it causes a white rot.

The fruit-bodies are quite striking and are readily recognized by their distinctive shape and warty, ribbed lower surfaces. They are tough and probably inedible for this reason.

Fruit-bodies mostly grouped on dead stumps, trunks or fallen branches of hardwood trees. *Cap:* Up to 180 mm across the widest part, thin, leathery to woody, bracket-shaped, fan-shaped or circular, somewhat depressed or almost funnel-shaped; adjacent caps frequently grown together, attach to substrate by a short, lateral to excentric stipe; margin thin, acute, wavy and unevenly bayed, at times appearing almost frayed from ridges pro-jecting beyond the intervening tissue. Upper surface usually completely covered with a dense, felt-like layer, overlying sharp, knife-edged ridges radiating from area over the stipe; pale fawn to tawny-brown to almost snuff-brown in the oldest parts, pale at the margin. *Stipe:* Rudimentary in fan-shaped forms, cylindrical in funnel-shaped forms, up to 50 x 10 mm covered with thick, felt-like hairs; fawn to brown, matt. *Hymenial surface:* White to pale beige or pinkish brown with age, ornamented with prominen branching folds radiating from the stipe and scantily to densely covered by short, wart-like spines. *Flesh:* Thin, pale wood-colour, tough-leathery, fibrous. *Spore print:* White to pale fawn. *Spores:* Hyaline, ellipsoidal to broadly ellipsoidal; 6-9 x 3,5-5 μm.

Laxitextum bicolor
Light-rimmed Crustcap

Laxitextum bicolor Thin, sessile fruit-bodies with snuff-brown upper surface, white margin and smooth, white hymenium.

Cymatoderma elegans showing brown upper surface, unevenly bayed margin, prominent ridges, and wart-like spines of white hymenial surface.

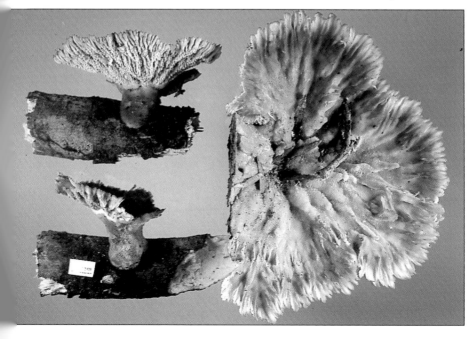

Inedible

135. Podoscypha parvula (Lloyd) Reid

Podoscypha parvula is known only from the eastern Transvaal where it occurs on dead branches of indigenous hardwood trees in contact with soil and in damp places. It is found in early summer on branches of 15-40 mm diameter and causes a white rot, the severity of which is unknown. This species is also known from tropical East Africa.

The fruit-bodies resemble those of *Stereum* species but can be distinguished by their hairless surfaces and thin, translucent appearance. They also differ in microscopic characters. The fruit-bodies dry to a horny consistency and are inedible.

Fruit-bodies grouped and clustered on dead hardwood. *Cap:* Up to 50 mm long and 5-75 mm wide, leathery, thin, strap-shaped to spoon-shaped or fan-shaped, plane or somewhat depressed and approaching funnel-shaped, arising from a narrow, reduced base or a short stipe attached to the substrate by a basal disc; separate but often growing together laterally and sometimes forming dense clusters; margin wavy, entire or lobed, acute, thin. Surface hairless, smooth, or with shallow, radiating grooves, zonate in older parts; pale orange-brown to golden-brown, lighter coloured to pale ochreous at the margin. *Hymenial surface:* Smooth or reflecting surface grooves, cream to pale cream at the margin. *Flesh:* Thin, less than 1 mm, pale brownish; without a distinctive odour. *Spore print:* White. *Spores:* Hyaline, ellipsoidal to broadly ellipsoidal to almost subglobose, thin-walled, often with one guttule; 3,2-4 x 2-2,5 µm.

Inedible

136. Stereum australe Lloyd   *Bleeding Crustcap*

Stereum australe is known to occur in Natal and in the north-eastern, eastern and central Transvaal. Its fruit-bodies appear on dead branches and logs of broad-leafed trees from summer to autumn. It causes a white rot in the wood. This species does not seem to be very common and its importance in the decay of wood is unknown.

The thin, leathery fruit-bodies with smooth hymenial surfaces are characteristic of *Stereum* species but its 'bleeding', dark-coloured hymenium distinguishes it from *S. ostrea*. At present most mycologists consider it to be a form of *S. ostrea*.

S. australe is considered to be inedible because of the thin, tough fruit-bodies. (*Afrikaans:* Rooibruin Kruiphoed.)

Fruit-bodies solitary or more often grouped on dead logs of broad-leafed trees. *Cap:* 30-50 mm wide and 20-40 mm radius, leathery, fan-shaped and attached by a reduced base; often grown together laterally, occasionally imbricate, or partly resupinate with cap reflexed and attached to a narrow, spreading base; margin thin, entire, wavy. Surface concentrically furrowed and zoned with velvety hairs, reddish brown to light yellow-brown to greyish in colour, wearing off and leaving smooth ridges with age. *Hymenial surface:* Smooth or reflecting the surface furrows, reddish brown when moist, dark greyish to greyish buff, 'bleeding' red when bruised or cut when fresh. *Flesh:* Very thin, less than 1 mm, leathery, tough, yellow-brown, pale under surface hairs; without distinctive odour or taste. *Spore print:* White. *Spores:* Hyaline, ellipsoidal, smooth, thin-walled; 5-6 x 2,5-4 µm.

Podoscypha parvula

Podoscypha parvula
Fruit-bodies showing narrow attachment and smooth upper and hymenial surfaces.

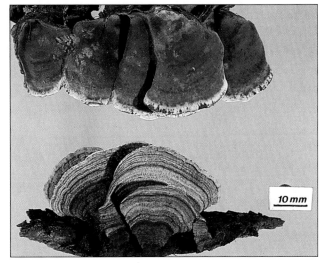

Stereum australe **Bleeding Crustcap** Fruit-bodies showing brown-zoned cap surface and smooth, brown hymenial surface bleeding red at the pale margin.

10 mm

Inedible

137. Stereum hirsutum (Wild.:Fr.) S.F. Gray   *Hairy Crustcap*

Stereum hirsutum is widely distributed throughout southern Africa. It is one of the most common wood-rotting fungi and is an early colonizer of dead stumps, logs and thicker branches of broad-leafed trees, especially oak and *Eucalyptus*, in contact with soil. It causes a severe white rot of the wood. The fruit-bodies can survive dry conditions but do not survive from one season to the next. Because of their tough consistency they are inedible. (*Afrikaans:* Harige Kruiphoed.)

Fruit-bodies in dense clusters on dead stumps and logs of broad-leafed trees. *Cap:* 7-50 mm wide or more, 10-40 mm radius from attachment, leathery, sessile, often grown together laterally, bracket-shaped, or effused-reflexed, or semi-resupinate and attached to substrate by an umbo, often imbricate; margin thin, entire, wavy to lobed. Surface covered with bundled or matted hairs, with concentric zones and grooves, greyish, light yellow-brown or reddish-brown. *Hymenial surface:* Smooth, cream-coloured to buff-cinnamon or light orange. *Flesh:* Very thin, leathery, tough, pale yellowish brown; without distinctive odour or taste. *Spore print:* White. *Spores:* Hyaline, cylindrical, occasionally slightly curved, smooth; 6,4-8 x 2,4-2,6 µm.

Inedible

138. Stereum ostrea (Blume & Nees: Fr.) Fr.   *False Turkey Tail*

Stereum ostrea is widely distributed throughout southern Africa. The fruit-bodies mostly form in groups on dead logs and stumps of broad-leafed trees, often in indigenous forests. Like *S. hirsutum* it causes a white rot of the wood. It differs from *S. hirsutum*, however, in the habit, size and colour of its fruit-bodies but may be confused with the multicoloured, thin fruit-bodies of *Coriolus versicolor* on casual observation. *C. versicolor* has pores in the hymenial surface.

The thin, tough fruit-bodies are inedible. (*Afrikaans:* Vals Elwebankie.)

Fruit-bodies grouped on dead logs of broad-leafed trees. *Cap:* 40-100 mm radius, leathery, wedge- to fan-shaped, attached by a reduced base and usually without a resupinate part, mostly grouped, often grown together laterally; margin thin, wavy, entire to somewhat lobed or splitting. Surface with thin, velvety layer of short, matted hairs that rub off in old specimens, concentrically furrowed and zoned, some zones hairless, mostly grey or greenish grey with light yellow-brown to reddish-brown, hazel or chestnut zones. *Hymenial surface:* Smooth or reflecting surface furrows, cream to pale buff. *Flesh:* Very thin, less than 1 mm, yellowish, tough; without distinctive odour or taste. *Spore print:* White. *Spores:* Hyaline, cylindrical, unilaterally depressed to broadly ellipsoidal, smooth; 5,3-8 x 2,7-3,3 µm.

Stereum hirsutum **Hairy Crustcap** Clustered fruit-bodies with smooth, orange-yellow hymenium.

tereum ostrea
alse Turkey Tail

Stereum ostrea showing narrowly attached fruit-bodies with multicoloured, zonate upper surface and smooth, pale buff hymenial surface.

Inedible

139. Hymenochaete ochromarginata Talbot

The specimens described here were found on a dead log of an indigenous, broad-leafed tree in the Tsitsikamma Forest National Park. The fruit-bodies occurred after good rains in early November. *H. ochromarginata* was first described from the eastern Cape and has also been found in Natal but it appears to be uncommon and is little known.

H. ochromarginata occurs on hardwood logs in which it causes a white rot like other species of this genus. It does not appear to be important in the decay of timer because of its rare occurrence.

A related and very similar species, *H. rubiginosa*, occurs in the same areas but does not have the ochre margin of *H. ochromarginata*, and its upper surface turns black with age. The two species also differ in micro-scopic characters. The tough fruit-bodies of *H. ochromarginata* are inedible.

Fruit-bodies effused-reflexed

Fruit-bodies grouped on dead hardwood logs. ***Cap:*** Up to 60 mm wide and projecting outwards up to 25 mm, tough, rigid, narrowly resupinate, upper part reflexed to shelf-like, imbricate and growing together laterally, bright yellow-brown to rusty-brown, with upper surface velvety and concentrically furrowed. Margin acute, wavy, bright ochreous, especially on the hymenial surface, in 1 mm wide band. ***Hymenial surface:*** Warm brown, smooth and slightly reflecting the surface furrows. ***Flesh:*** Thin, less than 1 mm, deep yellow-brown, unchanging; without distinctive odour. ***Spore print:*** White. ***Spores:*** Hyaline, oblong-ellipsoidal, smooth, thin-walled; 3-4 x 2-3 µm.

Inedible

140. Rhizopogon luteolus Fr. & Nordh. emend Tul. *Pale Brown False Truffle*

Rhizopogon luteolus occurs in the south-western and eastern Cape and in the Transvaal where it is associated with pine trees. It does not appear to be common but this is probably because the inconspicuous, partly buried fruit-bodies are easily overlooked. The fruit-bodies are formed from autumn to early winter under pine trees with which the species forms mycorrhizae.

The species is distinguished by the hard, potato-like fruit-bodies which are covered with dark, adhering mycelial threads. A related species, *R. rubescens*, also occurring under pines, can be distinguished by its fruit-bodies which are cream-coloured when underground but become tinged with red on exposure to air or when touched while fresh. Also, the spore mass of this species remains firmly soft and may be easily cut even when old and dark-coloured.

R. luteolus is inedible but *R. rubescens* is regarded as a delicacy in the Far East. The latter species has also been reported to be dug up and eaten by buck in pine plantations in the eastern Transvaal. (*Afrikaans:* Bruingeel Vals Truffel.)

Fruit-bodies single to clustered and partly buried in sandy soil under pine trees. ***Fruit-body:*** 20-60 mm across longest dimension, subglobose to egg-shaped or tuber-like, honey-yellow to pale ochreous brown, finally olive-brown, covered by tawny, reddish-brown or dark brown mycelial strands which are closely appressed at the sides but loose at the base; outer skin tough, thick, drying very hard and ochreous brown to bay-brown or umber with lighter patches; deliquescing in wet weather into a greenish-yellow mass with an unpleasant odour. ***Spore mass:*** Pale yellowish brown at first, darkening to cinnamon-brown to dark amber-brown, arranged in small, subglobose, ellipsoidal, or somewhat irregular internal cavities, 2-5 mm, separated by thin, colourless partitions; drying hard. ***Spores:*** Ellipsoidal to ovoid, pale greenish brown, smooth, thin-walled; 4-8,5 x 3-4 µm.

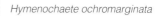

Hymenochaete ochromarginata

Hymenochaete ochromarginata
showing dark brown fruit-bodies
with ochre margin.

10 mm

Rhizopogon luteolus **Pale Brown False Truffle** Potato-like fruit-bodies partly covered by soil and pine needles.

141. Phallus rubicundus (Bosc.) Fr. *Yellow Stinkhorn*

Inedible

Phallus rubicundus is known from the south-western, southern and eastern Cape Province, Orange Free State, Natal and Transvaal. It grows mostly in lawns and other grassy localities and is probably involved in the decomposition of organic debris. It may be quite common during certain seasons with good rainfall but the fruit-bodies shrivel and disappear within a few hours when growing in sunny places. The fetid odour attracts flies which aid the dispersal of the spores.

This fungus is very distinctive in appearance and seems to be the most common and widespread species of the genus in southern Africa. The short-lived fruit-bodies are inedible. (*Afrikaans:* Geel Stinkhoring.)

Fruit-bodies single or scattered in grassy places. **Fruit-body:** When mature consisting of a golden-yellow, buff, salmon-orange or apricot-coloured stalk, 80-150 x 8-15 mm, cylindrical or slightly tapered towards the top; soft and spongy in texture and appearance, arising from a white, egg-shaped, membranous structure immersed in the soil. Apex surmounted by a membranous, conical to thimble-shaped, whitish cap, 15-28 x 8-14 mm with more or less longitudinal, irregular ridges and covered by a brownish-olive, mucilaginous spore mass which emits a strong, fetid odour. **Spores:** Subhyaline, broadly ovoid, smooth, thin-walled; 4-5 x 2-3 μm.

142. Itajahya galericulata Möller *Jacaranda Stinkhorn*

Inedible

Itajahya galericulata has been recorded from around Pretoria only. It is usually found under jacaranda trees and can occasionally be seen emerging from cracks in the asphalt or concrete slabs under the street trees. This fungus was described from South America originally, the home of the jacaranda, and it would seem that a mycorrhizal relationship with this tree might exist. It might also occur in other areas where jacarandas grow.

I. galericulata is the only species known in this genus. It is clearly related to the other stinkhorns but the intricately branched, cauliflower-like processes on which the spores are borne are unique to this fungus. The fetid odour attracts flies which disperse the spores. The fruit-bodies are short-lived and inedible. (*Afrikaans:* Jakaranda Stinkhoring.)

Fruit-bodies single, grouped or clustered on soil. **Fruit-body:** Consisting of a globose to egg-shaped, whitish, membranous sac, 30-80 mm diam., attached underground by a white mycelial cord; sac splitting irregularly at the apex to allow the emergence of a stalk and spore cap. **Stalk:** White, cylindrical or slightly tapered, straight or curved, 70-160 x 16-40 mm; spongy, hollow, brittle; apex bearing a smooth, white, solid, centrally depressed cap with an irregular margin; cap bearing externally folded and branched structures which form small, white, cauliflower-like processes which bear a dark spore mass. **Spore mass:** At first dark grey with a mottled appearance from the white, cauliflower-like processes of the cap, soon greenish black, mucilaginous and emitting a strong, fetid odour. **Spores:** Hyaline, broadly ellipsoidal, smooth, thin-walled; 4 x 2 μm.

Phallus rubicundus Yellow Stinkhorn

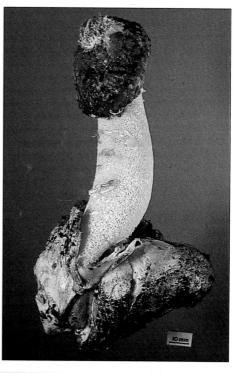

10 mm

Itajahya galericulata
Jacaranda Stinkhorn
Mature fruit-body with
white stipe and grey
spore mass arising
from membranous sac.

Itajahya galericulata Immature
sacs clustered on the soil.

143. Aseroë rubra Labillardiére *Star Stinkhorn*

Inedible

Aseroë rubra has been reported from the south-western and eastern Cape and from southern Natal, among pine needles in pine plantations. It has also been seen growing on wood shavings in a tree nursery near Johannesburg. The species seems to play some part in the decomposition of plant remains to humus. The fruit-bodies appear in early to late summer and are quite conspicuous because of their bright colours. Their presence is usually indicated by the strong, fetid odour of the slimy spore masses. This attracts flies which serve to disperse the spores.

The reddish fruit-bodies with the radiating arms which fork towards the ends are characteristic of this species. They are very fragile and watery, seldom lasting more than a few hours. Fruit-bodies of *A. rubra* are inedible. (*Afrikaans:* Sterstinkhoring.)

Fruit-bodies single or scattered on ground often under pines. *Fruit-body:* Arising from a globose, whitish, membranous sac up to 30 mm diam., consisting of an erect, cylindrical or flaring stipe, 36-60 x 10-20 mm, white below and deep pink towards the apex, hollow, cellular; apex of stipe covered by a horizontal, yellow to reddish, disc-like structure – the diaphragm – which extends inwards to form a central pore, and outwards into a rounded expansion from the margin from which five to nine arm-like processes radiate; arms up to 35 mm long and 6 mm wide at the base, longitudinally grooved, smooth or rough, each splitting about 15 mm from the base into two thinner arms, typically orange to red, tapering towards the ends. *Spore mass:* Mucilaginous, dark greenish brown to black, covering the upper surface of the diaphragm, disc expansion and adjoining basal portions of the arms; with fetid odour. *Spores:* Hyaline or pale greyish black, cylindrical, smooth, thin-walled; 4-5,5 x 1,5-2 µm.

144. Clathrus archeri (Berk.) Dring *Red Stinkhorn*

Inedible

Clathrus archeri, formerly known as *Anthurus archeri*, occurs in the south-western, southern and eastern Cape after good rains in summer and autumn. It commonly grows in the leaf-litter of broad-leafed trees, especially oak and *Eucalyptus*, decomposing it to humus. The unpleasant odour emitted by the black, slimy spore mass attracts flies which disperse the spores.

The fruit-bodies are quite conspicuous and resemble those of *Aseroë rubra* but *C. archeri* has thicker arms which do not fork into two thinner ends and often appear to lie directly on the surface of the leaf-litter.

The fruit-bodies are inedible and usually shrivel and disappear within a few hours. (*Afrikaans:* Inkvisstinkhoring.)

Fruit-bodies scattered or grouped on ground under broad-leafed trees. *Fruit-body:* Arising from a whitish, globose or ovoid, membranous sac which splits irregularly at the apex and consists of a short, brittle, cylindrical or flaring stalk. Stalk 10-50 mm x 10-25 mm, hollow, with spongy, cellular walls and roughened by transverse ridges; white at the base, reddish above, dividing at the top into four to six subcylindrical, arm-like processes at first united at their apices, soon free and spreading. Arms up to 140 mm long and 15 mm at the widest part, but tapering towards the apices; spongy, brittle, cellular, strongly transversely ridged over the bright red and rounded inner (upper) surface, and with a central groove along the reddish to white outer (lower) surface. *Spore mass:* Borne on the inner surface of the arms, greenish black, mucilaginous; with a penetrating, putrid odour. *Spores:* Faintly greenish, cylindrical, smooth, thin-walled; 6-7 x 2-2,5 µm.

Aseroë rubra
Star Stinkhorn

Aseroë rubra showing
split arms with blackish,
slimy spores at centre,
and stipe arising from
membranous white sac.

athrus archeri **Red Stinkhorn** Fruit-body
owing slimy, black spores scattered over
e red, spreading, radial arms.

145. Clathrus transvaalensis Eicker & Reid

Clathrus transvaalensis was described for the first time only recently. It is known only from the vicinity of Pretoria at present but, because the fruit-bodies are quite short-lived, may occur unnoticed in other areas. Other species of *Clathrus* with net-like fruit-bodies have been reported from other parts of southern Africa. *C. transvaalensis* appears after good, soaking rains following a hot dry spell in January and February. The fragile, short-lived nature of the fruit-bodies makes collection, preservation and study of specimens very difficult with the result that little is known about these fungi in southern Africa.

Species of *Clathrus* may play some part in the breakdown of organic matter to humus but this is largely unknown. The fruit-bodies are not edible.

Fruit-bodies single or grouped among grass or in leaf-litter of broad-leafed trees. *Fruit-body:* 80-100 x 45-55 mm, ellipsoidal, consisting of eight, ascending, fragile, spongy columns, 50-70 x 6-10 mm, branching apically; branches uniting in a net-like structure, with openings in the 'mesh' circular to elongate, 5-10 mm across. Columns white to yellowish or cream below, darkening upwards to pale pinkish brown over the upper parts, transversely grooved, with spore-bearing organs on their inner surfaces, mostly at the junctions of the arms; spore-bearing organs consisting of cushion-like swellings with net-like meshes ending in lobed processes which ooze olivaceous, mucilaginous masses of spores and emit a strong, fruity odour of granadilla and pineapple. Entire structure arising from a whitish 'egg' which remains as a white, smooth, membranous cup with an irregularly lobed margin; partly immersed in the soil to which it is attached by means of a few rhizoid-like threads. *Spores:* Subcylindrical, olivaceous; 4-4,5 x 1,5 μm.

146. Scleroderma cepa Pers.   *Smooth Earth-ball*

Scleroderma cepa is widely distributed and fairly common in the south-western, southern and eastern Cape Province, Natal and Transvaal, where it occurs from mid-summer to late autumn. The fungus grows under trees, hedges and in open grassy or gravelly places. It does not appear to form mycorrhizae with trees but may be involved in the decomposition of plant litter to humus.

S. cepa may be distinguished from other species by its smooth, pinkish skin and small column of white mycelial threads at its base. This species is inedible. (*Afrikaans:* Bobbejaansnuif.)

Fruit-bodies solitary, grouped or clustered on ground. *Fruit-body:* 15-80 mm over largest part, subglobose, often somewhat flattened over the top, irregularly compressed when clustered, with a column of white mycelial threads at the base, attaching it to the soil. Outer wall pinkish buff, pale brown to ochreous, smooth when young, later slightly scaly to warty, especially over apical area; thick at first, later thinning to 1 mm or less, leathery, brittle, finally splitting irregularly over apical part to liberate the spores. *Spore mass:* Internal, at first watery white, soon darkening to nearly black with a violet tinge, finally olive-grey with a violet tinge, powdery. *Spores:* Subglobose, brownish, strongly echinulate, echinulae long; 10-15 μm diameter.

Clathrus transvaalensis showing erect, spongy columns united in a net-like structure in their upper parts.

Scleroderma cepa
Smooth Earth-ball

Scleroderma cepa Subglobose fruit-body with basal column of mycelial threads.

Poisonous

147. Scleroderma citrinum Pers.   *Common Earth-ball*

Scleroderma citrinum, known previously as *S. aurantium*, is widely distributed in the wetter parts of southern Africa. In South Africa it is more common
in the Transvaal than in the Cape Province. It occurs under pines with which
it forms mycorrhizae and the fruit-bodies appear in late summer to autumn.

This species is reported to be edible when young, and occasionally fruit-
bodies that have been nibbled by small animals like porcupines are seen
in pine plantations. However, mature fruit-bodies are poisonous when eaten
raw and may cause stomach upsets even when cooked. The species is
best avoided. (*Afrikaans:* Vratjie Snuifbal.)

Fruit-bodies single or grouped, occasionally clustered, on ground under pine
trees. *Fruit-body:* Up to 80 mm diam., more or less spherical or with a flattened base, hard, lemon-yellow at first, later ochre to brownish. Surface
covered with large, irregular, flattened, wart-like protuberances or smaller
warts, especially over the upper part, but warts may be so small as to be
nearly smooth. Base constricted to a narrow column of yellow, root-like
threads; bright lemon-yellow when fresh. *Wall:* 1,5-3 mm thick, leathery,
white, turning pinkish when cut while young, later corky, hard woody, and
finally cracking irregularly at the top to release the spores. *Spore mass:*
Internal, chocolate-brown to olivaceous grey at maturity. *Spores:* Globose,
dark brown, covered by reticulate ridges; 13-17 µm diam.

Edible

148. Scleroderma verrucosum (Bull.:Pers.) Pers.   *Scaly Earth-ball*

Scleroderma verrucosum is known to occur in the south-western, southern
and eastern Cape, Natal and Transvaal but is less common than *S. cepa*
which is found in the same areas. The fruit-bodies appear on sandy soil
among leaf-litter of broad-leafed trees and shrubs from late summer to late
autumn. This species seems to be involved in the decomposition of organic
material to humus.

S. verrucosum may be recognized by the thin, pale brownish wall which is
evenly covered with small, dark brown scales or warts, and by the relatively
thick, well-developed rooting base of the fruit-body.

The fruit-bodies are reported to be edible while the spore mass is young
and still white but a bitter taste develops as the spores mature. (*Afrikaans:*
Aartappel Snuifbal.)

Fruit-bodies solitary, grouped or clustered on ground. *Fruit-body:* 10-50 mm
diam., subglobose, flattened globose to somewhat pear-shaped, contracted
at the bottom into a thick, short, stem-like base, usually prominently ribbed
and attached to the soil by numerous whitish mycelial threads; surface pale
brown to yellow-brown or darker and covered with small, darker brown
scales or flattened warts; wall thick at first becoming thin and leathery at
maturity and splitting irregularly over the top to liberate the spores. *Spore
mass:* Internal, white at first, soon dark grey to almost black with a violet
tinge, finally stone-grey to greyish brown or olivaceous grey-brown, powdery. *Spores:* Globose, brown, coarsely echinulate; 9-15 µm.

☠ *Scleroderma citrinum* **Common Earth-ball**

Scleroderma citrinum showing yellow, warted, thick wall, basal column of root-like threads, and dark grey internal spore mass.

Scleroderma verrucosum **Scaly Earth-ball** Subglobose, brown, scaly to warty fruit-body with thick, stem-like base and purplish-brown internal spore mass.

Inedible

149. Pisolithus tinctorius (Pers.) Coker & Couch   *Dye Ball*
Pisolithus tinctorius, known in Europe as *P. arrhizus*, is common throughout southern Africa. It is mostly associated with *Eucalyptus* trees with which it forms mycorrhizae. It also occurs with black wattle, *Acacia mearnsii*, and occasionally in dry, sandy or gravelly soil without trees. The fruit-bodies appear from mid-summer to late autumn, and the basal rooting part with some spores attached may survive into the following season.

The species is readily recognizable by its characteristic appearance and internal structure. The young fruit-bodies yield a dark, brown-staining liquid when squeezed or cut which was used in the manufacture of various dyes. This fungus is not edible. (*Afrikaans:* Kleursnuifbal.)

Fruit-bodies solitary, scattered or grouped on soil or under broad-leafed trees. *Fruit-body:* Large, up to 200 mm tall and 170 mm diam., variable in shape, subglobose, egg-shaped or pear-shaped, often irregularly lobed, usually narrowing gradually or abruptly into a stout, root-like base immersed in the soil and attached underground by yellow, rhizomorphic strands; firm and solid when young. Outer layer thin, smooth, shiny, ochreous or bright yellow at first, darkening to greyish brown and to dark grey with dark brown markings producing a snake skin effect. Rooting base yellow at first and with a rubber-like texture, later dark brown, hard and woody. Outer skin breaking away irregularly to expose spores at maturity. Spores internal, in egg-shaped or irregularly polygonal cavities, 1-4 x 1-2 mm, separated by thick, black, persistent walls; spore cavities whitish at first, producing a mottled effect when cut through, later darkening to olive-brown to umber as spores mature, and becoming powdery as separating walls disintegrate. *Spore mass:* Olive-brown to umber, powdery when mature. *Spores:* Globose, pale olivaceous brown, strongly verrucose; 5-10 µm diam.

Edible

150. Lycoperdon perlatum Pers.   *Gem-studded Puff-ball*
Lycoperdon perlatum, previously also known as *L. gemmatum*, occurs in the Cape, Natal and in the eastern Transvaal. It occurs in late summer to autumn, among the leaf-litter of broad-leafed trees. It does not appear to be common but the mature fruit-bodies blend well with their environment and may be overlooked.

A variety of this species which has white fruit-bodies with greyish upper surfaces covered with short, dark grey to blackish spines, has been collected under pine trees in the eastern Transvaal recently. This variety and the species described below are both very similar to the European species which is pure white when young. Until the identity and naming of these forms have been resolved, the name *L. perlatum* is used for both varieties.

The fruit-bodies are edible when the spore mass is still white and firm. The flavour is reported to be excellent. (*Afrikaans:* Pêrelstuifbal.)

Fruit-bodies solitary, grouped or clustered on ground among leaf-litter. *Fruit-body:* Up to 50 mm tall and up to 30 mm diam., pear-shaped to top-shaped or inverted egg-shaped, with mycelial threads attached to the base white at first, thickly studded with tiny, persistent, straw-coloured warts and granules over the apical part, interspersed with more pointed, umber, erect warts which soon disappear to leave small, light-coloured depressions producing a net-like pattern over the spore-sac; spore-sac buff, greyish-brown to olive-brown, opening by means of a torn, raised, apical pore. Basal part sterile, often elongated, stalk-like. *Spore mass:* At first firm, white, changing to golden-brown and at maturity greyish-brown, olive-brown to chestnut-brown and powdery. *Spores:* Globose, olivaceous, finely verrucose, 3,5-5 µm diam., pedicellate, pedicels deciduous, hyaline and up to 10,2 µm long.

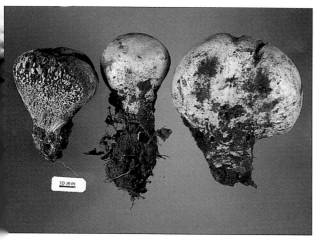

10 mm

Pisolithus tinctorius **Dye Ball**

Pisolithus tinctorius showing yellow, rooting base and internal spore cavities.

Lycoperdon perlatum showing umber warts and light-coloured depressions over upper surface.

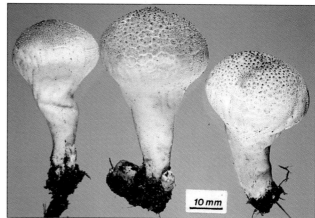

10 mm

Lycoperdon perlatum
Gem-studded Puff-ball

151. Calvatia lilacina (Berk.) Henn. *Lilac Puff-ball*

Edibility unknown

Calvatia lilacina is widely distributed throughout southern Africa. The fruit-bodies appear in autumn and often grow in groups, even in fairy rings. They develop and disintegrate within a short period of time so that only the purplish-brown, inverted conical base remains for a few weeks after the disappearance of the spores. The species appears to be active in the decomposition of organic debris.

C. lilacina is recognizable by the purplish-brown spore mass which is covered at maturity by the thin, fragile, chocolate-brown or purplish-brown outer layer of the fruit-body. The persistence of the purplish-brown base after the disintegration of the fruit-body is also characteristic.

The edibility of the species is unknown. It might be edible while young and firm if no unpleasant flavours are present. Some other species of *Calvatia* are edible. (*Afrikaans:* Lila Stuifbal.)

Fruit-bodies solitary, scattered or grouped on ground among grass. *Fruit-body:* Up to 150 mm diam., subglobose to pear-shaped with a short, thick, basal stalk attached to a branching, rooting structure; subglobose upper part firm-spongy at first, creamy white or ochreous and finely downy but changing to buff and finally chocolate, umber or bay-brown; smooth, sometimes areolately cracked and soft, the outer layers thin, fragile, breaking up and exposing the spore mass. *Spore mass:* Yellowish grey in young stage, darkening to purplish grey to purplish brown; firm at first, becoming floccose and disappearing until finally only the inverted conical, purplish-brown, sterile base remains. *Spores:* Globose, verrucose, yellowish to bay-brown with purplish-brown epispore; 4-6,8 μm.

152. Vascellum pratense (Pers.) Kreisel *Common Puff-ball*

Edible

Vascellum pratense, known earlier as *Lycoperdon hiemale*, is widely distributed and very common throughout southern Africa. It appears repeatedly through summer and autumn after good rains in grassy, open places where plant litter or compost is abundant in the soil, and seems to be involved in the decomposition of plant litter to humus.

This species is edible, the cooked fruit-bodies tasting like cooked sheep' brains. It should be eaten in the immature state only, while the flesh is still firm and white. (*Afrikaans:* Oueltjie.)

Fruit-bodies scattered or grouped or clustered in lawns and grassy places. *Fruit-body:* 15-30 mm diam., occasionally up to 50 mm high, more or less top-shaped to almost spherical, slightly flattened on top or laterally flattened when clustered, later more irregular; white, the surface covered with small warts which are largest over the top; base anchored in soil by short, root-like threads; firm at first, later softening and developing a pore at the top from which spores are puffed out when touched. Outer wall darkening, becoming thin, membranous and finally disappearing to leave a yellow-brown, powdery spore mass. *Flesh:* Firm, white when young, becoming soft, mushy and yellowish, finally drying into yellowish-brown to olivaceous-brown spore powder. *Spores:* Globose, pale olivaceous brown, almost smooth to coarsely verrucose; 3,5-4,2 μm diam.

Calvatia lilacina **Lilac Puff-ball**
Mature fruit-body with lilac spores; inverted conical, sterile base of disintegrated fruit-body; and immature, creamy white fruit-body.

Vascellum pratense Young and mature fruit-bodies with root-like basal threads.

Vascellum pratense
Common Puff-ball

153. Geastrum triplex Junghun   *Collared Earth-star*

Geastrum triplex is fairly common in the Cape, Natal and Transvaal, occur-ring even in the drier areas of these provinces. The fruit-bodies appear from summer to autumn in the summer-rainfall regions and during winter in the south-western Cape. They always grow among leaf-litter of broad-leafed trees and hedges in well-composted soil. The species is involved in the decomposition of organic material to humus.

   G. triplex is readily recognizable as an earth-star but the thick, cracking, fleshy layer and recurving rays of the exoperidium distinguish the species. These characteristics are very variable however, and it is often difficult to distinguish this species from *G. saccatum* which has a felty exoperidium and a spore sac mouth without a surrounding disc-like area.

   The spores are puffed out and dispersed when raindrops strike the ripe spore sac. The species is inedible. (*Afrikaans:* Gekraagde Aardster.)

Fruit-bodies grouped on ground among leaf-litter. **Fruit-body:** Consisting of a globose spore sac resting upon a star-shaped bed of tissue formed by the expanded outer layers, the exoperidium; attached to the substrate by numerous white mycelial threads. In young stages exoperidium is dirty white to ochreous, smooth, hairless, completely enclosing the spore sac and forming a prominent point at the apex; later splitting into four to eight sharp-pointed rays and expanding; rays curving backwards, up to 40-80 mm diam., their inner (upper) layers thick, fleshy, pale ochreous, darkening to cinnamon or reddish brown, usually cracking across the curvature and in this way leaving a collar of tissue around the spore sac. **Spore sac:** Sub-globose, 15-30 diam., smooth, grey to brownish to reddish brown with age, with an apical pore surrounded by fibrils forming a low, conical ring and arising from a narrow disc-like area. **Spore mass:** White at first, firm, turning dark brown to umber and powdery. **Spores:** Globose, brown, verrucose; 3,5-4,5 µm.

154. Myriostoma coliforme (Pers.) Corda   *Saltshaker Earth-star*

Myriostoma coliforme occurs in the Cape, Natal and the Transvaal but does not appear to be common. It is usually found among the leaf-litter of broad-leafed trees, often in rather dry localities in association with indigenous *Acacia* species, and seems to be involved in the decomposition of leaf-litter and other organic material to humus. The fruit-bodies appear from later summer to autumn.

   This species is distinguished from related *Geastrum* species by the pres-ence of more than one pore mouth on the spore sac which is supported upon a number of thin columns. Falling raindrops cause the spores to be puffed out. *M. coliforme* is inedible. (*Afrikaans:* Peperbus.)

Fruit-bodies grouped on ground among leaf-litter. **Fruit-body:** Consisting of a globose spore sac set upon several short stalks connected to a spread-ing, star-shaped structure formed by the outer layers of the fruit-body, the exoperidium. Mature exoperidium with five to nine, tapering, pointed rays curving backwards and spreading, 50-90 mm diam., smooth, brownish, membranous, the inner (upper) layers fleshy, pale but darkening later to greyish brown. **Spore sac:** Subglobose, 10-50 mm diam., often somewhat flattened, rough, greyish brown, with four to 15 irregular, circular or elliptical pores scattered over the upper surface; supported on several, short, colum-nar supports over the central, upper part of the spreading exoperidium. **Spore mass:** White, firm when young, changing to umber and powdery. **Spores:** Globose, pale brown, strongly verrucose; 3-7 µm diam.

Geastrum triplex
Collared Earth-star

Myriostoma coliforme
showing spore sac supported
by several small columns.

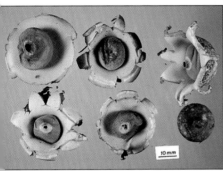

Geastrum triplex showing fruit-
bodies in different stages of
development, and cracked,
fleshy layer of rays forming
collar around spore sac.

Myriostoma coliforme
Saltshaker Earth-star
showing elliptical pores
over top of spore sac.

155. Battarrea stevenii (Liboschitz) Fries

Battarrea stevenii has been recorded from the Cape, Orange Free State, Transvaal and Mozambique. The fruit-bodies occur from March to June in the different localities, in both exposed and sheltered conditions. The fungus seems to prefer sandy soils in areas with low rainfall but has also been found in heavy, clayey soils.

This species is quite distinctive with its tall, shaggy stipe bearing a convex, rust-brown spore mass over a woody, convex base. In many specimens only the stipe and spore base remain, the spores having been blown off. The role of this species in nature and its edibility are unknown.

Fruit-bodies solitary or occasionally grouped in open, sandy places.
Cap: 25-70 mm diam., 20-50 cm high, bell-shaped to convex cushion-like, firm at first, covered by a glossy, white to cream or ochreous membrane attached to a thin, concave, cream to buff-coloured base. Surface membrane splitting at maturity to fall away in one, cap-like piece, leaving the powdery, greyish-brown to rusty brown spore mass disintegrating over the upper surface of the base; finally leaving it bare. *Stipe:* Central, cylindrical to elongate-ovoid, narrowing towards its base, 110-400 x 7-30 mm, dovegrey to ochreous to dull brown, deeply grooved and shaggy with elongate, membranous scales; woody fibrous, hollow; without ring; surrounded by a leathery, rusty brown, sheath-like volva at its base. *Spores:* Globose, subglobose to slightly irregular, pale rust-coloured, finely verrucose, thickwalled; 4,5-7 µm diam.

156. Podaxis pistillaris (L.:Pers.) Morse   *False Ink Cap*

Podaxis pistillaris is widely distributed throughout southern Africa, frequently occurring in the arid regions of the northern Cape, western Transvaal and Orange Free State. The fruit-bodies appear from late summer to autumn, often on mounds of the harvester termite, *Trinervitermes trinervoides*. It is not cultivated by termites as is the case with the *Termitomyces* species.

Although having a distinctive form which allows easy recognition, the fruit-bodies vary in size and appearance. Recent studies have shown that more than one species is referred to as *P. pistillaris* in southern Africa. Two of these, *P. africana* and *P. rugospora*, can only be distinguished with certainty from *P. pistillaris* on microscopic characters.

The dark brown spore powder has been used in folk medicine in the treatment of cancer. It has also been used in a mixture with unsalted fat as a salve for the treatment of nappy rash in infants. Species of *Podaxis* are not generally regarded as edible. (*Afrikaans:* Slangkop.)

Fruit-bodies single or in small groups on soil or on termite mounds.
Fruit-body: Tall, 100-320 mm high, consisting of an elongated, egg-shaped spore sac, 20-150 x 15-70 mm, surrounding and attached to a stipe. Spore sac initially covered with large, brownish scales which come off easily to leave a silvery white rind, up to 4 mm thick; rind soon turning greyish brown to umber, becoming brittle, tearing away from stipe at its lower edges and splitting along the margin to liberate the spores. *Stipe:* Concolorous with spore sac, straight or curved, cylindrical, 130-320 x 10-40 mm, extending to the apex of the spore sac; longitudinally grooved, often covered with overlapping scales; enlarged at the base into a bulbous or tuberous structure consisting of mixed fungal threads and soil particles. *Spore mass:* Firm at first, whitish, changing to greenish brown to almost black, powdery.
Spores: Broadly ovoid to subglobose, or somewhat irregular; olivaceous brown to dark reddish brown, finely roughened; 5-17 x 4-12 µm, sometimes with short pedicels.

Battarrea stevenii showing bare cap base on scaly stipe and powdery, rusty brown spore mass on cap base, exposed by separation of covering membrane from base.

Podaxis pistillaris **False Ink Cap**
Fruit-body on termite mound (below left), and with disintegrating spore sac and dark reddish-brown spore mass (below right).

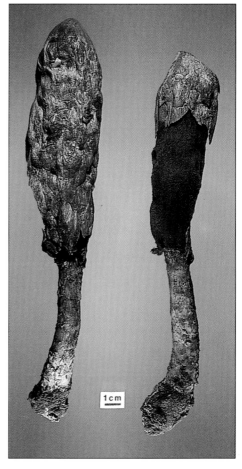

157. Tulostoma albicans White

Tulostoma albicans is known from collections around Pretoria, Kimberley and central and eastern Orange Free State. The fruit-bodies appear from summer to autumn. Fourteen species of *Tulostoma* are known to occur in southern Africa, growing mostly in sandy soil among leaf-litter and apparently involved in the decomposition of plant remains to humus.

Species of *Tulostoma* are distinguished mainly on the microscopic characters of the spores. *T. albicans* is recognizable by the very pale, almost white spore sac of the young fruit-bodies and by the size and surface ornamentation of the spores. It is inedible.

Fruit-bodies scattered in sandy soil. *Fruit-body:* Consisting of a subglobose spore sac raised above soil level on a dark-coloured stalk, partly immersed in the soil. *Spore sac:* 8-15 mm diam.; outer wall bay-brown to reddish brown, encrusted with soil particles, breaking away from the upper parts and exposing the inner wall which is attached around its base to a shallowly depressed cup-like section of the outer wall; inner wall, dirty white to grey or pale beige, smooth, tough, membranous with a circular, apical pore on a short, tubular ridge. *Stipe:* Dark reddish brown, grooved, cylindrical, 20-45 x 2-5 mm, with adhering soil grains, widening into a basal bulb 3-7 mm diam. *Spore mass:* Rusty brown, powdery, puffed out through the apical pore when spore sac is depressed by raindrops or other means. *Spores:* Globose to subglobose, golden brown but epispore darker, sparsely verrucose; 4-7 µm diam.

158. Cyathus olla Pers. *Grey-egg Birds' Nest Fungus*

Cyathus olla is widely distributed throughout southern Africa. It is common in some seasons, and occurs in wet places from mid-summer to autumn on wood and in soil rich in decaying plant remains. It is apparently one of the species involved in the breakdown of plant remains to humus.

C. olla is one of a group of similar species which resemble birds' nests, the spores of which are dispersed when the 'eggs' are dislodged from the 'nest' by raindrops. In some, such as *C. poeppigii*, the 'nests' have grooved inner surfaces. The small fruit-bodies of *C. olla* are inedible. (*Afrikaans:* Gladde Voëlnesswam.)

Fruit-bodies grouped on dead wood, decayed plant material, or on soil. *Fruit-body:* Small, 5-15 mm high, goblet or inverted bell-shaped, tapering downwards to a substipitate base; mouth incurved at first, later straight or typically flared in mature specimens; outer surface light brown at first, later greyish brown and covered with woolly, appressed hairs; inner surface even, smooth, leaden grey, greyish brown or silvery brown containing several 'eggs' (peridioles containing the spores). Peridioles 2-3,5 mm diam, lens-shaped, pale grey at first and covered with a thin, white membrane, changing to dull olive-brown to blackish when mature; attached to the fruit-body by a thin, white, detachable thread (funiculus). *Spores:* Hyaline, broadly ellipsoidal to obovoid, smooth, thin-walled; 6,8-13,6 x 5-7 µm.

Tulostoma albicans showing greyish spore sac with apical pore in cup-like upper part, and reddish-brown stalk with bulbous base.

10 mm

Tulostoma albicans

Cyathus olla **Grey-egg Birds' Nest Fungus**
Goblet-shaped fruit-bodies containing greyish 'eggs' – the spore sacs.

10 mm

159. Rhizina undulata Fr.   *Pine Fire Fungus*

Inedible

Rhizina undulata, also known as *Rhizina inflata* (Schaeff.) Karst., was reported in southern Africa from Knysna in 1944 for the first time. It has since been found in the eastern Cape, Natal, eastern Transvaal and Swaziland on 10 different species of pines. The fruit-bodies appear from spring to autumn among dead needles under pine trees, often near stumps. *R. undulata* is a serious pathogen of young pines and has caused extensive damage to some newly planted sites. The burning of plant debris before replanting is a source of the problem as the ascospores germinate by way of heat from the fires. The disease can therefore be controlled by avoiding fire or by delaying the planting of new seedlings after fire. The fruit-bodies are readily recognizable by their unusual shapes. They are inedible. (*Afrikaans:* Dennevuurswam.)

Fruit-bodies single, scattered or grouped on needle layers under pines. *Fruit-body:* Consisting of a crust-like, irregularly shaped, shallow inverted cup, 40-150 mm across widest part, 10-60 mm thick, firm; in age hard-horny; margin irregularly lobed, ochreous while growing, later concolorous with surface. Surface chestnut-brown at first, gradually changing to blackish brown and to black in age, uneven, matt, occasionally cracking in age; lower surface lighter in colour, uneven, with irregular depressions and protuberances giving rise to numerous pale-coloured rhizoids attaching the fruit-body to the substrate. *Flesh:* Reddish brown, fibrous, turning hard-leathery under a blackish surface layer about 0,3-0,5 mm thick. *Ascosopores:* Hyaline, fusiform, minutely verrucose, with two or more oil droplets; 22-40 x 8-11 μm.

160. Terfezia pfeilii Henn.   *Kalahari Truffle*

Edible

Terfezia pfeilii occurs in the northern Cape from Kakamas, Prieska and Kimberley northwards into Botswana and Namibia in sandy soil and in the reddish sand-dunes found in these areas. The fruit-bodies form 5-40 cm underground from late April to early June after good, recurrent, seasonal rains. Their presence is indicated by cracks in the surface, often near tussocks of bushman grass (*Stipagrostis* species), grey camel thorn, (*Acacia haematoxylon*), candle-pod (*Acacia hebeclada*) and other thorn tree species A mycorrhizal relationship between *T. pfeilii* and these plants has been suggested but has not been proven yet.

Choiromyces echinulatus Trappe & Marasas, a pale cream-coloured fungus resembling *T. pfeilii* but with a more convoluted surface and softer texture, grows in the same region; its whitish flesh marbled with dark brown veins has an unpleasant taste and is considered inedible. *T. pfeilii* is edible with an excellent flavour and texture. (*Afrikaans:* n'Abba.)

Fruit-bodies underground, single or in small groups under cracks in sandy soils. *Fruit-body:* Subglobose, top- or pear-shaped, 25-65 x 25-58 mm, with a basal attachment scar, pale yellow-brown to dark brown, smooth; enclosed by toughened rind (peridium) up to 1 mm thick; surface somewhat uneven or with occasional vertical grooves; darkening and occasionally cracking irregularly in age. *Flesh:* Whitish to creamy white at first, with a faint, marbled appearance when cut, later yellowish with more conspicuous white, marbled veins; emitting a strong, pleasant, mushroomy odour. *Spores:* Embedded in flesh. *Ascospores:* Globose, at first hyaline, darkening to pale brown at maturity, wall two-layered, 16-26 μm diam., densely covered in minute spines 1-2 μm tall.

Rhizina undulata
Pine Fire Fungus

Terfezia pfeilii **Kalahari Truffle**
Crack in sand indicating
presence of fruit-bodies.

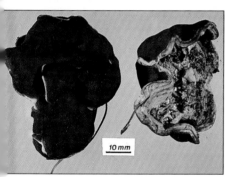

Rhizina undulata showing
upper and lower surfaces
fruit-bodies.

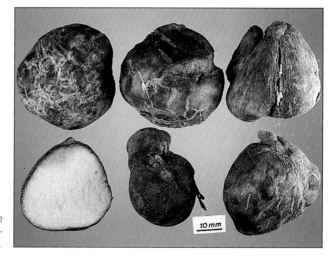

Terfezia pfeilii Mature
fruit-bodies showing attachment scar and white flesh.

COLLECTING AND PRESERVING MUSHROOMS

Before you can legally collect mushrooms from a forest in South Africa it is necessary to obtain a permit from the Director General: Department of Water Affairs and Forestry. If you intend collecting mushrooms from a nature reserve, however, it is necessary to apply to the Director of Nature Conservation of the province for a permit.

When collecting mushrooms, irrespective of whether they are intended for eating or for scientific study, two principles must be scrupulously observed, namely, cleanliness and orderliness. Soil and other debris adhering to mushrooms are clearly undesirable if the mushrooms are to be eaten and in scientific study can interfere with microscopic examination of the specimens. Also, when photographing mushrooms, debris or soil may impart colours or markings to the specimens which are not true to the species. Orderliness will prevent different species from getting mixed with others which could be dangerous if some of the specimens are for eating. A collection in which different species have become mixed is useless for scientific purposes.

The equipment required for collecting is simple: a wide, shallow, flat-bottomed basket or a corrugated cardboard box to which convenient ropes for carrying have been fitted; paper bags of various sizes; a pencil; a 10-15 mm paint brush, and a sturdy, narrow, steel gardening trowel. When a group or scattered individual specimens of mushrooms are found in the field, first examine them to determine whether or not they are too old or too young. A range of fruit-bodies from immature to mature is most desirable for collecting. Select a suitably sized paper bag and write notes on it regarding the habit of the fruit-bodies (whether they are solitary, grouped or tufted), the substrate, colours of the fruit-bodies and any other relevant observations. A collection number should also be written on the paper bag. Use the gardening trowel to remove the specimen, ensuring that you do not damage any part of it and that the entire base of the stipe is exposed. Use the paint brush to remove any soil particles and other debris, and then carefully place the fruit-body into the marked paper bag. Fruit-bodies from the same group may be placed together in the paper bag provided that they do not rest on top of and crush one another. Fleshy species growing on wood may be removed by means of a sharp, sturdy knife, taking care to remove some of the underlying wood as well so that the type of decay and wood can be determined. A separate paper bag must be used for each collection so as to avoid confusion when identifying species.

If the specimens collected are required for scientific study, enter the data on the paper bag into a notebook, together with more detailed descriptions of the fruit-bodies, after the day's collecting. Data pertaining to size of the fruit-bodies, surface texture, shape and colour of the cap, lamellae, tubes, stipe, flesh, and colour changes in cutting or bruising should be written down, and sketches made if necessary. You can then proceed with identification of the species. If spore prints are required, specimens should be prepared as described on page 17. They are then preserved for future study and reference purposes by drying. Pore fungi are best dried with the pore surface turned upwards to prevent loss of spores.

If the collections are intended for eating, the fruit-bodies should be carefully compared with descriptions and illustrations to determine whether or not they are edible. Those that are not, or about which any doubt exists, should be discarded. If edible and poisonous species have been in contact with one another in the collecting basket, both should be discarded.

Preserving mushrooms
Mushrooms are short-lived and decay quickly after they have been collected. They can be preserved in various ways but the most practicable way for both eating and scientific study is by drying because the removal of water halts the life processes. During drying as much water as possible must be removed without causing undesirable changes, such as darkening of colours. This is best achieved by placing the specimens in a draught of warm air which need only be a few degrees higher (5-10 °C) than the ambient air temperature. Higher temperature may cause darkening of the colours, even scorching of the specimen and may damage some of the delicate microscopic structures necessary for identification and scientific study.

An effective way of drying mushrooms is on a drying rack, as illustrated. This can be constructed using four uprights (10 x 10 x 3 mm angle iron or 12 mm square tubing, each 70 cm long), four wire grids (35 x 45 cm) obtained by removing the connecting links and handles of

two folding barbecue handgrids, and a sheet of unbleached linen or canvas (0,65 x 1,75 m) fitted with hooks and eyes, press studs or a zipper.

Attach the wire grids to the uprights to form four shelves, the first one level with the top ends of the uprights, the second one 8 cm below this, the third 10 cm below the second one and the bottom one 10 cm below the third, so that the bottom shelf is 40 cm above floor level. The warm air can be supplied by means of a small single-bar electric heater (750-900 watt). Position this on the floor with its bar parallel to the longer sides of the rack and below the middle of the bottom grid, or place it to one side of the rack in the event of overheating. Wrap the linen sheet around the rack so that its lower edge is about 5 cm above floor level, and suspend it from the top shelf by means of hooks. Hold the overlapping ends together by means of a zip fastener, hooks and eyes, or press studs. This opening allows fresh specimens to be placed on the shelves or dried specimens to be removed without interrupting the drying of others. The linen covering creates a chimney effect which speeds up the circulation of air rising from the heater and being drawn in through the bottom opening. The drying rack and heater are best placed on a concrete floor or a piece of asbestos sheeting away from flammable materials.

Specimens to be dried are laid on the shelves, the larger ones on the lower shelves, the covering is closed and the heater is switched on and left overnight or longer, until all the specimens feel dry right through to the centres.

The drying rack is described in basic terms and may be altered and adapted in various ways to suit individual requirements. It can be constructed in such a way that it can be dismantled quickly to allow easy transport and storage in a small space. A drying rack may even be improvised by firmly supporting a metal grid from an oven or refrigerator some distance above a convection- or blower-type electric heater. This can be quite satisfactory for drying a small number of specimens.

Mushrooms intended for eating may be cut up into slices about one centimetre thick, or less, in order to allow rapid drying. Store the dried slices in small quantities sufficient for one portion, in tightly closed or sealed containers. If stored in a large container which is opened repeatedly, the mushrooms are liable to infestation by insects and possible spoilage by moulds or bacteria. Dried mushrooms may be kept for months, even years, if kept dry and insect free, for use in soups and other dishes. The thick, fleshy fruit-bodies of *Boletus edulis* and some of the larger *Termitomyces* species are well suited for preservation in this way as they retain their flavour. Dried slices are rehydrated by pouring boiling water over them and allowing them to soak for 15-30 minutes before use.

Specimens intended for preservation for scientific study must be carefully selected to include undamaged individuals in various stages of development; overmature specimens should not be used. Dry and preserve the specimens intact if possible, although thick, fleshy fruit-bodies may be cut longitudinally into 10-15 mm slices to allow rapid drying with minimum risk of damage. The slices must be regarded as one collection. Because specimens intended for scientific study may be required to last indefinitely, it is most important that they be dried thoroughly as a first step towards satisfactory preservation. Thereafter, proper storage in which they are protected against mechanical damage, heat, moisture and insect attack, is essential.

Storing mushrooms

The prime objective in storing mushrooms is to protect them against damage, be it mechanical, weather-related or as a result of insects. Mechanical damage is best prevented by keeping specimens in suitable cardboard boxes of different sizes, each collection in its own box so that only one need be disturbed at a time. Store the boxes in a suitable wooden or metal cupboard fitted with a tightly closing, lockable door to protect them against damage by water or condensation and against excessive heat. In some coastal areas high levels of humidity would result in the absorption of moisture which in turn may cause mould growth. This can be prevented by placing a cotton sachet of silica gel in the cupboard. When the crystals appear colourless through absorption of moisture, heat them gently in a warm oven to drive off the moisture, and return them to the cupboard once they are dry (having changed to a deep blue colour).

Insects can ruin stored specimens very quickly. A small brown beetle, the herbarium or cigarette beetle, is particularly destructive as it burrows inside preserved specimens, reducing them to a little pile of frass. Certain species of mushrooms and many species of bracket fungi with hard, woody fruit-bodies are particularly susceptible to attack by these insects. Fortunately there are chemicals which will deter insects or exterminate an infestation already in progress. Naphthalene flakes or moth balls are cheap and fairly effective; paradichloro-benzene, also sold under the brand name *Extermoth* is another good deterrent and dichlorvos, the active ingredient of several common insect deterrents, is very effective. These preparations should be placed with the specimens when kept in a closed cupboard and the supply should be renewed periodically. Remember, however, that these substances give off toxic fumes which are hazardous to health, and should be used only in cupboards with tightly fitting doors which will prevent the vapours from escaping into working or living areas.

FUNGUS COLLECTIONS AND HERBARIA

When you begin collecting mushrooms, you may decide to keep some specimens for future reference or because they are particularly interesting in some way. This may be the start of a collection in which you have a personal interest. You may become more interested and collect mushrooms to satisfy personal curiosity and may retain rare or particularly interesting ones as trophies to be shown proudly to other interested people. This could be the start of a personal collection of mushrooms which may acquire considerable scientific value with time, provided that the specimens are carefully maintained. Many such collections have found their way to recognized herbaria and have been of great value to professional mycologists.

A herbarium is a collection of dried plant or fungus specimens intended for reference pur-poses and scientific use. New collections are constantly being added and, together with older ones, are preserved for use by professional workers. An essential requirement of a herbarium is that all collections are properly catalogued and accompanied by full, detailed records which then become valuable sources of information on distribution of species, host associations and other important aspects of fungal biology.

A number of fungus collections and herbaria exist in the region. Each of the universities has one within the departments of Botany and Plant Pathology. These collections include dried specimens of mushrooms and other large fungi, as well as dried specimens of leafspots, stem cankers and other plant diseases caused by fungi. At some universities, herbaria – mostly of flowering plant specimens – have been developed as centres of active research which are recognized by international scientific organizations. Some, such as the H.G.W.J. Schweikerdt Herbarium at the University of Pretoria, also include a collection of fungi.

Certain regional herbaria which now operate within the National Botanical Institute (NBI), such as the R.H. Compton Herbarium at Kirstenbosch and the Albany Museum in Grahamstown, also have collections of fungi and mushrooms. The main herbarium for fungi in South Africa is the National Collection of Fungi which is administered by the Plant Protection Research Institute of the Agricultural Research Council in Pretoria. A staff of trained mycolo-gists are actively engaged in fungi research, and information is available to interested mem-bers of the public. The public is also welcome to send or take mushrooms to this institute for identification. Interested persons are indeed encouraged to bring in good specimens, as rare or even unknown species may come to the notice of the scientists in this way, and new infor-mation on the occurrence, distribution and appearance of different species is thus made avail-able to science.

As relatively little is known about the mushroom flora of southern Africa, interested persons can make contributions to our knowledge and at the same time develop a useful and satisfying interest in nature.

GLOSSARY

Adaxial surface Side of basidiospore next to long axis of basidium.
Adnate Broadly attached to stipe (as in lamellae).

Adnexed Narrowly attached to stipe (as in lamellae).

Appressed Closely pressed to surface.
Agaric Mushroom, one of the Agaricaceae; fleshy fungus with lamellate hymenium.
Allantoid Sausage-shaped (as in spores).
Amyloid Turning blue to blue-black in Melzer's (iodine-based) reagent.
Anastomosing Forming an angular network by dividing and rejoining (ridges; lamellae).
Annulus Ring on stipe; remains of partial veil membrane on stipe.
Apical At the tip or apex.
Apiculate Having an apiculus.
Apiculus Short projection on spore by which it is attached to the sterigma.
Appendiculate Pertaining to cap margin which appears fringed with tooth-like remains of veil.

Applanate Flattened.
Apud According to, in the work(s) of.
Areolate Divided by cracks into small areas.
Ascus (pl. asci) A microscopic, sac-like structure which contains spores (ascospores) of the Ascomycotina.
Ascomycotina Fungi which produce spores in asci; the largest group of Fungi.
Basidiomycotina A major group of Fungi which form spores on basidia.
Basidium A microscopic structure which bears spores (basidiospores) of the Basidiomycotina.
Bleeding Producing a fluid, usually red in colour.
Blushing Changing to a diffuse reddish colour.
Bolete A fleshy mushroom of the Order Boletales, the hymenium of which is in tubes.
Bulbous Bulb-like; swollen at the base.

Button Young, unexpanded mushroom.
Campanulate Bell-shaped.
Cartilaginous Tough flexible; like cartilage.
Clavate Club-shaped.
Clustered/Tufted Pertaining to a group of mushrooms united at the base of their stipes.
Compound Made up of a number of parts; individual fruit-bodies united into one structure.
Concolorous Having the same colour.
Coprophilous Growing on dung.
Crenate Edge with rounded teeth.

Crenulate Delicately crenate.
Crispate/Crisped Finely wavy.

Cristate Finely divided, crested.
Crustose Covered by a crust.
Cuticle Outermost layer of cap or stipe.

Deciduous Falling off at the end of the growing season.
Decurrent Running down the stipe (as in lamellae).

Deliquescing Liquefying after maturing.
Dentate/Denticulate Toothed.
Dextrinoid Spores turning reddish-brown in Melzer's (iodine) reagent.
Dichotomous Branching into two equal parts.
Disc/Disk Central part of cap surface.
Distal Farthest from the origin or attachment.

Echinulae Fine spines on spore surface.
Echinulate Covered with small spines.
Ectomycorrhizae Mycorrhizae formed by various mushrooms on root surface of forest trees.
Effused-reflexed Spreading over the surface with margin turned away from surface.
Ellipsoidal Elliptical in optical section; shaped like a rugby ball.
Endospore Innermost layer of spore wall.
Epispore Thick layer of spore wall which determines spore shape.
Excentric/Eccentric Off-centre.
Exoperidium Outermost wall of fruit-bodies of puff-balls, earth-stars and similar fungi.

Fairy ring Rings of mushrooms formed mostly in grasslands.

Fasciculate Tufted; growing in tufts or bundles.

Fibril Fine thread.

Fibrillar/fibrillose Covered in threads.

Fimbriate Fringed; delicately toothed.

Flabellate Fan-shaped.

Flexuous Bent repeatedly; winding.

Floccose Cottonwool-like; covered with little woolly tufts.

Free Not attached to stipe (as in lamellae).

Fungus comb Cellular, convoluted clay structure on which some termites grow their fungus gardens.

Fusiform Spindle-shaped.

Fusoid Somewhat fusiform.

Gasteromycetes A group of fungi the basidiospores of which ripen in a spore-bearing tissue enclosed in a toughened outer layer (peridium).

Germ pore Thin area on spore wall through which germ tube emerges.

Gill Lamella of an agaric.

Glabrous Hairless; without ornamentation.

Globose Spherical or globe-shaped.

Glutinous Sticky; covered with a substance which turns sticky when wet.

Granular(-ose) Covered with small particles.

Grouped Individual fruit-bodies growing close together but not united.

Guttulate Containing one or more oil-like droplets (as in spores).

Guttule An oil-like droplet.

Hirsute Covered with long hairs.

Host Living organism harbouring a parasite.

Hyaline Clear; colourless.

Hygrophanous Having a water-soaked appearance when wet.

Hymenium Spore-bearing layer of a fruit-body.

Hypha (pl. **hyphae**) One of the filaments comprising the mycelium.

Imbricate In overlapping tiers like tiles on a roof.

Infundibuliform Funnel-shaped.

Innate Immersed; bedded in.

Involute Rolled inwards.

Labyrinthiform Maze-like.

Laccate Shiny, lacquer-like; appearing varnished.

Laciniate As if cut into bands.

Lamella A plate-like appendage on the underside of the cap of a mushroom and bearing the hymenium; gill.

Lamellate Having lamellae.

Lateral At the side.

Lenzitoid Elongated, maze-like.

Lignicolous Growing on wood.

Ligulate Strap-shaped.

Lobate Lobed.

Marginate Having a well-marked rim.

Mushroom The fruit-body of an agaric or bolete, especially an edible one.

Mycelium The collection of hyphae forming the vegetative part of the fungus.

Mycorrhiza Symbiotic association of a fungus with the roots of a plant.

Mycosis A fungal disease of man and animals.

Obconical Inversely conical.

Oblong Twice as long as wide.

Obovoid Egg-shaped with the narrow end below. (opposite of ovoid).

-oid A suffix meaning like or similar to.

Olivaceous Olive-coloured.

Ovoid Egg-shaped; with the broad end below.

Papilla A small, rounded process.

Papillate Having a papilla.

Partial veil A membranous tissue of certain agarics connecting the cap margin to the stipe and remaining as the ring or annulus on the stipe after expansion of the cap.

Pedicel Short stalk.

Pedicellate With a small stalk.

Perennial Living over a number of years.

Perforatorium Umbo on cap of fruit-bodies in species of *Termitomyces*.

Peridiole Small, lens-shaped, spore-containing body of certain Gasteromycetes.

Peridium Outer wall of fungal fruit-bodies.

Perithecium Microscopic, subglobose or flask-shaped fruit-body of some Ascomycotina.

Peronate Like or having a closely fitting sheath.

Plane Flat.

Plicate Pleated; deeply furrowed.

Polyporaceae (polypores) Larger fungi in

which the hymenium is borne inside tubes on the underside of the mostly tough, corky or woody fruit-body.

Pore The orifice of the hymenium-bearing tube of a bolete or polypore fungus; opening in spore-sac of some Gastromycetes.

Poroid Pertaining to lamellae joined by cross veins and so resembling pores.

Primordia Earliest developmental stage.

Pseudorhiza A root-like extension of the stipe as in *Termitomyces*.

Pseudosclerotium A compacted mass of mixed substrate held together by mycelium.

Punctate Marked with very small spots.

Pustulate Covered with small pimples or blisters.

Pyriform/piriform Pear-shaped.

Radiate Spreading from a centre.

Radicant Rooting.

Reflexed With margin turned upwards or backwards.

Refringent Refractive.

Reniform Kidney-shaped.

Resupinate Lying flat on the substrate with the hymenium on the outer surface.

Reticulate Net-like.

Rhizoid A thin, root-like strand.

Rhizomorph A root-like aggregation of hyphae, usually with a dark-coloured rind and apical growth tissue.

Ring *see* **Annulus**.

Saprophyte/saprobe An organism which obtains food by growing on dead organic material.

Sapwood Soft, new wood next to the bark.

Scabrous Rough, with short rigid projections.

Sclerotium A resting body composed of densely intertwined hyphae capable of surviving adverse conditions.

Seceding Pertaining to lamellae at first joined to the stipe but later tearing free.

Semi- A prefix meaning half.

Sensu lato In the broad sense.

Septum (pl. septa) Cross wall.

Serrate Edged with saw-like teeth.

Sessile Sitting; without a stipe.

Seta (pl. setae) Stiff, thick-walled hair.

Sinuate Pertaining to lamellae notched close to the attachment to the stipe.

Spathulate Spoon-shaped.

Spore Reproductive unit of fungi.

Spore print A deposit of basidiospores obtained by allowing spores from a fruit-body to fall on a sheet of paper placed under the tubes or lamellae.

Sporocarp Spore-bearing structure; fruit-body.

Squamose Scaly.

Stellate Star-shaped.

Sterigma A minute stalk bearing a spore or chain of spores in certain fungi.

Sterile Without spore-bearing structures.

Stipe Stalk.

Stipitate Stalked; having a stipe.

Striate Marked with fine lines or grooves.

Stroma A compact mass of hyphae, often hardened, on or in which spores are produced.

Stuffed Pertaining to a stipe, having the inner part of a different texture to the outer layers.

Sub- Prefix meaning under; almost or approximately.

Subglobose Almost spherical.

Substrate/substratum The material to which a fungus is attached or on which it is growing.

Substipitate Having a short, indistinct or poorly defined stipe.

Symbiont A partner in symbiosis.

Symbiosis The living together of unlike organisms often to mutual benefit.

Terrestrial Growing on the ground.

Toadstool The fruit-body of (usually) an inedible or poisonous agaric or bolete.

Tomentose Covered with soft, downy hairs.

Toxin A metabolic product produced by one organism which is injurious to another.

Truffle Subterranean fruit-body of certain Ascomycotina.

Truncate Ending abruptly as though cut off.

Tufted Clustered.

Turbinate Shaped like a spinning top; top-shaped.

μm Micrometre, that is $\frac{1}{1000}$ of a millimetre.

Umbo A central swelling or raised part on the upper surface of the cap.

Umbonate Having an umbo.

Undulate Wavy.

Ungulate Shaped like a horse's hoof.

Universal veil A layer of tissue covering the young, developing fruit-bodies of agarics and Gasteromycetes and remaining around the base of the stipe as the volva in some mushrooms.

Veil A covering membrane; *see also* **Partial veil** and **Universal veil**.

Velar Concerning the veil.

Ventricose Swollen around the middle.

Verrucose Covered with small, blunt, wart-like processes.

Vinaceous The colour of red wine.

Violaceous Of the colour violet.

Viscid Constantly sticky; *see* **Glutinous**.

Volva Cup-like remains of universal veil around the base of the stipe or receptacle.

Zonate Having concentric lines or bands of different colours and/or texture.

BIBLIOGRAPHY

Books

Ainsworth, G.C., Sparrow, F.K. & Sussman, A.S. 1973. *The Fungi: an advanced treatise. Vol. IVB. A taxonomic review with keys : Basidiomycetes and Lower Fungi.* Academic Press, New York, San Francisco, London.

Bottomley, A.M. & Talbot, P.H.B. 1954. *Common edible and poisonous mushrooms in South Africa.* Union of South Africa, Department of Agriculture Bulletin no. 324.

Bresadola, J. 1927 – 1941. *Iconographia Mycologica Vols. 1 – 27.* Societa Botanica Italiana. Musio Civico di storia Naturale di Trente, Mediolina.

Bresinksy, A. & Besl, H. *Giftpilze, mit einer Einführung in die Pilzbestimmung.* Wissenschaftliche Verlagsgesellschaft mbH., Stuttgart.

Buczaki, S. 1989. *New Generation Guide to the fungi of Britain and Europe.* Collins, Grafton Street, London.

Chaumeton, H. 1987. *Pilze Mitteleuropas.* Gustav Fischer Verlag, Stuttgart.

Courtenay, B. & Burdsall, H.H. 1982. *A field guide to mushrooms and their relatives.* Van Nostrand Reinhold Company, New York.

Dähncke,R.M. & Dähncke, S.M. 1982. *700 Pilze in Farbfotos.* A.T. Verlag Aarau, Stuttgart.

Dickenson, C. & Lucas, J. 1979. *The encyclopedia of mushrooms.* Orbis Publishing Ltd.: London.

Faulstick, H., Kommerell, B. & Wieland, T.L. 1980. Amanita *toxins and poisoning.* Verlag Gerhard Witzstrock, Köln.

Groves, J.W. 1962. *The edible and poisonous mushrooms of Canada.* Roger Duhamel F.R.S.C., Queens Printer and Controller of Stationary, Ottawa.

Hawksworth, D.L., Sutton, B.C. & Ainsworth, G.C. 1983. *Ainsworth & Bisby's Dictionary of the fungi.* Commonwealth Mycological Institute, Kew, Surrey.

Heim, R. 1977. *Termites et Champignons.* Société nouvelle des editions Boubée, Paris.

Kibby, G. 1979. *Mushrooms and Toadstools: a field guide.* Oxford University Press, Oxford.

Klan, Jaroslav. 1981. *Mushrooms and fungi.* Hamlyn Publishing Group, London.

Lange, M. & Mora, F.B. 1963. *Collins Guide to Mushrooms and Toadstools.* Collins, London.

Largent, D.L. *How to identify mushrooms to genus. 1 : Macroscopic features.* Mad River Press, Inc. Eureka, CA 95501.

Largent, D.L., & Thiers, H.D. *How to identify mushrooms to genus 11 : Field identification of genera.* Mad River Press, Inc. Eureka, CA 95501.

Largent, D.L., Johnson, D.D. & Watling, R. *How to identify mushrooms to genus. 111 : Microscopic features.* Mad River Press, Inc. Eureka, CA 95501.

Levin, H., Branch, M., Rappoport, S. & Mitchell, D. 1987. *A Field Guide to the Mushrooms of South Africa.* C. Struik (Pty) Ltd., Cape Town.

Lincoff, G.H. 1981. *The Audubon Society field guide to the mushrooms of North America.* Alfred A. Knopf Inc. New York.

Orton, P.D. 1986. *British fungus flora, Agarics and Boleti. 4/Pluteaceae : Pluteus & Volvariella.* Royal Botanic Garden, Edingburgh.

Pacioni, G. 1985. *The Macdonald encyclopedia of mushrooms and toadstools.* Macdonald & Co (Publishers) Ltd., London.

Phillips, R. 1981. *Mushrooms and other fungi of Great Britain and Europe.* Ward Lock Ltd.,London.

Rayner, R. 1979. *Mushrooms and Toadstools.* Hamlyn nature guides. The Hamlyn Publishing Group Ltd, London.

Reid, D.A. 1980. *Mushrooms and Toadstools.* Kingfisher Books, Ward Lock Ltd.: London.

Rinaldo, A. & Tyndalo, V. 1977. *Mushrooms and other fungi. An illustrated guide.* Hamlyn, Middlesex.

Ryvarden, L. & Johansen, I. 1980. *A preliminary polypore flora of East Africa.* Fungiflora, Oslo.

Schlechte, G. 1986. *Holzbewohnende Pilze.* Jahn & Ernst Verlag, Hamburg.

Singer, R. 1986. *The Agaricales in modern taxonomy. Fourth fully revised edition.* Koeltz Scientific Books, Koenigstein.

Stephens, E.L. & Kidd, M.M. 1953. *Some South African edible fungi.* Longmans Southern

Africa (Pty) Ltd., Cape Town.

Stephens, E.L. & Kidd., M.M. 1953. *Some South African poisonous and inedible Fungi.* Longmans, Green & Co., Cape Town.

Stuntz, D.E. *How to identify mushrooms to genus.* IV. *Keys to families and genera.* Mad River Press Inc., Eureka, CA 95501.

Svrcek, M. 1983. *The Hamlyn book of mushrooms and fungi.* Hamlyn, London.

Van der Westhuizen, G.C.A. 1983. *Sampioene en paddastoele/Mushrooms and toadstools.* Republic of South Africa, Department of Agricultural Technical Services. Bulletin no. 396.

Wasson, R.G. 1968. *Soma : Devine Mushroom of Immortality.* Harcourt Brace Jovanovich, New York.

Wieland, T.L. 1986. *Peptides of Poisonous* Amanita *Mushrooms.* Springer Verlag, New York.

Young, A.M. 1982. *Common Australian Fungi.* New South Wales University Press, Kensington, Australia.

Journal Articles

Bottomley, A.M. 1948. Gasteromycetes of South Africa. *Bothalia* 4, 473-810.

Doidge, E.M. 1950. The South African Fungi and Lichens. *Bothalia* 5. 1-1094.

Dring, D.M. 1980. Contributions towards a rational arrangement of the Clathraceae. *Kew Bull.* 35, 1-96.

Gorter, G.J.M.A. & Eicker, A. 1988. Gewone Afrikaanse en Engelse name vir die meer algemene Suid-Afrikaanse sampioene en ander makroswamme. *S.A. Tydskr. Natuurwet. & Tegn.* 7, 55-64.

Louwrens, B.A. 1964. Some mushrooms of the Transvaal. *Fauna & Flora* no. 15, 1-16.

Marasas, W.F.O. & Trappe, J.M. 1973. Notes on southern African Tuberales. *Bothalia* 11, 139-142.

Pearson, A.A. 1950. Cape Agarics and Boleti. *Trans. Brit. mycol. Soc.* 33, 276-316.

Pegler, D.N. 1968. Studies on African Agaricales : 1. *Kew Bull.* 21, 499-533.

Pegler, D.N. 1969. Studies on African Agaricales : 11. *Kew Bull.* 23, 347-412.

Pegler, D.N. 1977. A preliminary agaric flora of east Africa. *Kew Bull. Add. Ser.* VI. 1-615.

Pegler, D.N. 1983. The genus *Lentinus*, a world monograph. *Kew Bull. Add. Ser.* X, 1 – 281.

Pegler, D.N. & Piearce, G.D. 1980. The edible mushrooms of Zambia. *Kew Bull.* 35, 475-491.

Pegler, D.N. & Rayner, R.W. 1969. A contribution to the agaric flora of Kenya. *Kew Bull.* 23, 347-412.

Piearce, G.M. 1987. The genus *Termitomyces* in Zambia. *The Mycologist, Bull. Brit. mycol. Soc.* 21, 111 – 116.

Reid, D.A. 1965. A monograph of the stipitate stereoid fungi. *Nova Hedwigia Beih.* 18.

Reid, D.A. 1973. A reappraisal of type and authentic specimens of Basidiomycetes in the Van der Byl Herbarium, Stellenbosch. *J.S. Afr. Bot.* 39, 141-178.

Reid, D.A. 1974. A reappraisal of type and authentic material of the larger Basidiomycetes in the Pretoria Herbarium. *Bothalia* 11, 221-230.

Reid, D.A. 1975. Type studies of the larger Basidiomycetes described from southern Africa. *Contributions from the Bolus Herbarium* no. 7, 1-255.

Reid, D.A. & Eicker, A. 1993. South African fungi. 2. Some species of *Leucoagaricus* and *Leucocoprinus. S. Afr. J. Bot.* 59, 85-97.

Singer, R., Aranjo, I., & Ivory, M.H. 1983. The Ectotrophically Mycorrhizal Fungi of the neotropical Lowlands, especially Central Amazonia. *Nova Hedwigia Beih.* 77.

Talbot, P.H.B. 1951. Studies of some South African resupinate Hymenomycetes II. *Bothalia* 6, 1-116.

Talbot, P.H.B. 1954. The genus *Stereum* in South Africa. *Bothalia* 6, 303-308.

Talbot, P.H.B. 1958. Studies of some South African resupinate Hymenomycetes 1. *Bothalia* 7, 131-187.

Van der Bijl, P.A. 1922. A contribution to our knowledge of the Polyporaceae of South Africa. *S. Afr. J. Sci.* 18, 246-293.

Van der Bijl, P.A. 1924. Descriptions of additional South African Polyporaceae. *S. Afr. J. Sci.* 21, 308-313.

Van der Westhuizen, G.C.A. 1971. Cultural characters and carpophore construction of some poroid Hymenomycetes. *Bothalia* 10, 137-328.

Van der Westhuizen, G.C.A. & Eicker, A. 1988. Die sampioene van Pretoria en omgewing. *S.A. Tydskr. Natuurwet. & Tegn.* 7,15-25.

Van der Westhuizen, G.C.A. & Eicker, A. 1990. Species of *Termitomyces* (Agaricales) occurring in South Africa. *Mycol. Res.* 94, 923-937.

INDEX TO AFRIKAANS NAMES

INDEX TO COMMON NAMES

INDEX TO SCIENTIFIC NAMES